D. COLTHERD
9 - 10 - 2016

£2.50

D. COLTHERD
9 - 10 - 2016

LOST
TREASURE
SHIPS OF ✴ THE
TWENTIETH
CENTURY

LOST TREASURE SHIPS OF THE TWENTIETH CENTURY

NIGEL PICKFORD

PAVILION

First published in Great Britain in 1999 by
PAVILION BOOKS LIMITED
London House, Great Eastern Wharf
Parkgate Road, London SW11 4NQ

Designed by David Fordham
Picture editing by Jenny de Gex

A CIP catalogue record for this book is available
from the British Library.

ISBN 1 86205 079 1

Typeset in Galliard by MATS, Southend-on-Sea, Essex

Printed in Singapore by Imago
Origination by DP Graphics, England

2 4 6 8 10 9 7 5 3 1

This book can be ordered direct from the publisher.
Please contact the Marketing Department.
But try your bookshop first.

CONTENTS

INTRODUCTION

ABOVE: *Commendatore Quaglia, head of the Italian company Sorima, on board the salvage ship* Artiglio, *stares pensively at some of the gold bars he recovered from the* Egypt – *a landmark recovery as it witnessed the first really successful use of a grabbing system deployed from a surface vessel.*

TREASURE SHIP! The words exert a powerful mythic pull on the imagination but elude easy definition. For most of us they suggest Spanish galleons or Portuguese East Indiamen with billowing sails, wooden hulls and holds crammed with silver dollars or gold escudos. None of this has much to do with the giant passenger liners that plied between New York and Liverpool in the early years of this century, with their compound engines, steel rivets and electric lighting. And yet, surprisingly, it was the first fifty years of the twentieth century that witnessed the greatest and final flowering of the entire treasure ship era.

In terms of the sheer volume of gold and silver moved, the first half of the twentieth century dwarfs all other periods before or since. A shipment of 100,000 ounces of gold, or approximately three tons, would have been exceptionally large for a Spanish galleon. By comparison, shipments of seventy tons of gold were a regular feature of peacetime liners in the early years of the twentieth century, and shipments of nearly 300 tons of gold inside one hull were not unknown during the two world wars. Indeed, in one small convoy alone, codenamed Crackerjack, that sailed early in July 1940, far more gold was moved out of Europe and across to Canada and the United States (in excess of 700 tons) than was moved from the Spanish American colonies back to Spain during the entirety of its most productive decade from 1590 to 1600.

In respect of the ships themselves the early years of the twentieth century can also claim to be the pre-eminent period of the treasure ship. The years 1900–50 saw ships being built of a luxury and a magnitude that had never before been dreamed of and which have not been surpassed in the second half of the century. Ships like the *Titanic* and the *Lusitania* were constructed on a scale and with a concern for comfort and craftsmanship that were in keeping with a unique age of leisure and privilege.

Not that all the ships written about in this book fall into the category of luxurious liners. The exigencies of two devastating world wars saw gold being moved out of Europe and into the safe havens of North America on a scale and with an urgency quite unprecedented. In such an emergency all kinds of makeshift vessels were used for the transport of vast riches, which explains why the treasure ships featured here include humble vessels such as *Pilot Boat No.19* and heavily armoured warships like the *Edinburgh*, as well as fast liners.

OPPOSITE: *A diving helmet made by C. E. Heinke & Co Ltd. This is the type of hard-hat helmet that was used by divers in the early years of this century working on wrecks like the* Laurentic.

RIGHT: *The* Titanic *leaves Southampton on 10 April 1912. Its recent discovery and the subsequent salvaging of artefacts from the debris field has led to a worldwide debate on the role of the salvor.*

What is perhaps most surprising about this final development of the treasure ship era is its sudden and total ending. For several thousands of years people have been in the habit of moving their most valued possessions around the world by ship, and a fair proportion of those ships have ended up on the sea floor as a result of storm, war or other perils. But not any more. It is highly unlikely that there will be many more vessels stowed with gold and jewels sinking to the bottom of the ocean. This has nothing to do with increased ship safety. A surprisingly large number of ships still sink every day of the year, but because they are mainly freighters rather than passenger ships they receive little public attention. Changes in modes of transport provide part of the explanation. Such valuables now tend to be sent in planes rather than ships. But the crucial factors are the ending of the gold standard and the decline in the importance of precious metals as a prerequisite for international trade. In these days of instant electronic transfers of cash assets between one side of the world and the other there is a tendency to forget that until quite recently debts could often only be settled by the transfer of physical assets in the shape of gold bars or silver dollars. That system of exchange is unlikely to return. But the first half of the century was a glorious culmination to several thousand years of precious commodity transport, both the apotheosis and the finale of the entire treasure ship era.

For the purposes of this book a lost treasure ship of the twentieth century is simply any ship that was carrying a cargo of gold, silver or jewels during the relevant time frame and which sank or was lost in transit. There is, however, one important qualification to this definition. It is not always easy to know exactly what a ship was carrying when it sank, particularly during times of war. This crucial element of mystery has meant that a number of ships have lodged themselves in people's imaginations as treasure ships, for one reason or another, even though very little hard documentary evidence exists to prove beyond reasonable doubt that the ship concerned was in reality carrying a precious cargo. Of course a lack of solid evidence has never stopped treasure-hunters spending large sums of money in trying to recover a supposed precious cargo that is believed to lie somewhere in the wreckage of a particular hull. Nor does one failure stop other salvors trying their luck on the same ship, since it is rarely the case that any large liner can ever be completely searched, and also the treasure hunter's obsessive secrecy means that few know accurately what has or has not been recovered. Indeed, sometimes it seems that persistent salvage attempts actually encourage other salvors, just because the repeated searching of a particular sunken wreck creates for it a kind of legendary treasure ship status. A number of such mythic treasure ships are considered as well as others that were most definitely carrying treasure. Perhaps in the final analysis the only entirely satisfactory way to define a treasure ship is to say that a ship is a treasure ship if enough people believe it to be so.

DEVELOPMENTS IN DIVING

IF THE FIRST HALF OF THE TWENTIETH CENTURY was remarkable for the growth of its treasure ship fleets and the size of the shipments, the second half has been notable for the extraordinary technological advances which have enabled us to locate and salvage those ships that were lost *en route*. In 1900 most practical salvage was carried out by divers using equipment the prototype of which had been developed by Augustus Siebe for work on raising the cannons of the *Royal George* in 1840. (The *Royal George* sank off Spithead in 1782 and was the object of extensive salvage operations for many years afterwards.) Each diver's dress consisted essentially of a copper helmet with corselet that screwed on to a flexible waterproof suit. It is this equipment that has provided us with the stereotypical image of the diver much deployed in adventure books such as Jules Verne's *Twenty Thousand Leagues Under the Sea*. It is important to note that the copper helmet was not intended to withstand the pressure of the external water, allowing the diver to breathe at normal atmospheric pressure. If this had been attempted, either the glass viewing plate would have been crushed or the diver would have experienced an extreme rush of blood to the head. In this respect, Verne's hero, Captain Nemo, notoriously misunderstood the physics involved. What kept the helmet intact was the fact that compressed air was being pumped down a flexible tube into the inside of the helmet through a non-return valve so that the pressures inside and outside the helmet were equalized. If the pressure was too low, the suit would be squeezed uncomfortably inwards, restricting breathing. If the pressure became too high, the suit would inflate and the diver would find himself helplessly buoyant. As well as the copper helmet and canvas dress, the diver wore heavy lead boots, weighing about 40 pounds each, and lead weights of around 16 pounds at his back and chest to reduce his buoyancy and take him down to the sea floor. He also had a line attached to his chest by means of which he could be hoisted back to the surface. This line often contained a telephone line for verbal communication. The diver would ascend and descend by means of a rope, called the shot rope, with a heavy weight attached to the end to stabilize it, which helped the diver not to lose his way under water and also provided a useful means of sending objects up and down. This was the basic equipment used by the divers who worked on the *Laurentic* and the *Tubantia*.

Using this equipment the diver could reach a depth of about 200 feet. In 1907 the newly instituted Admiralty Deep Diving Committee set a safe limit of 210 feet. The

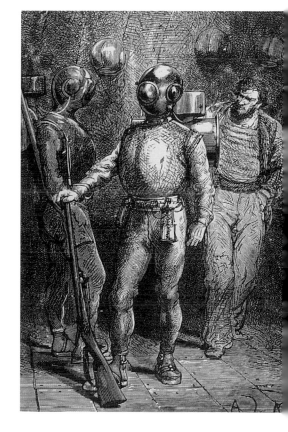

ABOVE: *Illustration of Captain Nemo from Jules Verne's best-selling book* Twenty Thousand Leagues Under the Sea. *If Nemo had dived to any significant depth wearing this equipment, his head would have been horribly crushed.*

limiting factor was not pressure of water but what was then known as compressed air sickness or 'the bends'. Breathing compressed air resulted in excessive quantities of nitrogen being dissolved into the blood stream. When the diver suddenly came to the surface after a dive the nitrogen came out of solution in a great rush of bubbles. The effect was excruciatingly painful and could cause paralysis or, in extreme cases, death. The problem had been known about for years, and the answer was for the diver to remain on the bottom for limited periods of time and to ascend slowly. The French physiologist Paul Bert established the theory for decompression in the late nineteenth century and J.B.S. Haldane refined it in the early twentieth, introducing the novel concept of the diver pausing altogether at certain predetermined depths rather than ascending in a slow but continuous mode as recommended by Bert. If a diver came up too quickly, for whatever reason, and developed sickness symptoms, he was either sent down again to the required depth in order to recompress, or else put inside a specially developed recompression chamber if one was available.

The problem with working at depths much greater than 200 feet was that the decompression times required became so great that the diver got very little work time on

BELOW: *A 1930s design for a supersubmarine capable of exploring underwater mineral deposits as well as sunken wrecks.*

UNDERSEA SALVAGER

The greatest unconquered frontiers on earth are the sea depths. This supersubmarine, built specifically for exploration and salvaging is scientifically constructed to withstand great pressure, capable of descending to depths as great as that achieved by Beebe's bathysphere. Retractable gear will insure solid foundation on any type sea bottom; special sea chambers will allow divers to work with assured safety. At super depths, salvage will be done from inside the ship, by retractable derricks, perhaps lifting whole ships to levels permitting divers to finish the job. Searchlights using ordinary light, infra-red light, and ultra-violet rays, coupled with a televisor periscope system permitting complete 360° vision, will allow scientific exploration of these realms of eternal night and mystery. See Page 145 for details.
© AMAZING STORIES 1939

the bottom and instead spent most of his time hanging unenviably on the shot rope. During the 1930s the engineer R.H. Davis developed a submersible decompression chamber in an effort to extend the diver's range, and make life more comfortable for the deep diver, but this did not greatly increase the depths that could be worked at.

Following the Second World War the focus for diving radically changed. Until then it had been entirely the province of the professional working on heavy industrial projects such as harbour walls and wrecks. In the late 1940s and 1950s the situation was revolutionized as a result of the activities of Jacques Cousteau and friends on the French Riviera. Cousteau and Emile Gagnan developed the first practical aqualung with a demand valve. Suddenly the diver was freed from all the cumbersome equipment – copper helmets, lead weights and lines – that had previously burdened him. The basic physics of the diver's situation was, of course, not altered. He still needed to breathe compressed air in order to avoid having his lungs crushed by the external water pressure, but the air was now supplied from a cylinder on the diver's back through a short length of tube, the other end of which he held in his mouth. The used breath, polluted with carbon dioxide, was expelled by the diver in a stream of bubbles. The idea of the diver moving around with his own self-contained equipment, freed from lines to the surface, was far from new, as Cousteau was the first to acknowledge. The inventor H.A. Fleuss had developed a self-contained breathing apparatus as far back as 1878. This, however, was of the rebreather type, where the exhaled carbon dioxide was purified and then recycled. Davis had refined Fleuss's invention during the First World War for work in poisonous atmospheres and for use by firemen. However, neither Davis nor Fleuss had available the toughened metal cylinder technology that allowed Cousteau to store enormous volumes of compressed air within the relatively tiny space of the aqualung.

It was the simplicity of Cousteau's innovation that led to diving becoming a mass sport rather than an arduous and arcane job undertaken by just a few intrepid professionals. It also led indirectly to an enormous growth in the general public's interest in shipwrecks and resulted in a number of small, dedicated groups of enthusiasts with limited finance launching their own salvage projects. Most of these amateur salvage efforts were concentrated on shallow-water wrecks and went on largely unregulated.

Cousteau, and the Mediterranean divers who are associated with him, quickly came up against a new physiological limit to diving, one which had been observed by earlier practitioners using the copper-helmet technology, but never fully explored or understood – this was known as nitrogen narcosis. It was noticed that when divers approached depths of 300 feet they tended to show signs of drunkenness, hysteria, mental imbalance and loss of judgement. Oxygen also proved to be potentially poisonous when under a pressure greater than 300 feet of water. It seemed for a while that the limit for diving had been reached at fifty fathoms.

In the 1960s and 1970s the need for the commercial diver to work at ever greater depths increased enormously with the growth of the underwater oil industry. This demand was underpinned, as almost all underwater exploration has been from the beginning of its development, by the interests of the world's military community. The American Naval Experimental Diving Unit had carried out a series of experiments during the late 1920s and 1930s and established that the use of helium instead of nitrogen in a carefully regulated combination eliminated many problems encountered by divers breathing compressed air.

RIGHT: *One of Jacques Cousteau's team diving in a cave off the Bahamas. Cousteau's development of the first practical aqualung, freeing up the diver from cumbersome and expensive equipment, turned diving from an arcane semi-industrial job into a worldwide leisure activity.*

Helium is virtually inert and did not dissolve in human blood and tissue as rapidly as nitrogen. It is, however, a very bulky gas, as well as very expensive, so there was no possibility of the diver carrying sufficient supplies of it on his back. The alternative of supplying it from the surface by means of tubes was considered impractical and dangerous because of the lengths of tubing required. The solution was to develop a rebreather system, on the same model as the original rebreathers developed by Fleuss, in which the carbon dioxide was eliminated by passing the gas through a filter such as lythium hydroxide, or beralyme. Using oxygen helium gas mixtures, divers were able to get down to 500 and 600 feet during experimental dives in the 1950s. The dangers of nitrogen narcosis were avoided, but work time on the bottom was still limited because of extended decompression requirements.

Another significant development took place in the early 1960s, when Cousteau developed a series of habitats on the sea bottom at depths of up to 100 feet out of which divers lived for a week at a time, thus avoiding the need for constant compression and decompression. The United States followed up with its own Sealab programme, largely pioneered by Captain George Bond. By 1970 it had been proved that the basic concept of divers living and working out of a habitat on the sea bottom at a depth of 600 feet for a week or longer at a time was viable. All the elements of what was to become known as 'saturation diving' were in place.

Today, divers 'in saturation' enter the bell on board ship and undergo compression, or 'blowing down', to whatever depth they will be working at. The bell is then lowered through the ship's moon pool in the centre of the hull. The deployment of this technology clearly requires specially designed ships known as dive support vessels.

Even saturation diving has proved to have its physiological limits. At depths of 500 feet or more divers begin to suffer from what is known as High Pressure Nervous Syndrome. This condition is mitigated by a slow rate of compression, but at depths of 1,500 feet even slow compression does not seem to eliminate it. Another new threshold has been reached for the 'free' diver, which has yet to be overcome. In practice saturation diving rarely occurs at depths greater than 1,000 feet, and even in shallower waters it is still an enormously expensive activity, appropriate only for extremely high-value cargoes or vital pipeline installation work.

Submersibles

Throughout the twentieth century there has been an alternative line of development for underwater exploration which employs an entirely different technology from that traced above. The basic concept behind this alternative is that a person is protected from the pressure of water at depth by being encased within some form of hull strong enough to resist whatever stress it is put under. Either air is supplied from the surface or, more usually, the enclosed hull contains within it a sufficient quantity of air for the planned duration of the dive. The latter characteristically involves some form of recycling. In both scenarios, air is being breathed at normal atmospheric pressure, which eliminates all the physiological compression and decompression problems.

The history of submarine inventions goes back as far as the early seventeenth century and Drebbel's underwater galley powered by twelve submerged rowers, a galley which apparently took tourists up and down the Thames. It was not until the beginning of the twentieth century that the first submarines were used in a significant and practical way, and by then the emphasis was very much on the submersible as a weapon of war rather than as a means of exploration and retrieval. Then, in the 1920s, interest turned again to the idea of putting a person inside a robotic suit of armour, capable of withstanding the external pressure of the water, with articulated arms and legs which would allow simple mechanical operations to be carried out on the seabed, with its own air supply that could be breathed at atmospheric pressure. In 1923 Neufeldt and Kuhnke developed the first of these 'iron men', as they were known, and soon afterwards Peress invented a slightly modified version, the joints of which were sealed with a lubricant. The Neufeldt model came to fame when it was used to assist with the salvage work on the *Egypt* in 1932. However, none of the iron men proved very practical for carrying out the nuts and bolts

ABOVE: *The* Alvin *was funded by the US Navy and built by Litton Industries. Completed in 1964, it had a depth rating of nearly 2,000 metres. It was upgraded in the 1970s with a titanium hull which enabled it to go to over twice this depth.*

OPPOSITE: *The small submarine* Delta *examines the rudder of the* Lusitania.

of salvage work. The limbs were too heavy and clumsy and could only be made to work at all in currents of one knot or less. Where the suit of armour did prove very useful was as a simple observation chamber, used for example for guiding a grab deployed from a ship on the surface. By the 1930s observation chambers had become an essential part of the salvor's equipment. The articulated arms and legs, however, were a failed encumbrance that quickly atrophied, only to be redeveloped in another form some 50 years later.

Inventions in deep-water exploration have a habit of coming full circle and then being reborn a second time in a new guise. The technology behind the iron man, the submarine and the deep observation chamber have all come together in the development of the manned submersible. Americans were the first to use submersibles like the *Alvin* and the *Aluminaut*. More recently these have been superseded by the pioneering work of Russian and French engineers. The manned submersible is in essence a small submarine with a titanium hull capable of withstanding pressures down to 20,000 feet. It has a built-in carbon dioxide recycling system so that the occupants can stay submerged for up to three days. It has its own power source and so is not dependent on a cable from a mother ship. It also is equipped with robotic arms that can be manoeuvred by the pilots from within

RIGHT: *The remotely operated vehicle* Jason Junior *was used on the* Titanic *in 1986 and obtained some rare film footage. It is shown here exploring the starboard forecastle deck of the* Titanic *its lights picking out one of the* Titanic*'s bollards.*

the submersible to pick up small objects or operate tools. It was developed primarily as a scientific resource and as a military accessory, but it has also been used commercially in a salvage situation. A famous example is the recovery of artifacts from the *Titanic* debris field by the French submersible *Nautile*. Its limitation as a salvage tool is that it does not have the power or lifting capacity to remove large objects without attaching airbags, which is not always practicable. Also it cannot penetrate inside an enclosed steel hull without great risk to itself and its occupants.

SURFACE CONTROLLED SYSTEMS

THERE IS A THIRD LINE OF DEVELOPMENT which does not involve putting a man below the surface of the sea, either as a diver breathing compressed air or inside a submersible using robotic tools, but instead relies on deploying the necessary technology from a ship on the surface. From the beginning of the century, salvage ships were equipped with lifting gear for winching sections of a wrecked ship's superstructure away from the area of the salvage operation in order to assist in clearing a route to the target area. To start with, this method relied on a diver attaching the necessary wires. By the 1930s, 'grabs' were being used to clamp the metal sections and drag them away. Once a route had been cleared, the grab could also be used to bring up the cargo. The role of the diver in this situation was reduced to that of a pair of eyes within an observation chamber for guiding the grab. The man in the observation chamber would be in constant telephonic communication with the salvage master operating the grab. This was the salvage system used with great success by companies such as Risdon Beazley and Sorima throughout the first twenty-five years after the Second World War and which came to be known as 'smash and grab'. In more recent years the man inside the observation chamber has been superseded by cameras attached to remotely operated vehicles, or RoVs as they are known. These vehicles are linked by cable to the surface ship from where they are controlled. RoVs can be equipped with robotic tools for the retrieval of small items, and are also very useful for activities such as preliminary survey work or the placing of explosives.

The early grab systems were limited in their uses as the ship had to be securely moored in order to remain on station over the wreck, which was impossible in very deep water. This meant that it was difficult to operate a conventional grab system at depths greater than 1,000 feet. During the 1980s a company called Blue Water Recoveries, in conjunction with the French research foundation IFREMER took the grab concept a stage further by developing a hugely powerful tool that was deployed on the end of a drill pipe slung from the centre of an oilfield drilling ship. The ship was dynamically positioned, which meant that it was no longer dependent on mooring but was kept on station by the constant use of bow and stern thrusters, which were controlled by a computer linked to a satellite navigation system. The rigidity of the drill pipe reduced unwanted movement of the grab at great depths, as well as supplying enormous strength. The grab itself was equipped with its own cameras and batteries of lights, providing those on the mother ship with a visual image of what was happening below. It was also equipped with its own thrusters so that it could be precisely positioned to within a metre of accuracy. This system was developed to operate at depths of up to 15,000 feet with a lifting capacity of 100 tons (see *John Barry* chapter).

LOCATION SYSTEMS

In many respects the advances made in the ability to find objects on the sea floor have been even more startling than the technical developments that allow their recovery. At the turn of the century, a lost ship with a valuable cargo could only be discovered, presuming that no masts stood above sea level, by means of dragging a wire or net and waiting until it snagged. Clearly, even when two or more ships were employed dragging a net stretched between them, this was a very slow and inefficient method of locating a wreck. If the search area was greater than a square mile or two, the task was virtually impossible.

The art of searching for sunken ships was revolutionized by the development of Asdic, an acronym for Anti Submarine Detection Investigation Committee. This was a joint Anglo-French agency set up in 1918 to investigate a remote mechanism for detecting submerged submarines from surface ships. Essentially it consisted of a transducer attached to the hull of the ship that emitted high-frequency sound pulses which travelled through the water until they bounced back off the first solid surface they came into contact with. A receiver on the ship's hull would then pick up the echo. Any sudden change in the shape of the solid surface below, or in the depth of water through which the sound pulse had to travel before it met the solid surface, would result in a change in the frequency of the echo, and this change could be translated into a graphic recording. It was a brilliant invention for defence purposes, but it was soon discovered to have other useful applications as well. By the 1930s the echo-sounder had been developed for non-military applications such as establishing the depth of water below a hull. It was far more exact and much faster than the traditional method of lowering a log line. It soon also became evident that a changed pattern on the echo-sounding recording paper would occur when the sound pulses passed over an object on the sea bottom such as a shipwreck. A skilful interpreter of these sonar patterns would be able to tell what aberrations might have been caused by non-geological factors. The *Lusitania* was one of the very first ships to be discovered using an echo-sounding technique after many years of failed efforts using the traditional wire sweeping methods.

During the 1960s, side-scan sonar was developed. This technique uses the same basic principle of acoustic pulsing but sends out a wide fan of pulses from both sides of the ship or, more usually today, the towed 'fish'. By this means a far wider swathe of water is searched in one pass of the ship than can be achieved with the traditional echo-sounder. Also, by towing a fish near the sea bottom it is now possible to carry out a search at far greater depths of water. The only limiting factor is the length of the cable and the size of the winches. Two other recent developments have also greatly enhanced the utility of side-scan sonar search systems. The first is computerization. The pulses that are received back can now be digitized, fed into a computer program and displayed in conventional graphic images, making them much easier to interpret. All the voluminous data can also now be stored and analysed on disc. The second important advance is the improvement in navigational systems. Clearly, when carrying out a search in a given area it is of the utmost importance to know exactly where you have been and what part of the area still remains to be covered. In the absence of landmarks, even the most experienced navigators could well miss a patch as a result of drift or some other slight aberration. Even when a sonar had picked up a change of frequency that might indicate a wreck, it was not always easy to relocate exactly that anomaly on the sea bottom. Today, with the advent of satellite global positioning systems, a ship knows exactly where it is to within a few metres. As a result one can not only be certain of the areas covered but can also return to any detected anomaly with a high degree of accuracy.

Thanks to these advances it is now possible to consider searching for a lost ship in an area of up to 500 square miles. An initial survey using a modern side scan of an area of this size would take approximately a month. Before the advent of sonar, to search any area larger than a few square miles was out of the question. Today's systems are a great advance but they are still not entirely foolproof. Even a skilled interpreter of sonar images cannot always distinguish objects of geological origin from those that are made by humans. This means that during any search a large number of anomalies will have to be dived on or examined by use of RoVs, and most of these anomalies will turn out to be rocks. Eliminating geological anomalies can be a very time-consuming business. Sonar is also very limited if the target ship happens to be lost in an area of sea bottom that is mountainous and full of ravines. Under these conditions it may be necessary to make passes from several directions in order to try to build up an accurate picture of the seabed, and even then there is always a possibility that the wreck will remain acoustically hidden. Another limiting factor that is not always appreciated is that in most searches the target is a particular wreck, not wrecks in general, and often it is necessary to investigate and discard twenty or thirty similar but wrong wrecks in a given search area before the correct target is found. Sometimes a wreck will be entirely buried beneath the sand or mud on the sea bottom, in which case the sonar will not pick up the image even if the beams pass over the top of it. Since its development in the 1950s, a magnetometer has often been used in these cases, either in conjunction with the sonar or by itself. The principle is that ferrous objects have a magnetic field which will be detected by the magnetometer as they come into its range. It is possible to calculate the likely magnetic signature of a particular wreck that is being searched for on the basis of the total weight of iron objects contained in it, most usually iron cannon, anchors and nails, although with more recent wrecks clearly the volumes of ferrous metals will be much larger. The earth has its own natural

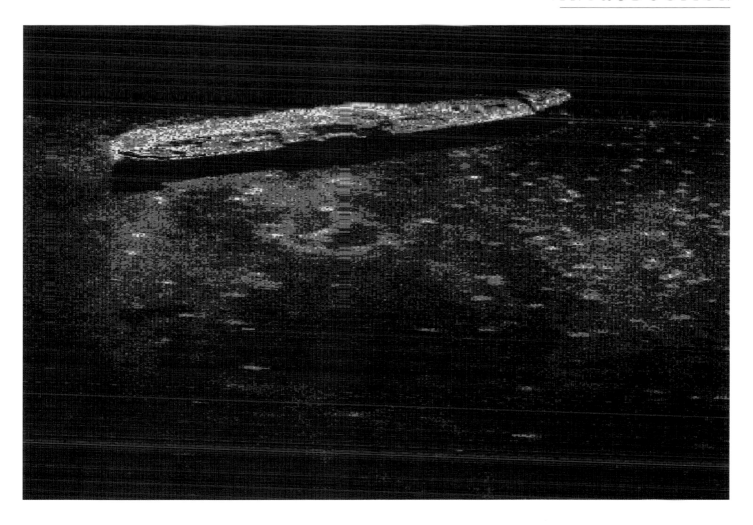

magnetic field, which is itself always subject to change and distortion, and it is necessary to try to eliminate this factor in order to obtain accurate recordings for any other anomolous ferrous objects that might be in the search area. To assist in this, sometimes two magnetometers are towed. In this procedure it is assumed that the natural background reading for both magnetometers will be the same and that any difference between their readings should indicate some local anomaly. The magnetometer is a very useful search tool, but it too has its drawbacks, not the least of which is the fact that in many areas individual rocks also have strong magnetic fields. As with sonar it is usually necessary to identify and discard a large number of potential targets before the right one is found. Magnetometers are particularly important when searching for small wooden wrecks, which might not show up on a side-scan sonar.

An important search tool that has recently come into existence is the sub bottom profiler. During sonar trials it was discovered that low-frequency acoustic signals were capable of penetrating the sedimentary layers on the sea bottom, providing a cross-section view of what was below the surface. By this means objects buried in mud or sand could be imaged. The lower the frequency of the acoustic signal, the further down through the earth the signal would penetrate. Low-frequency signals gave a poorer resolution of image

ABOVE: *A side-scan sonar image shows the wreck of the* Shinsan Maru *on the sea bottom.*

than high-frequency ones, however, and a compromise had to be achieved between clarity and depth of penetration. The sub bottom profiler can only provide an image for a small area of the seabed surface at a time and therefore it is not of much use as a search tool in the first instance. It comes into its own once the target wreck has been found, in helping to locate objects which might have sunk out of view beneath the surface. It could be useful, for instance, on a project such as finding the remaining gold bars lost with the *Fort Stikine*.

SHIPWRECKS AND THE LAW

THE LAW SURROUNDING THE OWNERSHIP of shipwrecks and the cargoes they hold, together with rights of salvage, is extremely complex. The sources of this complexity are various. Wrecks lying in the territorial waters of individual nations are subject to the laws of those nations. The laws of Indonesia, for instance, an area rich in wrecks, provide that all wrecks in its waters are the property of the state regardless of any prior rights of ownership. Any company wishing to search for and salvage a wreck must first come to an agreement with the Indonesian government. Britain and the United States on the other hand recognize continuing rights of ownership, where ownership can be proved, but also acknowledge that the salvor is entitled to a salvage award.

In international waters there is no agreed law. The United Nations Convention on the Law of the Sea (UNCLOS), to which many but not all Western states are signatories, does not cover the issue of shipwrecks, indeed it specifically excludes it. There have been numerous attempts in recent years both by Unesco and the EEC to draft legislation covering the salvage of wrecks in international waters, but so far all attempts at getting an agreement among the various parties have failed. A salvor who operates in international waters is not entirely beyond the reach of the law, however, because it is ultimately necessary to land the recovered cargo somewhere, and when salvaged cargo is landed the salvor comes under the jurisdiction of the country into which it has been taken.

Salvage law is complicated by the fact that different nations have different views on how far their territorial waters extend. Some nations, such as Britain, work on the basis of twelve miles, which is increased a further twelve miles by what is now known as the contiguous zone, a kind of half-way house between territorial waters and international waters. Territorial waters are not to be confused with economic zones, which under UNCLOS extend to 200 miles. A shipwreck can lie in a nation's economic zone but still be in international waters. Other countries that are not signatories to UNCLOS take the view that their territorial waters extend to 200 miles or more. An already confused scenario becomes further muddied by the fact that a number of nations, the United States pre-eminently among them, insist that they have absolute rights of ownership over their lost warships wherever in the world they are sunk and will protect that right, if necessary by force. Notoriously, however, this did not stop the CIA, at the height of the Cold War, from sponsoring the salvage of a Russian nuclear submarine lost in international waters at a depth of 7,000 feet – the most expensive salvage project ever undertaken. This principle of absolute sovereign rights over warships bears interestingly on the proposals of Paul Tidwell to salvage the Japanese submarine *I.52*. In practice many warships have been salvaged by nationals of other countries. Even the definition of a warship can become somewhat hazy. For instance, how heavily armed does a requisitioned merchant ship have to be to become a warship?

Another complication is the fact that most wrecks have many owners. First, there is a distinction between the owners of the hull, that is of the ship itself, and the owners of the cargo. To confuse matters further, on most ships there are usually the private belongings of crew and any passengers that might have been aboard. When one takes into account the fact that cargo, hull and personal belongings may or may not have been insured with multitudinous different insurance companies that subsume rights of ownership on paying out on claims, one can begin to appreciate the difficulties involved when sorting out issues of ownership. In certain extreme cases owners will even deliberately take legal measures to abandon their property in order to relinquish any responsibilities they may have with regard to that property, because a sunken wreck can be a liability as well as a potential asset.

In many cases ownership remains unknown. In these instances, any cargo or artifacts landed in Britain that derive from a shipwreck, where the owner is unknown and where there is therefore no salvage agreement with the owner, have to be deposited with the Receiver of Wreck, who keeps them in safe custody for a year and a day, taking appropriate measures to publicize their existence. The reason for the year and a day rule is to give any owners time to come forward and prove their claim. If at the end of this period no owner has come forward, then the recovered items become the property of the Crown if they have been recovered in British territorial waters. The Crown in turn usually makes a generous salvage award to the salvor to encourage salvors to come forward rather than conceal their finds. If the salvaged items came from outside territorial waters, then the Crown does not have a claim, in which case the entire property belongs to the salvor. This was the decision reached by the British courts in the Lusitania case. The Lusitania case, however, has become further complicated recently by the Irish Government's claim that the wreck is not in international waters but lies within Ireland's territorial waters.

When considering the law relating to shipwrecks it is important to realize that salvage law, throughout its long history, has primarily been concerned with the salvage of ships that are in distress, not ships that have already been wrecked or foundered. Historically, British Admiralty salvage law was formulated in order to encourage one ship to give assistance to another during times of distress or difficulty. Salvage of goods or hulls after loss was only a minor part of the law of salvage's remit.

Salvage law, as it developed, established the principle of 'no cure no pay', which is to say that if the assistance provided was not effective, then no liability existed on the part of the person to whom assistance had been rendered. The captain of the ship that was in distress also had the right to refuse any proffered assistance. If, on the other hand, assistance was offered and accepted, and proved effective in saving property, then the salvor had a right to a salvage award and had a lien over any property salvaged until that claim had been satisfied. A lien, however, was only a claim against the salvaged property, while the property itself still belonged to the original owner.

Another important concept was that of 'salvor in possession'. This elaborated the idea that the first salvor on the scene had a right to carry out the salvage unless he was proved to be incompetent. The principles of 'salvor in possession' and 'no cure no pay' extended to cargoes and ships that were already lost as well as those that were simply in distress. The law of salvage was encoded by the various nineteenth-century merchant shipping acts, and in 1910 there was an attempt to internationalize the agreement among maritime nations with the Brussels Convention. The force and guiding principles behind the elaboration of salvage law were essentially concerned with the preservation of property and life.

Shipwrecks and archaeology

Since the 1970s another entirely different set of principles has been brought into play. These relate to the shipwreck not as a piece of property but as a part of our cultural heritage that requires scientific investigation and conservation. A number of countries have now written laws regulating the activities of the salvor, laws which override issues of property ownership and which in many cases are intended to stop the commercial salvage of shipwrecks altogether. The United States introduced the Abandoned Shipwreck Act of 1988, which passed control of shipwrecks in US national waters from the federal government to the individual state and so helped to remove the shipwreck from the arena of salvage law to the domain of cultural heritage laws. The previous American concept of 'finders keepers' under salvage law, which was employed where no original owner came forward to make a claim, was no longer regarded as acceptable. Ownership was now clearly vested in the individual state itself. The British Historic Shipwrecks Act of 1973 was slightly different. Its concern was to regulate and license the excavation of historic shipwrecks and ensure that excavation and salvage were carried out according to proper archaeological principles. Ownership rights, however, were essentially unchanged. One must bear in mind that these new American and British laws

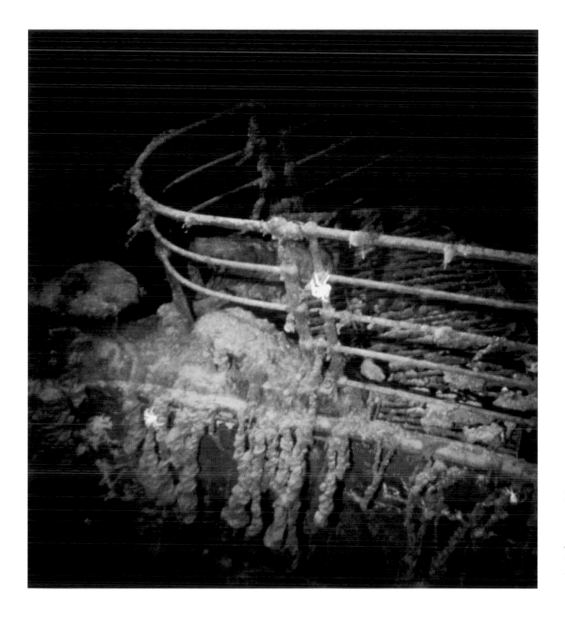

LEFT: *The curved forward bow railing of the* Titanic *immortalised by images from James Cameron's film showing Kate Winslet and Leonardo DiCaprio leaning over it in the manner of latterday figureheads.*

apply only within their respective territorial waters, and that other countries have developed their own laws for the cultural preservation of shipwrecks, some of which are more restrictive on the activities of the salvor, others less so. At present the situation in international waters remains unchanged by these laws.

There is, needless to say, much debate about when a shipwreck becomes historic and therefore worthy of archaeological interest. This debate has particularly come to the fore with the discovery of the *Titanic* and the consequent furore that developed about the raising of artifacts. The world's archaeological community has in general been fiercely opposed to the raising of artifacts from shipwrecks by anyone except archaeologists, arguing that only archaeologists are capable of understanding the full significance of the unique arrangement of these artifacts on the seabed. Some archaeologists even object to other archaeologists raising artifacts because that would be destroying the unique arrangement for future generations of archaeologists who may also wish to carry out their own excavations and studies.

A factor in this difficult debate that often does not seem to be taken into account by the archaeological community is that the bottom of the sea is not a benign environment where a shipwreck's remains will stay perfectly preserved for ever. It is not just the commercial salvor that interferes with virgin shipwreck sites. There are other far more destructive factors at work. Probably the most significant is deep-bottom trawling, which can drag wrecks apart and spread the artifacts over wide areas of seabed in a totally random, unrecorded manner. Added to this are the highly corrosive forces of nature itself. The scouring action of currents and sand movements and the pounding of artifacts against rocks are clearly perils for wrecks in shallow water. But even wrecks in deep water are subject to slow destruction through the activity of bacteria eating away the ferrous metal of the hull and creating deposits of rusticles.

There is also a numerical issue. What frequently seems to be glossed over in the archaeology versus commercial salvage debate is the sheer quantity of wrecks that lie beneath the sea. There are literally millions of them. Several thousands of steel ships were lost during the two world wars alone. Are they all to become protected sites? Out of the very large number of wrecks that are lying on the sea bottom only a very small percentage are of interest to the commercial salvor. To give an example, I was recently involved in a search in the Bay of Biscay for an iron wreck built around the turn of the century. In the course of our investigations, which took several years to complete, approximately ten wrecks of exactly the same period and style were located, examined and rejected before we finally came upon the right one. And this was within a limited search area of some 100 square miles. The other nine wrecks would be of no interest to a commercial salvor, but they would be of interest presumably to an underwater archaeologist. However, they are all in relatively deep water and would be very expensive to excavate. There is really no shortage of potential sites. What there is a shortage of is the resources to find and investigate them. Which is why, of course, it tends to be only the potentially commercially valuable wrecks that are searched for and discovered. One would have thought that this was a perfect opportunity for co-operation between commercial enterprise and state-funded university departments of underwater archaeology. Unfortunately, progress on this has so far been painfully slow.

SHIPWRECKS AS GRAVES

THERE ARE THOSE who accept that the case against the commercial salvor with respect to twentieth-century wrecks does not stand up particularly well on the basis of a consequent loss of scientific knowledge. They still object just as strongly, but their objections tend to take a different form. The essence of the argument is that the twentieth-century shipwreck should be saved from the depredations of the commercial salvor because it is a grave site. Again the *Titanic* has been very much the focus for these arguments, and it is essentially the reason given by Dr Robert Ballard for his objections to the raising of its artifacts.

The grave-site argument is a powerful one, raising as it does all kinds of deep psychic taboos relating to respect for the dead, though it is also fraught with illogicalities. The idea of a grave suggests an intention to bury and commemorate, and the deliberate

ABOVE: *The bell of the* U-20 *submarine which sunk the* Lusitania *off the southern coast of Ireland.*

choosing of a specific place for that ritual to be enacted. A shipwreck is, on the contrary, the random site of an accident, often terrible and the cause of great human suffering but an accident all the same. Fatal accidents happen all the time. If they take place on land the emergency services clear up after them. We do not leave wrecked cars by the edge of roads as grave sites. Nor do we leave wrecked ships in busy shallow waterways as grave sites. When the *Herald of Free Enterprise*, for instance, sank in a busy waterway off Holland with the loss of several hundred lives, it was quickly cleared away. The hull itself was in fact repaired and put back into service under a different name. It is only when ships are lost in deep water or in remote locations that they are abandoned and in later years develop the mystique of being a grave site. It is also worth pointing out that very few wrecks – sunken submarines tend to be the exception – have skeletons within them. Most bodies float away from the ship as it sinks. It is only when a ship sinks very fast and people are trapped somewhere within the hull and unable to escape that skeletons are likely to be found.

The theoretical idea of the shipwreck as a grave is not entirely logical, and in practice the attitude of the authorities to the concept has been notoriously inconsistent. The British Admiralty, for instance, has for a long time fostered the idea of the war grave to discourage diving on warships containing human remains. However, only warships lost on active service during the two world wars were deemed to be war graves. The term was not extended to the much more numerous merchant ships also lost during the two world wars, many of which sank after having been requisitioned. The British government was also quite prepared to overlook its own scruples when it was felt to be in its interests to do so, as for instance with the salvage of HMS *Edinburgh*. It is interesting to note that until quite recently the concept of the war grave was simply an administrative convenience and had no legal backing. In 1986, however, the British government introduced The Protection of Military Remains Act to toughen up its position on interference with war graves, particular because of certain activities which were known to have taken place on the wreck of HMS *Hampshire*. The new act gives the Secretary of State for Defence the power to designate known warship wreck sites as 'controlled sites', making any interference illegal without a licence, and also gives the minister the power to designate warships which have not yet been found as 'protected places'. The act also covers aircraft remains. Interestingly, it covers wrecks in both territorial and international waters, but because there is no internationally agreed law on wrecks in international waters, as discussed above, the act has the curious effect of discriminating against British companies and British nationals. This is because, while the act can prevent British citizens or companies from interfering with British warships in international waters, it cannot prevent citizens or companies of other countries from interfering with such wrecks because it has no jurisdiction over what foreign nationals and foreign companies do in international waters.

It is evident that law surrounding salvage is extremely complex. Issues of ownership and abandonment, archaeology and war graves, combined with conflicting or non-existent legal jurisdictions, all conspire to create a potential legal nightmare. In the light of this it is hardly surprising that so many salvage operations have ended up in the courts. What *is* surprising is that there are still sufficient adventurers prepared to give treasure hunting a go, in what can be a most frustrating business.

THE KLONDIKE NEWS

VOL. I — DAWSON, N.W.T. APRIL 1ST, 1898. — NO. I

OUTPUT FOR 1898 $40,000,000.

FROM Nº 8 EL DORADO.
PROPERTY OF CHAS. LAMB.
VALUE $315ᴹ

SCHMIDT L. & LITH CO. S.F.

DISCOVERER,
GEO. W. CARMACK.

THE LARGEST GOLD NUGGET.
FOUND ON EL DORADO CREEK Nº 36 BY M. KRUSTER
WEIGHT 35 OUNCES VALUE $530⁵²

THE ISLANDER
ICE GOLD

IN AUGUST 1896 A DETERMINED prospector by the name of George Carmack succeeded in panning gold from a small creek of the Klondyke River, itself a tributary of Canada's mighty Yukon River. From that day on it became known as Gold Bottom Creek and the last of the great nineteenth-century gold rushes had begun. In many ways it was to be the most spectacular and craziest of them all. At the western edge of Canada, near the Alaskan border and approximately 200 miles from the Arctic Circle, the Klondyke is in one of the most inhospitable and least accessible corners of the world. Nevertheless, miners, dance-hall girls, crooks and dreamers were soon pouring in by the thousand and large new towns like Dawson City sprang up overnight. The end-of-the-century stampede for quick riches was on.

ABOVE: *George Carmack, the first man to pan gold from the Klondyke River.*

LEFT: *The main street in Dawson City on 4 July 1899. Dawson sprang up overnight with the stampede for gold.*

OPPOSITE: *The Klondyke was the last, the toughest and the shortest lived of the great nineteenth-century gold rushes.*

RIGHT: *A view of Skagway which was preferred to Dyea as a port because of its wharves.*

In the early years the only way into the Klondyke was by ship to Skagway, followed by the long trek over the mountains either on foot or horseback to Lake Lindemann, before picking up the shallow draft boats or scows that navigated the lakes and rivers that led eventually to Dawson City. It was the kind of journey that would have deterred all but the most intrepid or the most foolhardy. But from the moment that a tiny steamer called the *Portland* docked in Seattle on 17 July 1897 with two tons of Alaskan gold nuggets in its holds the doubters were vanquished, the faithful were vindicated, and eager thousands flocked to these frozen gold-fields to try their luck. The transportation companies could not cope with the sudden demand, and ships northbound along the British Columbia coast were frequently overcrowded. One ship, the *Williamette*, carried 800 people and 300 horses and yet was only equipped with a dining-room for sixty-five passengers. A passenger aboard another steamer, the *Amur*, described conditions on board as 'a floating bedlam, pandemonium let loose, The Black Hole of Calcutta in an Arctic setting'. Under such circumstances shipwreck and disaster were not infrequent. The *Nancy G*, the *Whitelaw*, the *Clara Nevada*, the *City of Mexico*, the *Corona* and many others were all lost in the icy waters off the northwest coast of America and Canada. But the most famous loss of the era is indisputedly that of the Canadian steamship the *Islander*.

The *Islander* was a small steamship of 1,495 gross tons, 240 feet long and 42 feet wide, built by Napier Shanks & Bell of Glasgow for the Canadian Pacific Navigation Company in 1888. For twelve years it plied between Victoria, British Columbia, and Skagway, and was regularly used by the first of the Klondykers, before the giant corporation Canadian Pacific Railway Company took over Canadian Pacific Navigation on 11 January 1901. The *Islander* did not survive long under new ownership – on 19 August that year the following cable from Reuter was received in Victoria:

The Skagway steamer *Islander*, belonging to the Canadian Pacific Alaskan Line, struck an iceberg near Juneau, Alaska, at 20 minutes to 2 in the morning of Thursday last, and foundered in 20 minutes. 65 of the passengers and crew were drowned, including the Captain. The steamer was less than a mile from the shore at the time and the water was perfectly calm. A number of bodies have already been recovered. 107 of the passengers and crew were saved, and have been brought to Victoria by the steamship *Queen* last night. Among those reported lost are the wife, daughter and niece of Mr Ross, Governor of the Yukon Territory, who were returning home after visiting Dawson City, Mr Andrew Keating and his two sons, lately arrived from England, Dr John Duncan, of Victoria, and Mr Douglas, a wholesale merchant of Vancouver. A returning miner strapped 8,000 dollars in gold round his waist. The weight of the money made the life-preserver topple over and he was drowned. A million dollars in treasure went down with the ship.

In the days that followed, further grim details of the disaster emerged. The *Islander* had left Skagway at six o'clock on the evening of 14 August. At two a.m. the following morning, as it was leaving the Lynn Canal, just off the southwest coast of Douglas Island, and running at its full speed of fourteen knots, the *Islander* had struck a submerged floating iceberg. At the time of the collision the ship was in the charge of the pilot, a Frenchman known variously as La Blanc and La Blonde. He later claimed at the inquest that if he had been allowed to beach the ship at the nearest point of land about half a mile away, all the lives could have been saved. Captain Foote, not realizing the severity of the situation, insisted on heading his ship further down the coast to where the beach was less precipitous. In no time

ABOVE: *Home-made gold panning equipment called a 'grizzly' by the prospectors.*

BELOW: *A rare photograph of the* Islander *built in 1888 by Napier Shanks & Bell of Glasgow for the Canadian Pacific Navigation Company.*

RIGHT: *The Al-Ki was another of the early gold carriers plying between Seattle and the gold ports of Alaska.*

at all the ship began to sink, bows first. There was a rush for the lifeboats and discipline broke down. A man went berserk with an axe. Some of the passengers were trapped in their cabins, the impact of the collision having distorted the structure of the ship. One survivor, a Mr Hinde-Bowker, recalled how he slid down a rope to a life-raft that was already in the water with eight to ten people on it. When the *Islander* sank, the raft was sucked under the water – when it re-emerged, there were only two or three people left clinging to it. A Dr Phillips of Seattle described how he had watched helplessly as his wife and child had been sucked down the ship's huge ventilation tube as it began to plunge beneath the water. He would have suffered a similar fate himself if his head had not caught the rim, enabling him to resist the tremendous downward rush of water into the doomed ship. Many of the passengers who survived mentioned how they had had to abandon a fortune in gold. Mr Brumbauer of Portland, Oregon, left behind $14,000 in gold dust in his satchel rather than jump with it and risk making a hole in the bottom of the lifeboat through the force of his landing. A Mr D.H. Hart lost $40,000, Mr Manlin of Winnipeg $4,000, and a friend of his a further $3,000. One miner was reported to have taken his portmanteau containing $40,000 of gold nuggets from the care of the purser and jumped into the sea still holding it. Captain Foote stayed on the bridge, as captains are supposed to, until his ship sank. He was one of those drowned. One eyewitness told of how the captain swam to a life-raft, but realizing there were already too many clinging to it, swam away again saying, 'I see there are too many here, so goodbye, boys.'

Afterwards Captain Foote came in for much criticism. He was blamed for not heading the ship for the nearest land and for not immediately lowering the lifeboats. Information later emerged, however, that went some way towards exonerating his behaviour. He might well have expected the ship to float longer than it did, it was said, because he was unaware that the door to the watertight bulkhead that sealed off the foremost compartment, the forehold, had been opened. Apparently, when the ship's bows struck the iceberg, there had been a stowaway in the forehold. When water rushed in, the man had immediately started hammering and yelling to be released, and a sailor on the deck above, hearing his cries, went below and opened the watertight door. Immediately, water rushed through, throwing both men to one side and making it impossible to close the door again. Stowaways were very much a feature of the period – after the collision it emerged that there had been as many as ten on board.

A more pertinent question that seems not to have been asked at the inquest was why the *Islander* was travelling at such speed when an iceberg had already been sighted shortly before the collision and, by the pilot's own admission, the weather was cloudy. According to several of the survivors, at the time of the accident a dense fog surrounded the ship, making it very difficult for the boats to locate the land except by sound. In such conditions, along a narrow channel, a speed of fourteen knots was most certainly far too high.

In the aftermath of the tragedy there was no talk of salvage. The *Islander* had gone down in forty fathoms (240 feet) of water, beyond the limits of contemporary salvage. The *Skyro* and the *Alfonso* had both been partially recovered in 1890s, but they had sunk at a depth

LEFT: *Crates of Klondyke gold being loaded on board ship. The total value was 1.5 million dollars.*

of approximately thirty fathoms, and even then the divers had had great difficulty in reaching the valuable cargo and had had to abandon their attempts half-way through. There is a report that $4,000 worth of gold was salvaged in 1904, but the details are vague. The *Islander* was soon forgotten. Other, bigger tragedies captured the public's imagination and filled it with horror, most notably the loss of the *Titanic* in 1912.

By the 1930s the era of the Klondyke Gold Rush was already a distant memory. But the *Islander* treasure lived on in local bar-room gossip in Seattle, transit point for many of the earlier shipments. Diving technology had moved on during the last thirty years, and thirty fathoms was no longer considered such a forbidding depth. An enterprising local salvor named Frank Curtis was not intimidated. Convinced that the *Islander* held $3 million worth of gold, he set out on 25 May 1931 with a barge and diving bells to search for the rotting hulk. The bell was a giant steel-cast shell with powerful lights and its own air purifier.

By March 1932 the wreck had been located and various artefacts recovered to prove conclusively that Curtis had found the right ship, including an 'SS Islander' nameplate from a cash register. The Curtis team had also recovered a leather pouch containing $5,000 of gold, a small taste of what they expected to find. The salvors' plan was not to salvage the ship where it lay on the seabed, however, but to slip a huge steel cable beneath the wreck, lift it with powerful tugs, and beach it nearby. This salvage concept had been in use for thousands of years, but not with an iron ship of the size and gross tonnage of the *Islander*. The salvors spent two years overcoming a variety of technical problems before the damaged structure was finally freed from the clinging suction of the seabed. It was not just the laws of physics that the divers had to contend with. Senior diver Charles Huckins of Seattle gave a graphic account of his battle with a giant octopus at a depth of 365 feet:

> One day while working at the stern of the ship in darkness caused by sand being pumped out, I straightened up and my helmet came into clear water. Three feet away was a monstrous devil-fish. I drove my spear into his body. He was about 16 feet across. He scuttled away, tentacles waving. Later I was being lowered through murky water to the wreck deep in the ocean, when I stepped on something soft and slimy. I was feeling around to locate my cable when something wrapped around my right leg. I grabbed a blade of the port propellor and tore myself loose and went to the surface. I came back with my spear and started hunting for him. I happened to glance upward and there on the upper blade of the starboard propellor, four feet above me, was an octopus at least twice as large as the one I had stepped on. I slashed at him. The spear glanced off the propellor blade, but ripped a hole a foot long in him. His tentacles groped 15 feet reaching for me. I realized he would be 28–30 feet in diameter. I had never seen one of such great size in Alaskan waters. Well, I stabbed him and he finally went for deep water.

Making use of each high tide, the *Islander* was moved inch by inch towards the shore. It was finally beached on Admiralty Island at the beginning of August 1934. It was a great technical triumph. The whole operation had cost $200,000 – an immense sum of money in those days – but the salvors were confident that their outlay would soon be recompensed many times over.

ABOVE: *An aerial view of the Yukon River.*

With the ship now on the shore, it became obvious that the decks had collapsed as a result of the collision with the iceberg. The salvors' task now was systematically to cut through the remains of the ship in order to locate the $3 million fortune in gold that was supposedly contained within the hull. Although far easier to accomplish on dry land than at a depth of forty fathoms, it was still a relatively arduous and unpleasant task as the hull was full of mud and barnacles and the odd human bone. Small parcels of gold did come to light. Gold and currency worth $8,000 were found in the ship's safe, and several other small amounts were recovered, reaching a total of $50,000. It was not, however, the enormous reward the salvors had anticipated.

The results were disappointing. But salvors as a breed are stubbornly optimistic. If the gold was not within the section of the ship that had been recovered, then it had to be somewhere else. It was recalled that the salvage operation, while a technical success, had not gone entirely smoothly. As the hull had swung suspended from steel cables between the two salvage ships there had been a fierce storm which had caused the already stoved in bow of the *Islander* to tear apart and drop off. The bow still lay in 190 feet of water some 2,000 feet from Admiralty Island. The salvors now focused all their hopes of salving further treasure on that bow section. Investors, however, are not always as optimistic as salvors. It is not clear from surviving reports how thoroughly the bow section was investigated, if at all. What is evident is that no more gold was recovered and what remained of the *Islander* was allowed to rest in peace.

ABOVE: *Gold in its nugget state. It was in this form that gold was shipped on the* Islander.

33

MARUNOUCHI HOTEL
TOKYO

Cable Address: "MARUHOTE" TOKYO
TEL: (23) 0271~9・4161~9

6. I have made a provisional booking with BOAC to leave here on Sunday 12th September in flight BA 963/771 arriving London Terminal 1730 Sept 16th. This is of course if I have had any success with the main object of my visit, sh should you think I should stay on in connection with A.Nakhimoff please cable me on receipt of this letter.

Yours sincerely

G H A Williams.

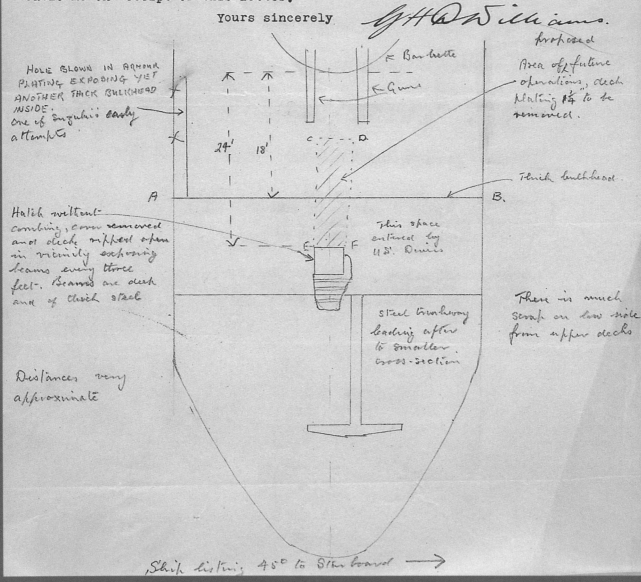

HOLE BLOWN IN ARMOUR PLATING EXPOSING YET ANOTHER THICK BULKHEAD INSIDE.
One of Suzuki's early attempts

proposed
Area of future operations, deck plating 1¼" to be removed.

← Barbette
← Guns

Thick bulkhead.

Hatch without combing, cover removed and deck ripped open in vicinity exposing beams every three feet. Beams are deck and of thick steel

This space entered by 45' Davis.

There is much scrap on low side from upper decks

Distances very approximate

Steel trunkway leading after to smaller cross-section

Ship listing 45° to Starboard →

THE ADMIRAL NAKHIMOV

TREASURE ON TAP

ABOVE: *Admiral Togo who commanded the Japanese Imperial fleet at the battle of Tsushima in 1905.*

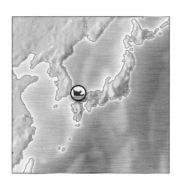

O N 14 OCTOBER 1980, eighty-three-year-old Ryoichi Sasakawa, a prosperous businessman and Chairman of the Japanese Shipbuilding Industry Foundation, held a press conference at the Tokyo Press Club. Next to him on the podium was a small grey ingot. Made of platinum, it was stated that the ingot had been salvaged from the Russian armed cruiser *Admiral Nakhimov*, sunk on 28 May 1905 by the Japanese fleet during the Russo-Japanese war. The ingot itself was fairly insignificant, but it was reported to be only a tiny part of treasure worth £1,000 million that had already been raised according to newspaper reports. The total value of the treasure to be recovered was expected to exceed £1,700 million. There was mention of 5,500 boxes, each containing 5,000 British gold sovereigns, together with 30 platinum bars and 48 gold bars. It was a spectacular start for an operation that had only begun some two months beforehand, especially given that fifty years of previous salvage efforts that had reaped no rewards at all. The *Nakhimov* immediately became the richest treasure ship of all time – or the most hyped. There were articles in *Time* magazine and *Newsweek*. The Soviet ambassador in Tokyo, Boris Zinovjev, promptly called on the Japanese Foreign Ministry and claimed that the lost treasure belonged to the USSR. Sasakawa then infuriated the Russians by offering to give them the entire cargo of the *Nakhimov*, if they in turn promised to give back the Kurile Islands, which they had seized at the end of the Second World War. A state of diplomatic impasse ensued.

The story of the Admiral Nakhimov began in February 1904 when, provoked by recent Russian territorial expansionism in the East, Japan carried out a surprise torpedo attack on the Russian Far Eastern Fleet in Port Arthur. The Russo-Japanese War had begun. The early months of hostilities were inconclusive, but by October a Russian reinforcement fleet that included four new Borodino-class battleships was ready to depart from the Baltic Sea. Tsar Nicholas II hoped that deploying a strengthened navy would reassert Russian control over the Eastern seas. One of the older ships was the *Admiral Nakhimov*, an armed cruiser of

ABOVE: A *letter from a Tokyo Hotel in the 1950s by British shipwreck researcher Commander G.H.D. Williams. It shows the state of that part of the wreck where it was thought the treasure had been stowed.*

RIGHT: *The* Admiral Nakhimov *was built in 1885. It was the most important ship in the Russian fleet, but was, however, one of the faster ships and for this reason it may have been selected for a special mission.*

BELOW: *Part of the Russian fleet followed the Cape of Good Hope route to the Far East around the Southern tip of Africa, others came through the Mediterranean Sea and the Suez Canal as shown in this illustration.*

8,524 gross tons, 333 feet long, with a crew of 567. Built in 1885 and then largely reconstructed in a British shipyard in 1899, the *Nakhimov* had eight 6-inch guns and ten 4.7-inch guns. It was an unspectacular war vessel, but it did have a top speed of 17.5 knots, and it was for this reason that it had been selected for a special mission.

The Russian fleet, under Admiral Rozhdestvensky, entered the North Sea on 20 October 1904. The competence of its command quickly came into question when, on 22 October, Russian guns opened fire on the Hull fishing fleet in the mistaken belief that they had run into Japanese torpedo boats – a fairly unlikely proposition in the North Sea. The result was the sinking of four innocent trawlers. In the general confusion the Russians even managed to fire on their own ships. It was not a good omen. There were those in the British Admiralty who wanted to launch an immediate attack on the Russian fleet as a reprisal, but more pacific counsel prevailed, and the Russian fleet passed through the English Channel without further incident. They followed the Cape of Good Hope route round the southern tip of Africa, pausing in Madagascar as they waited for further supplies to come through the Suez Canal and down the east coast of Africa.

On 27 May 1905, some eight months after setting out, the Russian fleet was in the Tsushima Strait between Korea and Japan, *en route* to Vladivostok, when it sailed within range of the guns of the Japanese Imperial fleet, lying in wait for them under the command of Admiral Togo. The Japanese fleet was smaller than the Russian but it had state-of-the-art design and equipment thanks to British technical assistance. Their superior manoeuvrability, combined with better-trained crews, resulted in one of the most disastrous and humiliating defeats inflicted on any nation in maritime history. Within twenty-four hours the Russians had lost all eight of their battleships and four cruisers. An enormous number of personnel were killed or drowned. The *Admiral Nakhimov* was among those ships damaged during the initial mêlée. It was discovered by two Japanese destroyers the following day, off the island of Tsushima. Most of its crew were taken off, and the *Admiral Nakhimov* sank almost immediately afterwards in over 300 feet of water.

The *Admiral Nakhimov* was far from being the most important of the various ships lost on that day. It is the ship, however, that has repeatedly been the subject of heated discussion in subsequent years. The explanation for this is quite simple – the lure of gold. Stories of fabulous sunken treasure aboard the *Admiral Nakhimov* began to surface soon after the battle, but salvage was not technically feasible at that time. Almost twenty years later, an ambitious teacher in the Japanese Naval School, by the name of Suzuki, began to dream about the *Admiral Nakhimov*. In 1905 he had been on the training staff in one of Admiral Togo's ships, having spent the previous three years learning navigation in England. In early 1932 he met Hishida, an old friend, in a Tokyo restaurant. That meeting was to change Suzuki's life. He would spend the rest of his days, over thirty years, in an unending quest for the *Admiral Nakhimov* treasure. Even though he never succeeded in salvaging a single penny Suzuki's faith in the treasure never once wavered. His belief was based on the information provided by his friend Hishida.

Hishida told Suzuki that another friend, Tanaka, had recently been approached by two Russian survivors of the battle, the 2nd Paymaster of the *Admiral Nakhimov*, Suzanov, and Rear-Admiral Natralof from the Russian flagship *Suvorov*, with a proposal for salvaging the gold and platinum on board the *Admiral Nakhimov*. There were various further items of supporting evidence. The Japanese government had received reports on 25 October and 19 November, from their embassies in Paris and Berlin respectively, that the Russians had succeeded in selling foreign bonds for 700 million French francs and 800 million German marks, all of which had apparently been converted into pounds sterling and placed on board the *Admiral Nakhimov*. In 1905 the Japanese Army Information Office had been informed that a Russian warship had left Libau with £20 million sterling on board.

LEFT: *The Russian warship* Petropavlovski *is shown sinking. The Japanese inflicted a severe defeat on the Russians who lost in total eight battleships and four cruisers within twenty-four hours.*

There was also a wealth of anecdotal evidence. Ninety-nine members of the *Admiral Nakhimov* crew were landed at Mogihama on Tsushima Island. All of them carried gold sovereigns – some £20,000 worth. Some of the Russian prisoners disclosed to a Mr Saibe, a villager on the island, that the *Admiral Nakhimov* had carried great sums of gold. Mr Saibe had attempted his own salvage operation soon after the *Admiral Nakhimov* sank, but one diver from the island had already died in the attempt and the wreck had not been found. Even the *Admiral Nakhimov*'s behaviour during the battle was considered suspicious. It had tried to flee from the main mêlée and make for Vladivostok. The Captain had then attempted to blow the ship up. When the Japanese boarded, they were forbidden to go below deck. The stories proliferated. Suzuki was even convinced that he knew exactly where the gold had been stowed. He had made the acquaintance of a tortoiseshell merchant called Eiso Ezaki, from Nagasaki City. Ezaki moved extensively in Russian circles, had friends in high places and had even constructed a model of the *Admiral Nakhimov* out of tortoiseshell for the Tsar. According to Ezaki the gold was stowed in the aft section of the third deck.

In August 1932 a team of 100 men began the search for the *Admiral Nakhimov*, deploying eight boats and dragging wires between them. At 11.00 a.m. on 16 January 1933 their efforts were finally rewarded. A large iron and steel vessel, fitting the dimensions of the *Admiral Nakhimov*, was discovered six miles east of Kami Tsushima on Tsushima Island. Salvage operations began almost immediately and continued until September. It became clear that the *Admiral Nakhimov* was not going to be an easy ship to penetrate. The hull was covered in fishing nets and the aft end was a mass of tangled steel plates. It all had to be blown up by means of carefully placed explosives and removed section by section. The team did not have the necessary financial resources, nor did it have adequately trained divers. The project was suspended pending refinancing.

Suzuki spent the next four years studying deep diving technology. The Japanese government were unable to provide assistance because the technical limit for diving at that time was 200 feet. Undeterred, he set about developing his own deep diving system. By 1937 he had a team of trained divers capable of descending 320 feet. He had also chartered a specialist salvage vessel and purchased a high-pressure compressor for feeding compressed air to his divers when at depth. Operations continued from 1938 to 1942. The diving logs for these years are a monument to human tenacity. The statistics for 1938, for instance, indicate 89 days worked, 349 dives made, using six divers and 22 back-up crew. In 1939, 121 days worked, 566 dives made, using eight divers and 19 back-up crew. In 1940, 107 days worked, 636 dives made, using eight divers and 23 back-up crew. Methodically and painstakingly, the wreck was removed piece by piece. Divers could only spend ten minutes working on the bottom and could only make one dive every twenty-four hours. Each diver was working in a tangled maze of collapsing decks, shafts and armoured plating, with a maximum visibility of twelve feet. Furthermore, dives could only be made at times of slack tide when the weather was good. Progress was slow.

When Japan entered the Second World War, operations were suspended and all the divers and crew were conscripted into the Japanese navy. All work on the *Admiral Nakhimov* was stopped. In February 1944 the Japanese government itself ordered Suzuki to recommence operations for salvaging the gold on the *Admiral Nakhimov* and financed the operation to the tune of $500,000. Within a few months of renewed operations, aerial bombardment by the American airforce became so severe that again all salvage work had to be suspended.

LEFT: *A tortoiseshell model of the* Admiral Nakhimov *given to the Tsar by a tortoiseshell merchant called Eiso Ezaki. Ezaki apparently had friends in Russian court circles who had told him that the gold had been stowed in the aft section of the third deck.*

After the war Suzuki was advised not to restart operations until the peace treaty with the United States had been signed. This meant a further delay until 1953. Then, with political considerations finally out of the way, Suzuki started once again on his quest for the *Admiral Nakhimov* millions, this time in a joint venture with an American corporation, the Pacific Far East Salvage Company Inc. Suzuki was asked some sceptical questions by the company. Why was so much gold sent by a long and perilous sea route when it could have been sent overland? Suzuki's answer was that the Trans-Siberian railway was insecure because the Tsar had only shaky political control over various parts of the hinterland, making the sea route the only sensible possibility. But why was so much gold being sent in the first place? Again Suzuki had a plausible explanation. The Tsar was anxious to build up Vladivostok as a major port with its own arsenal and shipyards. The American investors, like most of the others who met him, found Suzuki a thoroughly convincing and impressive character. They soon agreed to participate.

One of Pacific's promoters, a Mr Swatosh, went over to Tsushima to observe operations at first hand and, in a letter to the shareholders, provided a fascinating account of Suzuki's operational methods.

> We arrived at the salvage ship at 1130 hours on 8 October. The salvage ship is a 56 foot converted diesel fishing boat of about 35 tons, with a 14 foot beam. The ship was at anchor and there was an air of relaxed waiting aboard, with very little evidence of activity. We went aboard and I asked Mr Hamada, Chief Engineer, why they weren't diving. He took me to the rail of the ship and pointed out a piece of chalk line that extended out from the ship at an angle of about 60 degrees. He explained that there was a weight on the end of the line to determine the amount of tide. He said that if the surface wind remained as it was they would be able to start diving in about two and one half

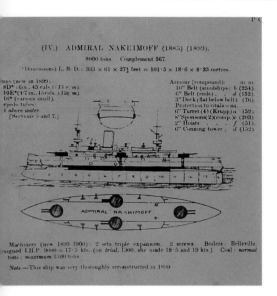

(IV.) ADMIRAL NAKHIMOFF (1885) (1899).

8000 tons. Complement 567.

ABOVE: *Line drawing of the Admiral Nakhimov showing the placement of the 8, 6 inch guns and the 10, 4.7 inch guns, all of which had been renewed in 1899 in a British shipyard.*

hours. Then we lowered a weighted 6 inch white disk into the water to determine the clarity and we could see it at 85 feet which, he said, was better than usual. By 1300 hours the chalk line had sunk to an angle of about 20 degrees and the conditions were determined suitable for diving. We spectators were moved into the Captain's quarters for our own safety, the anchor was weighed and the process of placing the ship over the wreck was begun by lines to each of the four anchors. By slacking off on any line and taking in on the opposite one it was possible to move the ship to the exact spot desired.

. . . I noted the divers on their raised platform aft getting dressed for their dives. Each diver put on two or three pairs of white coveralls. Some divers wrapped a thin blanket around their torso between the pairs of coveralls. They wore Japanese sneakers and white knitted gloves. Honestly, if I had not observed the diving with my own eyes I would have found it extremely difficult to believe. But, there I was watching a man prepare to go down more than three hundred feet. Two men lifted up a heavy semi-circular lead belt which was secured to the front of the diver's waist and supported by web suspenders. They placed a folding knife in his breast pocket, and handed him a face mask which covered only his eyes and nose, and looked like the ones they use on the coast in the US for underwater fish spearing. There was a small tube connected to each side of the mask and to a valve that was held in the mouth. The air tube to the surface was connected to this valve. By biting on the valve the air was released into the mask. The theory of Mr Suzuki on deep diving is that below 180 feet a suit is more of a hindrance than a help because it prevents the water from keeping equal pressure on all parts of the body. He has lost no divers in many years of operations. As the diver is lowered the pressure of the air he breathes is increased as the water pressure increases on his body. After a briefing on the situation blackboard the first diver went over the side and started sliding down the lead in rope. The man at the rail called off the depths marked on the line secured to the diver, and Captain Kagimoto sat with one hand on a valve regulating the pressure of the air the diver was breathing. At 320 feet he was breathing air at a pressure of 200 pounds per square inch. In two minutes the diver was on the bottom and starting his work. He made a survey of the after deck and secured another lead in line to a predesignated beam. In four minutes he signalled to come up. The reverse procedure went into effect, with six men hauling in on the line and three men on the air hose, with the Captain, standing by the air valve, reducing the pressure as the man came up. The diver climbed aboard, removed his mask, and began to talk.

The next diver down placed a charge. The charge was fired electrically and the next man surveyed the damages and reported results. One 5 foot by 7 foot deck plate was knocked loose and also a brass porthole cover which was brought up by a later diver.

Sadly, Mr Suzuki's good accident record did not last for long after this report was filed. In June 1954 the superintendent of the divers, Mr Yoichiro Oshii, lost his life when his air tube became entangled with a gun.

By 1955 the Americans were beginning to lose confidence in the project. Doubt centred not so much on the original existence of the gold on board the ship as on the question of stowage. New theories were beginning to proliferate. Perhaps the gold was not stowed at the aft of the third deck. Perhaps it was in the magazine room beneath the aft gun turret. Ingenious theories were put forward to support this contention, such as the supposed fact that the aft guns were never fired during the battle, presumably because there was no ammunition in the aft magazine. But by 1956 no amount of clever theorizing could induce stockholders to come forward with more money. The *Admiral Nakhimov* project was once again suspended, and although Suzuki continued trying to resurrect the project to his dying day, he had run out of willing financiers.

From the perspective of the end of the twentieth century it is still difficult to know quite what to make of the *Admiral Nakhimov*. Did Sasakawa genuinely recover the enormous quantities of gold that he claimed, suggesting that Suzuki had been correct all along, or was the press conference nothing more than a massive publicity stunt as some have suggested? As always with treasure ships, the truth is difficult to get at. There are certain substantive historical facts, however, that do support the *Admiral Nakhimov* treasure theory. A loan to Russia issued by the Banque de Paris for 800 million francs, or £32 million sterling, was genuine enough, as was a German one for 500 million marks, or £25 million sterling. The German loan was most probably issued too late for it to have been used for gold loaded on the *Admiral Nakhimov*, but the French loan, issued on 13 May 1904, could well have been used in part for sending out to the East. Interestingly, a book by Sydney Tyler entitled *The Japan Russia War* and published in the US in 1905, long before treasure stories about the *Admiral Nakhimov* began to circulate, mentions Russia losing $75 million in gold. Unfortunately, he does not state which ship the gold was supposed to have been on.

What we can say is that the long years of *Admiral Nakhimov* exploration and salvage did produce one tangible benefit, for which the citizens of Fukuoka at least should be grateful. In 1938 one of the *Admiral Nakhimov*'s propellor shafts was pulled to the surface. It was made of a metal alloy consisting of 85 per cent copper, 7 per cent tin and 7 per cent zinc. It was bought by Fukuoaka City Waterworks Department and used to manufacture 30,000 taps for the houses of its citizens. It is not everyone who can claim to have a historic relic for a tap.

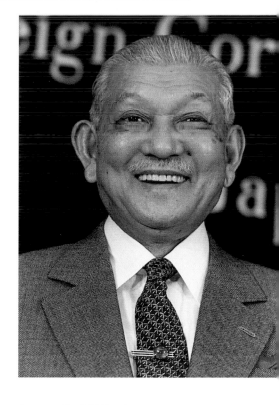

ABOVE: *Ryoichi Sasakawa masterminded a salvage operation on the* Admiral Nakhimov *in 1980, after which it was reported that treasure in excess of £1 billion in value had been recovered.*

LEFT: *A typical platinum ingot of the kind that Sasakawa presented to the world's press in 1980.*

THE REPUBLIC

'CQD'

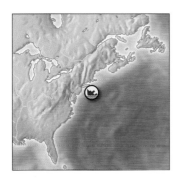

IN THE OPENING YEARS of the twentieth century the International Mercantile Marine Company, headed by the financier J.P. Morgan, bought up a number of rival passenger fleets including the White Star, Inman, Dominion and American Lines. In the space of just a few years IMM had established a dominant position in the transatlantic passenger trade. The *Columbus*, one of the Dominion Line's grandest ships, was purchased in 1904 and renamed the *Republic*. It had been built in 1903 by Harland and Wolff of Belfast, and, at 15,378 tons and 570 feet long, it was at the time of its fateful collision the largest ship ever to sink – a disaster record that was to be superseded by another White Star liner, the *Titanic*, three years later.

The *Republic* edged away from its moorings at three p.m. on Friday 22 January 1909 for its regular voyage between New York and the Mediterranean ports. On board were 228

ABOVE: *Captain Sealby of the SS Republic. Sealby stayed on board ship until shortly before it sank.*

LEFT: *At the time of its loss the SS Republic was the largest ship ever to sink. This unenviable record was overtaken by the Titanic only three years later.*

OPPOSITE: *Wireless operator John Binns with his Marconi apparatus pictured behind him. Binns spent fourteen continuous hours in an exposed and damaged wireless room, sending signals guiding the rescue ships to the sinking Republic.*

43

ABOVE: *The spacious boat deck of the* SS Republic. *The passengers were taken off the* Republic *by lifeboat in an orderly manner without mishap and transferred initially to the* SS Florida *until further assistance arrived.*

cabin passengers, 211 passengers in steerage and approximately 300 crew. The first-class passengers were mainly wealthy bankers and retired business people *en route* for luxury holidays in Egypt or Italy. Among their number were James Connolly, a famous writer of nautical stories, Alice Earle, an author, Mr W.J. Mooney, a wealthy Dakota banker, and General Brayton Ives. A few prospective passengers only joined the ship at the last moment. Mr and Mrs Hover arrived on the dockside at great speed in their new motor car just as the gangplank was being drawn up. Still more tardy, Dr Pietro Giliberti, the Italian commissioner, had to be ferried out to the moving liner on a tugboat. At 5.13 p.m. the *Republic* passed Ambrose Lightship, by which time it was travelling at its full speed of fifteen knots. It was already dark and shortly after its departure it ran into foggy weather.

As the *Republic* sailed eastwards, the Italian steamship *Florida*, owned by the Lloyd Italiano Line and much smaller at 3,231 tons, was travelling in the opposite direction. The *Florida* had only thirteen cabin passengers but carried 826 steerage passengers, mainly Italian emigrants, many fleeing from the Messina area after the disastrous earthquakes that had killed nearly 100,000 people there. The *Florida* also ran into thick fog, and as it approached Nantucket Island the 29-year-old Captain Angelo Ruspini was reduced to moving forward by means of taking regular soundings with the lead, searching out the thirty-fathom line and also looking for evidence of the sea bottom changing from sand to mud, both of which would help determine his position. The sea bottom to the west of Nantucket was muddy, sandy to the east. The drawback of this method of navigation was that, by following a contour line, the *Florida* was taken well to the south of the designated route for incoming liners.

Both Captain Ruspini and Captain William Sealby of the *Republic* were on their respective bridges, both ships had look-outs posted, and both ships were sounding their foghorns at regular intervals. The fog was so dense, however, that neither captain was aware of the other ship's existence until they were almost upon one another, by which time it was already too late. The *Republic* emerged out of the mist dead ahead of the *Florida*'s bows. The *Republic* turned to starboard and the *Florida* to port. There were those who later claimed that the *Florida* should have turned to starboard as well and that the move to port was a disastrous error on the part of its helmsman. But these accusations were fiercely denied by the *Florida*'s crew. The *Florida* accused the *Republic* of travelling too fast. Certainly the distance the *Republic* had covered since passing Ambrose Lightship would have suggested an average speed of fifteen knots, which was very fast for the conditions. But Captain Sealby stoutly maintained that he had cut his speed well before the *Florida* hove into view. Either way, the *Florida*'s sharp bow ploughed deeply into the *Republic*'s port side in the area of the engine-rooms, destroying, as it did so, five staterooms. The impact was so tremendous that thirty feet of the *Florida*'s bows were crumpled up. Three young Italian seamen were killed instantly. On the *Republic*, a Mr Mooney and a Mrs Lynch were also killed; her husband and a Mrs Murphy were seriously injured.

The hole gouged in the *Republic*'s side resulted in an inrush of water into the engine-rooms. Captain Sealby promptly ordered the bulkhead doors to be closed, which fortunately sealed off the damaged area from the rest of the ship and stopped the water from spreading. The engineers raked the fires down to prevent the boilers from exploding and then escaped up ladders with the water already three feet deep around them. Tarpaulins were draped over the ship's side in an attempt to slow down the ingress of water into the damaged area.

LEFT: *The* SS Republic*'s first class entrance and staircase. Many of the first class passengers were en route for luxury holidays in Egypt or Italy.*

The Marconi (wireless) operator John Binns immediately sent off a distress signal CQD (the code used before the adoption of SOS), meaning 'all ships danger', together with the *Republic*'s calling letters, KC. The *Republic*'s position was given as 40.17° North, 70° West. The message was picked up by the steamships *Baltic*, *Lorraine*, *Luconia*, revenue cutters *Acushnet* and *Gresham*, as well as the Nantucket wireless station and naval stations Newport, Woods Hole and Princetown. The reply signal G was received, meaning 'I am coming'. This was not actually the first time the wireless had been used in the circumstances of a sea disaster, as many of the newspapers erroneously reported, but it was certainly the first time it was to receive such massive publicity.

A number of passengers aboard the Republic recalled hearing two impacts, as if the *Florida* came forward twice before disengaging itself and drifting off, which is quite likely if the ship still had considerable speed on it at the point of impact. It was only when the lights went out that most of the passengers began to realize that there was something seriously wrong. It was 5.30 a.m. Soon the stewards were running along the corridors banging on doors and rousing everyone, instructing them to leave their cabins quickly without taking anything with them. General Brayton Ives was quickly to discover that his newly acquired and quaintly termed 'hand-held electric candle' was an extremely useful device in the circumstances. Captain Sealby assembled everyone on the promenade deck and calmed passenger fears. He told them that the damage was containable in the short term and that there was no immediate danger to life. He also explained that messages had already been sent off asking for help, and that he expected assistance to be provided shortly. The *Republic*, however, was already listing alarmingly to starboard.

On board the *Florida* it was evident that although the damage was serious there was little risk of the ship sinking. The forward bulkhead was holding, and again canvas had been draped over the damaged area to limit the ingress of water. As soon as his ship drifted off from the *Republic*, Captain Ruspini could no longer see it, but he could hear distress rockets being fired and the repeated short blasts on the horn that indicated that the other ship was in trouble. The engines of the *Florida* were still working, and so he was able to reapproach the *Republic* with all due caution. After a couple of hours spent re-establishing order on his own ship and then groping through the fog, he made contact again with the *Republic*. Messages were exchanged between the two captains and it was decided to transfer the *Republic*'s passengers by lifeboats to the *Florida*. According to the *Florida*'s purser, Maraviglia, the transfer began around 7.00 a.m. and continued until 10.00 a.m. The water was very calm and flat, and the passengers, including the injured, were removed without mishap.

When the CQD signal came through to the *Baltic*, this sister ship of the *Republic* was just approaching New York harbour. Captain Ransom had already been on the bridge for nearly thirty hours because of the dense fog. Without any hesitation, however, just as port was looming into sight, he immediately swung his ship round and set course for the position where the *Republic* was reported to be in difficulties, approximately twenty-six miles southeast of Nantucket Lightship.

On the *Republic*, Marconi operator John Binns was perched in his wireless room, three sides of which had been badly damaged at the time of the collision. The *Republic*'s power supply only lasted a couple of minutes after the engines were shut down, just long enough for Binns to get off the first distress signal. He had then gone below, to fetch the auxiliary

LEFT: *The* SS Republic, *settling slowly in the water, is photographed here by a passenger on board the Cunard ship* Luconia, *one of several ships that answered the CQD distress signal.*

batteries. The store room was already deep in water and Binns' clothes were drenched as he fished for the batteries among the floating debris. He succeeded in locating them, however, and, even more remarkably, the wireless apparatus still worked. He then spent the entire day and long into the evening shivering in his eyrie, constantly communicating with the various ships that were busily trying to find them, hidden in the dense fog.

By the middle of the Saturday afternoon the *Baltic* had reached the approximate position where the *Republic* was supposed to be, but the fog was so thick that it was impossible to see anything. The *Baltic* circled the area for hour upon hour without being able to discover the elusive *Republic*, which was meanwhile settling slowly in the water. Throughout this time the two ships were in continuous radio contact with each other, with Binns' messages becoming more and more desperate. Eventually, the *Baltic*'s foghorns could just be heard on the *Republic* through the mist. Binns now sent a series of signals of the blind man's buff variety. We're on your port side. You're getting hotter. You're getting colder. You're too close for safety. Eventually visual contact was made. Binns later stated: 'The most beautiful sight in the world is a ship at sea, especially when that ship is needed to supply a link between life and death.' It was now 7.30 p.m., fourteen hours after the collision.

For the next four hours the *Baltic* was alongside the *Republic*. The crew were taken off, but this would not have taken four hours. It was later admitted that the *Baltic* also salvaged from the sinking liner 3,200 sacks of mail. There was later to be some criticism that the White Star Line was wrong to prioritize the saving of its own property rather than attending to the welfare of its passengers. As well as mail-bags, there were also rumours that $250,000 worth of gold coin destined for Rear-Admiral Sperry's fleet at Gibraltar was removed at this point. At midnight the *Baltic* left the *Republic*'s side and began attending to the transfer of passengers from the *Florida*, both the *Florida*'s own and those that had earlier made the trip from the *Republic* to the *Florida*. The evacuation was carried out as it had been on the *Republic*. Women and children went first, followed by the men in first class, with the men in steerage left to the end. There was some suggestion that some of the first-class male passengers tried to push in before the women from steerage. James Connolly, the writer of sea stories, was criticized by a steward for cowardly behaviour, an accusation which he hotly denied. Some of the Italians also apparently drew knives but were dealt with firmly by the officers. As disembarkations go, it was more orderly than most and there was little panic. The transfer went on all through the night, the sea illuminated by the *Baltic*'s great searchlights, until about 7.00 a.m. the following Sunday morning. The injured Mr Lynch was in such pain that he refused to be transferred a second time, preferring to stay with the damaged *Florida*. He was to die from his injuries just a few days after finally reaching New York.

Late on the Saturday evening, Captain Sealby and a boat crew of some 35 men, including John Binns the Marconi operator, reboarded the *Republic*, which was still stubbornly refusing to sink. Their hope was that rescue tugs would shortly arrive and tow the liner into shallow water, enabling the ship to be beached and salvaged. It was about this time that the American whaleback steamer, *City of Everett*, owned by the Standard Oil Company, arrived on the scene, having also answered the *Republic*'s distress signals. The *City of Everett* was equipped with powerful pumps and towing gear and promptly offered to tow the *Republic* to safety. Captain Sealby refused the offer. The captain of the *Everett* was nonplussed. The refusal appeared to make no sense to him as he had a ship built for the job, though he may have been partly motivated by the lure of a handsome salvage award if he was successful. In any case Captain Sealby continued to refuse all assistance from the *City of Everett*. Sealby was awaiting the arrival of the two government cutters that he knew were on their way. It seems not improbable that Sealby was, in fact, acting on the orders of his White Star bosses. He had certainly been in radio contact with them throughout the crisis. Decisions regarding salvage were traditionally left to the captain alone, but interference from higher management was a likely if unpublicized consequence of the invention of the radio.

By 10.00 a.m. on the Sunday morning the second transfer had been completed and the *Baltic* headed for New York. The *Florida* also made for port, with the steamship *New York*, recently arrived at the scene of the collision, standing by in case of need. The Government cutter *Gresham* took the *Republic* in tow, and the steamship *Furnessia* took a line from the *Republic*'s stern to act as a rudder. During the previous twenty-four hours the *Republic* had drifted some sixteen miles closer to Nantucket Lightship and was now about ten miles to the south of it. The steamship *Lorraine*, which had also come to the rescue but had never managed to find the stricken ships, was informed by signal that its assistance was no longer needed.

The towing was painfully slow. By 4.00 p.m. on Sunday afternoon the bizarre little flotilla had made hardly any progress, and the *Republic* was settling ever lower in the water. Captain Sealby took the decision to abandon the ship a second time. The boat crew of thirty-five men were taken off. Sealby, however, refused to leave his ship and asked for a volunteer to stay with him. Second Officer Williams, the most senior unmarried man, volunteered. Captain Sealby arranged with the *Gresham* and the *Furnessia* that when he fired his pistol and lit two blue lights they would know that the *Republic* was going fast and they were to cut the lines immediately. If the escorts failed to cut the lines in time then they too would, of course, be dragged down with the sinking liner. The tow was recommenced, but progress was still very slow. At 8.15 p.m. the derelict destroyer *Seneca* joined the towing party, but by now it was already too late.

Meanwhile, Sealby and Williams decided on a last meal. Williams went down below and in the ship's pantry found a cake and a jar of marmalade. They smeared the marmalade over the cake and ate it all between them. Williams later described this delicacy as the best meal

ABOVE: *The crumpled hull of the* SS Florida *safely in dry dock in Brooklyn.*

"BALTIC." WHITE STAR LINE.

LEFT: *The White Star liner* SS Baltic, *sister ship of the* SS Republic, *was approaching New York Harbour when the* Republic's *distress message came through. The ship was turned around and was the first to discover the* Republic *in the thick fog*.

he could ever remember having eaten. At around 8.45 p.m. the *Republic*'s stern suddenly plunged downwards. Sealby turned to Williams and said, 'Well, old man, what do you think about it?' Williams replied, 'I have an idea it won't be a long race now, and when you are ready I am.'

Captain Sealby fired his pistol and lit the blue lights. The connecting hawsers were promptly severed with one blow from an axe that was kept ready for the purpose. Williams and Sealby both ran forwards. As the bow rose into the air, the deck quickly became too steep to climb up. Williams was thrown against the rails and dived over them. Captain Sealby climbed an amazing 100 feet up the foremast before he was washed off. Williams got hold of a piece of hatchcoaming and hung on to it. He was in the water for about twenty-five minutes before he was picked up by the boat from the *Gresham*. Sealby was in the water for a little longer before he too was picked up. Both men were cold and exhausted but otherwise fit and well.

As a result of all the radio messages that had been flying back and forth between the ships involved and the mainland, the public interest in the sinking was unprecedented. There were 5,000 people on the dockside when the *Baltic* finally steamed in. For days the papers were full of nothing else. Jack Binns and the wireless were the heroes of the hour. Senator Boutell of the House of Representatives stood up and claimed that 'Binns ought to be immortalized.' An editorial of the *New York Times* announced: 'The only gratifying feature of the incident is the proof it affords that the newest of man's inventions has greatly decreased the danger to human life at sea.' It was a reasonable observation in the circumstances, but in the light of the *Titanic* disaster three years later it sounds somewhat premature.

From early on there were many rumours that the *Republic* had carried gold, together with government stores. The source of the rumours was apparently a coastguard report. It was claimed that the gold was for the United States Battle Fleet. In this connection it is interesting to note that there was a report from Villefranche, in France, dated 24 January 1909, stating that 'as a result of the sinking of the White Star steamer *Republic*, fleet

RIGHT: *Martin Bayerle with some of the White Star china he salvaged from the wreck of the* Republic. *He has not altogether given up hope of one day recovering the gold supposed to be on board.*

paymaster McGowan left here hurriedly today for Marseilles.' The rumoured quantity was $250,000 in American eagle gold coins.

It was not until 1981 that the diver Martin Bayerle located the wreck of the *Republic* in 260 feet of water, 55 miles south of Nantucket Island. By 1987 his company Sub Ocean Salvors Inc. had raised $1.5 million to carry out a salvage project. An interesting collection of vintage wine bottles, White Star china and other artefacts were recovered, but no gold coins were found. In September 1987 the project was abandoned. It was considered that the strong currents in the area made operations too dangerous.

Whether the gold was ever on board, whether it was taken off by the *Baltic* or whether it is still somewhere inside the hull on the seabed is still unproven. What is certain is that a number of wealthy passengers lost considerable amounts of money and jewellery when the *Republic* went down. The White Star Line filed a claim for lost personal effects worth $305,000 on behalf of 136 of the first-class passengers. There were further personal claims running to more than another $200,000. The Scudder family, for instance, lost fifty pieces of personal luggage including valuable jewellery and a large sum of money. The unfortunate Mr Lynch lost a bag full of money, the whereabouts of which much preoccupied him during his last days alive. Many others lost similar amounts. It is unlikely that any of these valuables will ever be recovered.

OPPOSITE: *Two woven silk postcards of the ill-fated* Republic.

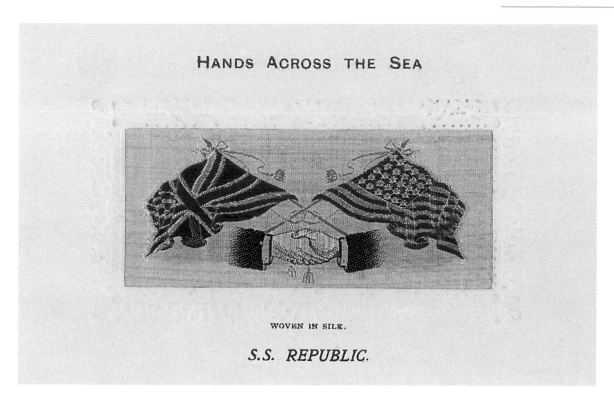

WOVEN IN SILK.

S.S. REPUBLIC.

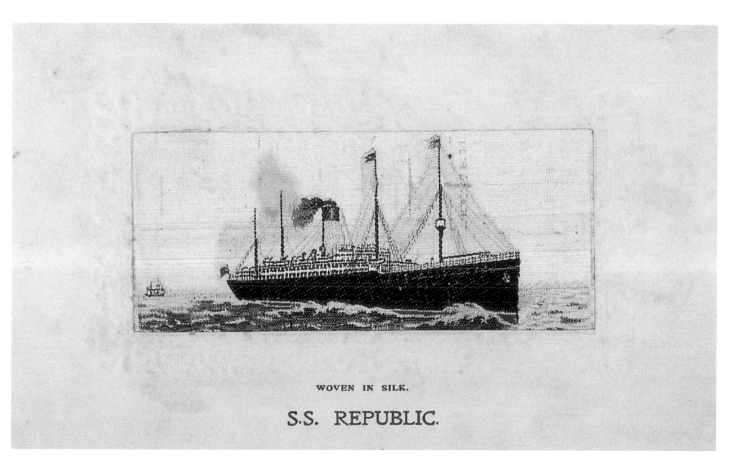

WOVEN IN SILK.

S.S. REPUBLIC.

THE TITANIC
THE END OF AN ERA

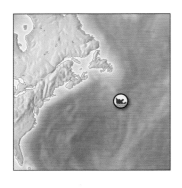

F ASCINATION WITH THE SINKING OF THE *TITANIC* appears to increase in direct proportion to our distance from the event itself. This growth of interest is partly explained, no doubt, by the discovery of the wreck on the seabed by a French-American team in 1985 and the superb photographic documentation that followed. Even this discovery, however, momentous as it was in terms of oceanic exploration, hardly explains the huge surge that the *Titanic* industry has undergone in recent years. The last decade has witnessed an opera, a Broadway musical and a new official inquiry, as well as many books, from a *Titanic* cookbook to a book claiming that the *Titanic* was not the *Titanic* at all but a completely different ship. Most importantly there has been James Cameron's $200 million blockbuster film, *Titanic*, a film about a legend which itself became a legend in the making and has broken all box-office records.

So why all the fuss? Even at the time of its sinking, the *Titanic* did not involve the largest loss of life in a shipping disaster. Nor was the cargo the most valuable ever carried – far from it. The sinking of the *Titanic*, however, ranks as highly in the public fascination as the assassination of President Kennedy or the death of Princess Diana. The comparison provides the clue. The *Titanic* story has those essential ingredients of death, glamour, money, heroism and treachery, as well as the allure of untold riches lying on the bottom of the sea, that are of such absorbing interest to us all.

After a year in the design stage, two years in the building by Harland and Wolff of Belfast, and a further year for fitting out and trials, the *Titanic* finally left Southampton at noon on Wednesday 10 April 1912 for its maiden voyage to New York. There were 1,842 people on board including both crew and passengers. This was just over half the liner's capacity, but its owners, the White Star Line, were still very satisfied with ticket sales. The *Titanic* was the largest and most expensive moving object ever to have been constructed, and this voyage seemed like a huge landmark in man's relentless technical progress.

ABOVE: *A rare contemporary watercolour of the* Titanic *in Harland and Wolff's Belfast shipyards in 1911.*

The first port of call was Cherbourg, in northern France, where a further 274 passengers boarded the ship. By 11.30 a.m. the following morning the *Titanic* had reached Queenstown in southern Ireland, where the final contingent of 120 passengers boarded, bringing the total number of people to be accounted for to 2,228. Eight people alighted at Queenstown – seven passengers, including Father Browne, whose photograph album of that first day was to provide a haunting document, and one crew member who had decided to abscond. He has a small place in history as probably the world's luckiest deserter.

The first four days of the voyage were uneventful. The *Titanic* gradually increased its speed as the new machinery bedded in, until it had reached a speed of 21 knots. Its top speed was 23–24 knots, a good two knots slower than the *Mauretania* but still swift by the standards of the time. The weather was good, the sea calm and there was much comment on how stable the *Titanic* felt. It was hardly like being on a ship at all.

At around 9.00 a.m. on Sunday morning, the *Titanic's* Marconi operators Jack Phillips and Harold Bride received a radio message from the *Caronia* warning of 'bergs, growlers, and field ice at 42° North, from 49° to 51° West'. The message was taken to the bridge, where Fourth Officer Joseph Boxhall read it and took no further action. It was not the first ice warning to be received, and throughout that Sunday numerous further warnings from various ships passing through the ice-field would be transmitted and logged on board the *Titanic*. It had been a warm winter and the ice floes were drifting further south than usual. At around 6.00 p.m. Captain Smith did order a slight change of course taking the *Titanic* slightly south of the normal transatlantic course. This was possibly done in the hope of avoiding the worst of the ice, but if this was the reason Captain Smith did not make his thinking on the subject explicit. At no time did the *Titanic* reduce speed. This was standard practice for liners in the vicinity of an ice-field at that time. Only when ice had actually been sighted was it customary to slow the ship, and the look-outs had seen nothing untoward.

It was early evening when those on board the *Titanic* felt the temperature suddenly drop – ten degrees in less than an hour. The weather was very calm and clear, almost supernaturally so. These conditions were not helpful when it came to spotting ice floes, because there was no breaking surf to be seen around the base of the berg, and the stars reflected so brilliantly off the flat water that it was difficult to distinguish between solid objects and the optical effects of phosphorescent sheen.

Towards 10.30 p.m. another westbound ship, the *Californian*, owned by the Leyland company and *en route* to Boston from Liverpool, saw a field of pack-ice ahead and came to a halt. As a precautionary measure, the *Californian*'s captain, Stanley Lord decided to spend the rest of the night stationary rather than risk collision with an iceberg. At around 10.55 p.m. Cyril Evans, the *Californian*'s Marconi operator, sent out a message warning of dense ice in the immediate area. His counterpart on the *Titanic*, Jack Phillips, heard the ice warning, and abruptly interrupted him to say that he was busy sending important commercial messages to Cape Race (in Newfoundland) and that Evans was jamming his signal.

At 11.40 p.m. Frederick Fleet, the look-out man in the *Titanic*'s tiny crow's-nest, positioned on the foremast some 50 feet above the deck, saw an iceberg dead ahead. He might have seen it earlier if he had had the usual binoculars, but for some reason this vital piece of equipment had been lost, mislaid or overlooked. However, at the subsequent Court of Enquiry, it was stated that the presence of binoculars would not have helped as they were only used to assist with identifying objects that had first been spotted with the naked eye. The warning bell was rung three times and on the bridge First Officer William Murdoch promptly ordered the wheel to be put 'hard-a-starboard', which had the effect of turning the ship's bows to port. The emergency bulkhead doors were shut to prevent the ingress of water throughout the entire ship, and the engines were ordered to be put full astern. The actions proved to have been made too late and the iceberg grazed along the side of the *Titanic*'s hull. Most of those on board hardly felt a thing. It seemed as if the great ship had given the merest shudder. The story was somewhat different in No. 6 boiler room, where stoker Frederick Barrett saw water gush in through a gaping hole in the ship's side. Unable to escape into No. 5 boiler room, he hastily climbed the emergency ladder to make his exit.

Captain Edward Smith, aged 62 and making his final voyage for his employers, was quickly on the bridge and ordered an immediate inspection of the damage. The *Titanic*'s hull was divided into sixteen watertight compartments by means of fifteen transverse bulkheads. The first five compartments – the forepeak, cargo holds 1, 2 and 3 and boiler room 6 – were all holed and flooding. The *Titanic* had been constructed so that damage to two watertight sections could be contained without endangering the stability of the ship. Damage to five sections was fatal. Captain Smith discussed the extent of the damage with Thomas Andrews, the *Titanic*'s senior designer, who was on board to smooth out any teething difficulties that might arise during its maiden voyage. Andrews calculated that the *Titanic* would only last between one hour and one and a half hours. It is one of the many ironies of the *Titanic* story that if the wheel had not been turned in an attempt to avoid the collision, probably only the first three compartments would have been crushed and the ingress of water might have been contained.

Captain Smith did not have the leisure to consider the ironies of the situation. He was responsible for 2,228 lives and had a lifeboat capacity of only 1,178. Even this number was

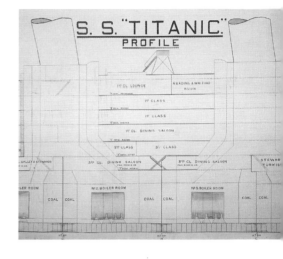

ABOVE: *Part of a longitudinal plan of the* Titanic *showing bulkheads between the boiler rooms.*

BELOW: *A telegram message from the* Titanic *received by* SS Birma.

BELOW: *A silver medal presented to the officers and crew of* RMS Carpathia, *the first ship to arrive at the scene of the* Titanic's *sinking having made great speed through the dangerous and shifting ice.*

significantly greater than Board of Trade regulations required. Fourth Officer Joseph Boxhall calculated the *Titanic*'s position as being 41.46° North, 50.14° West. Captain Smith went himself to the radio room and instructed his wireless operators to send out an emergency distress signal. The *Californian* was situated no more than twenty miles away, perhaps significantly less. The exact distance has been a subject of great debate by *Titanic* historians down the years. Cyril Evans, the *Californian*'s only wireless operator, had retired to bed, however, shortly before the *Titanic* sent out the first of its many, increasingly desperate distress signals.

During subsequent inquiries, both in Britain and the United States, it emerged that some of those on the deck of the sinking *Titanic* were convinced that they saw the lights of another ship. There were also those on the *Californian* who claimed to have seen the lights of another ship, and that they disappeared shortly after 2.00 a.m., around the time when the *Titanic* finally sank. Captain Lord had seen the lights himself and had asked to be kept informed of any movement. He also gave instructions for the duty officer to try to make contact with the strange ship by Morse code, using a lamp. This was unsuccessful; no reply was received. But duty officer Herbert Stone on the *Californian*'s bridge distinctly saw rockets being fired in the early hours which, with the benefit of hindsight, he realized could only have come from the *Titanic*. Captain Lord was informed about the rockets by Stone, but Lord dismissed them as probably being private signals. When further rockets were observed, a messenger was again sent to inform Captain Lord, who was by then asleep. Lord denied that he was ever given this message. He did recall the messenger coming to his cabin, but he claimed the man went away again without saying anything. Lord was to be severely criticized by the British Board of Trade inquiry for his failure to respond. The reputation of Stanley Lord has been a subject of great controversy ever since. His defenders claimed that there was another mystery ship in the vicinity that night, situated between the *Titanic* and the *Californian*, and that the presence of this ship had confused the situation. Interestingly, in 1962, fifty years after the sinking, a Norwegian captain called Henrik Naess admitted shortly before he died that his ship, the *Samson*, had been in the vicinity of the *Titanic* on the fateful night of 14 April. He had failed to respond to the distress rockets because he had been engaged in illegal sealing and he thought the rockets were signals for him to come to a halt and be searched.

Throughout the early hours of 15 April the *Titanic* continued to send out distress wireless signals that were picked up by numerous other ships over a range of several hundred miles. 12.26 a.m.: 'We have collision with iceberg. Sinking. Can hear nothing for noise of steam.' 12.36 a.m.: 'Sinking. Please tell Captain to come.' 1.25 a.m.: 'We are putting the women off in the boats.' 1.45 a.m.: 'Engine room full up to boilers.' After this the signals became indistinct, and at 2.17 a.m. they ceased altogether. A number of the ships which picked up the messages headed immediately towards the *Titanic*'s given position. The nearest was the *Carpathia*, under Captain Arthur Rostron, which was 58 miles away. Their usual top speed was fourteen and a half knots, but by firing up their boilers they managed to achieve seventeen knots through dense ice in the dark. It was a heroic effort and probably helped to save the lives of some who were already in the lifeboats but suffering from exposure. The *Carpathia* arrived on the scene of the disaster at approximately 4.00 a.m. – those on board were struck by the eerie silence of the debris-strewn sea.

The lowering of the lifeboats had started shortly after midnight, but the first boats to leave the ship were less than half full. The officers who survived explained that they had been

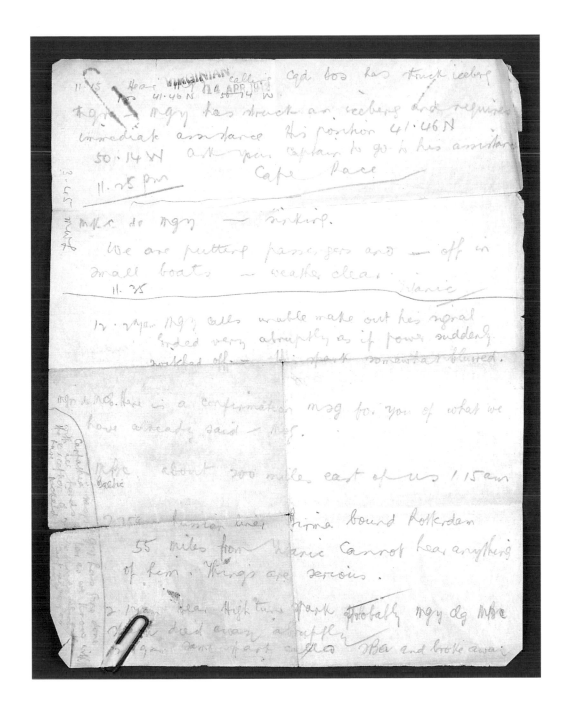

LEFT: *A hand-written radio signal received on board* SS Virginian

reluctant to fill the boats completely because of the strain on the davits during lowering. They had also expected that the boats would pick up more people out of the water. In fact, one of the great scandals of the *Titanic*'s sinking was that so few boats returned to the stricken ship once they had been safely launched. Sir Cosmo and Lady Duff Gordon in Lifeboat No. 1 came under particularly heavy criticism in the press because their boat had left with only twelve people in it, seven of whom were crew members, and yet they made no effort to return to pick up any of the drowning. The British Court of Inquiry, however, rejected these criticisms, upholding this behaviour as reasonable in the circumstances.

ABOVE: *A memorial picture of the* Titanic *musicians who died at their posts playing 'Nearer my God to Thee'.*

Another figure much pilloried in the American press was Bruce Ismay, the Chairman and Managing Director of the Oceanic Steam Navigation Company that owned the White Star Line. He was also one of the survivors. The *New York American* newspaper called him Brute Ismay. In his case the accusations of cowardice do seem somewhat misplaced. He did not leave the ship until 1.40 a.m., and up until then he had been helping others into the boats. He also claimed that when he got into a lifeboat there was no one else in the immediate vicinity wanting to get in.

There were other passengers, however, who certainly displayed great selflessness. Two such were Ida and Isidor Straus, major shareholders in Macy's, the world's largest department store. Ida refused a place in a boat, saying that she would stay with her husband. 'As we have lived, so we will die together' were said to be her final words on the subject. The couple, however, saw to it that their maid was put safely into a boat before going below decks to meet their end. Benjamin Guggenheim's behaviour in changing into evening dress for his final moments, together with his manservant Victor Giglio, was a similarly defiant and flamboyant gesture. But probably the most celebrated act of *Titanic* heroism was that of the band, under their leader Wallace Hartley, who continued playing right up until the ship's sinking, 'Nearer my God to Thee.' Statistics vary slightly, but out of the 2,228 people on board, only approximately 705 survived. Of the first-class passengers 94 per cent of women survived and 31 per cent of men. Of third-class passengers the percentages were 47 and 14 respectively.

The first talk of a salvage attempt came only a matter of days after the sinking. The Astor family were considering the recovery of the body of Colonel John Astor, who was among the victims. They approached the Merritt Chapman Wreckage Company, who considered that a salvage was feasible. Clearly they had no idea of the depth of water in which the *Titanic* had sunk, nor of the difficulties of finding a specific object such as a body inside a huge liner, even presuming that the body remained within the hull of the ship. The unlikelihood of the latter was quickly confirmed by Astor's body being recovered by the search ship the *Mackay Bennett*, sent to the area of the sinking with the remit to pick up as many floating corpses as they could find. The Astor family broke off discussions with Merritt Chapman. The *Mackay Bennett* picked up a total of 306 bodies, 116 of which were returned to the sea as being too disfigured for identification to be possible. Three other vessels picked up a further 22 bodies.

It was not until the 1970s that the idea of salvage again began to be taken seriously. There were by that stage a handful of underwater submarines that could reach the required depths, such as the *Aluminaut*, owned by the Reynolds Corporation, and the *Alvin*, owned by Woods Hole Oceanographic Institution. The idea was enthusiastically embraced by entrepreneurs like Douglas Woolley, who claimed that there was approximately £100 million in gold and silver aboard. Quite how such figures were reached was never fully explained. Equally vague was the evidence for the oft-repeated rumour that there was in excess of $5 million worth of diamonds in the strong-room. Woolley never managed to get a search expedition under way. The idea of finding the mammoth ship was very much in the air, however, and in the early 1980s Jack Grimm, a Texas oil millionaire, carried out what were the first serious, properly financed and scientifically credible searches for the *Titanic*, using a deep-towed side-scan sonar. Grimm organized three expeditions in total to the designated search area. There were numerous reports in the press that the *Titanic* had been found, but on each occasion detailed examination of the hopeful side-scan image proved negative. The

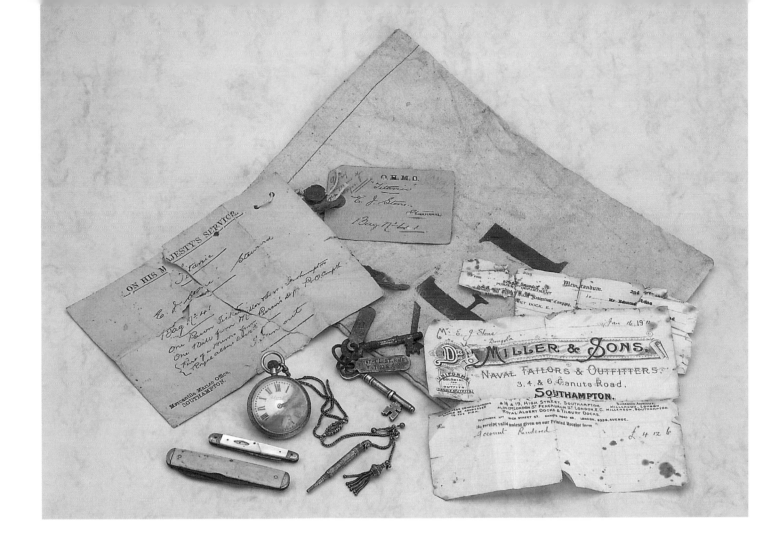

ABOVE: *A group of personal effects returned to the widow of Edmond J. Stone, one of the first class bedroom stewards on board the* Titanic.

business of finding the *Titanic* was becoming something of an international joke. There was even a suggestion that the giant ship must have been swallowed up by the huge ocean bed earthquake that took place in 1929, in the area where the *Titanic* was believed to lie.

As it happens the *Titanic* was not a treasure ship in the conventional sense. It carried in its holds a very run-of-the-mill mixed general cargo which included items such as wines, soap, rubber goods, golf balls, rabbit skins, cheeses, and so on. The total value of the cargo was less than £100,000 sterling and most of it was perishable. The specie room was stowed with opium rather than gold bars. And yet the name *Titanic* is synonymous with images of sumptuous wealth and splendour. Part of the explanation is to do with the ship itself. When, on 31 May 1911, it slid down its Belfast slipway into the water, the *Titanic* was, at 882 feet long and with a gross tonnage of 46,392 tons, the largest ship ever to be launched. It was also the most expensive, having cost its owners, the White Star Line, $7.5 million to build and to furnish. With swimming pools, gymnasiums, Turkish baths, a smoking room and its own library, the *Titanic* offered the ultimate in luxury to the transatlantic traveller. The grandest of the first-class suites cost $4,350 one way. The chandeliers on the famous grand staircase were supplied by Perry & Co. of Bond Street. The crockery in the à la carte dining room was Royal Crown Derby. The Goldsmiths and Silversmiths Company supplied the cutlery. When it came to soft furnishings, the ship was equipped with the very best that was available. In its massiveness and exorbitance the *Titanic* was the embodiment of that Edwardian love of solidity and comfort, and as such it was almost a floating denial of the very idea of a ship.

It was not just the structure and design of the *Titanic* that were lavish. Some of the passengers that boarded were equally flamboyant in their wealth. There were 337 first-class passengers on the *Titanic*'s fateful maiden voyage. Twelve of this number were multimillionaires. One of the richest was Colonel John Astor, recently divorced and now returning from a tour of Europe with his new, 18-year-old wife. When Astor's body was recovered, $2,000 was found in his pocket. It was because of these passengers, and the untold riches and jewels that they supposedly carried with them, that most of the subsequent rumours of treasure arose.

Certainly there were losses of jewellery and other valuables. Mrs Charlotte Cardeza's claim for lost jewellery, for instance, amounted to $104,753 and included two bracelets with fifteen diamonds in each, and a ruby ring bought from Tiffany's of New York. Hakan Bjornstrom-Steffanson lost a painting by Merry-Joseph Blondel, valued at $100,000, and William Carter lost his Renault automobile, valued at $5,000. All these losses are well documented. Other items, such as the fabled copy of *The Rubaiyat of Omar Khayyam*, the cover of which was sumptuously encrusted with gems, have a more legendary status. For salvors, however, the real value of the *Titanic* wreck probably lies not so much in the few scattered items of outstanding intrinsic value that could potentially be salvaged, as in the many thousands of small associative items for which the public has an insatiable appetite. *Titanic* memorabilia have commanded enormous prices in recent years. In 1994 a box of matches carried off the *Titanic* by one of the surviving crewmen fetched £1,450 at auction. The year before, a hip flask owned by Mr Hartley, the bandleader, and given to a woman as she got into a lifeboat, fetched £4,180. Third Officer Herbert Pitman's whistle fetched £3,410 in 1991, and in 1992 a set of 85 urgent wireless signals was sold for £66,000. The thousands of memorial cards, newspapers and other associative *Titanic* material are all keenly sought after by collectors.

In the early hours of 1 September 1985, the *Titanic*'s remains were finally discovered by a joint French-American project, led by Robert Ballard and Jean-Louis Michel of IFREMER, on board the Woods Hole research ship *Knorr*. The locator instrument used – *Argo*, owned by the American navy – worked as a deep-towed side-scan sonar, and carried cameras so that it supplied real-time pictures simultaneously with the sonar recording. The news of the find, together with the stunning visual images, took the world's media by storm.

The discovery of the wreck has answered certain technical questions that have long exercised the minds of *Titanic* devotees. We now know, for instance, that the ship did indeed break in two as it sank, confirming eyewitness accounts which the official inquiry had dismissed as unreliable. We also know that the collision with the iceberg did not cause a huge gaping hole, as was originally thought, and as was typically depicted in the many artistic versions of the calamity, but a series of quite narrow gashes. Similarly, we now understand that the steel used was particularly susceptible to fracture at cold temperatures. Information as to the exact longitude and latitude where the collision took place is now much firmer, and so we are in a better position to assess how feasible it would have been for the *Californian* to go to the rescue. The *Titanic* was in fact further off than was originally thought, though still near enough for the *Californian* to have covered the distance before the *Titanic* finally sank. However, the discovery of the wreck has also raised as many questions as it has answered, albeit questions of a different nature. They revolve around issues of ownership, the legality and appropriateness of salvage, shipwrecks as graves, and who, if anyone, should manage the cultural heritage of the seabed.

The *Titanic* is in international waters, and it is therefore open to anyone to search for it, film it and, should they so wish, salvage it, always presuming, of course, that they have the necessary technical and financial resources. There are two important caveats to this. First,

BELOW: *An artistic reconstruction of the submersible* Alvin *inspecting the bow section of the hull of the* Titanic. *It shows very graphically how the bow must have hit the seabed first and plunged deep into the soft mud crushing the metal plates.*

ABOVE: *One of the* Titanic's *deck benches photographed by a camera on the submersible* Alvin *strangely out of context on the seabed.*

whatever is salvaged still has a potential owner who has the right to come forward and lay claim to salvaged artefacts. In this case, however, the salvor is still entitled to a salvage award representing a percentage, usually a substantial one, of the value of what has been salvaged. Interestingly, Cunard, who eventually bought the White Star Line and who are therefore legally owners of the *Titanic*'s hull and fittings, have never made any claim to recovered artefacts. Secondly, any nation can, should it so wish, implement laws forbidding its citizens to salvage certain ships that lie in international waters or to prescribe in what manner that salvage is to be carried out.

The United States, as one of the leading players in international salvage as well as the main potential market for any salvaged items, was well aware of its responsibilities in respect of the *Titanic*. Almost immediately a bill was brought before Congress, 'To encourage international efforts to designate the shipwreck of the RMS *Titanic* as an international maritime memorial and to provide for reasonable research exploration and, if appropriate, salvage activities with respect to the shipwreck'. The bill was quickly passed into law, but attempts at coming to an international agreement got nowhere, and so as a means of regulation it proved totally ineffective. Congress was very aware that without international agreement any regulatory bill would be seen as discriminatory against American citizens, and so it has not pursued this route.

In 1987 RMS Titanic, the company that laid claim to the *Titanic* as salvor in possession, carried out a recovery of selected artefacts, in conjunction with IFREMER, the French Research Institute. IFREMER provided the technical expertise, including the services of its mini submarine *Nautile*, while RMS Titanic provided the finance. The salvors have been careful to record and catalogue the exact place from which each artefact was recovered as well as photograph and document each item in its pre-conserved and post-conserved states. The salvors have also pledged not to sell off and disperse recovered items. It would be difficult, therefore, even for the most non-interventionist of archaeologists, to criticize the salvage operation on the basis of a consequent scientific loss of knowledge. Nevertheless,

RIGHT: Titanic *Third Officer Herbert Pitman's whistle was sold by Onslow's, the auction house that specialises in* Titanic *memorabilia in 1991 for £3,410. Pitman was one of only three officers who survived the sinking.*

the salvage has caused outrage, particularly in the United States. The recovery process has been widely regarded as nothing short of the desecration of a holy place. Ballard, one of the original discoverers of the wreck, has been particularly outspoken in his condemnation. Ballard claims 'to have argued long and hard that the *Titanic* is a grave site that should have been left undisturbed'.

The objections have not stopped the salvage continuing. In 1996 RMS Titanic, again utilizing the scientific expertise of IFREMER, attempted its most ambitious recovery to date, bringing to the surface a section of the hull weighing several tons. The operation ended in failure. Rough weather caused the huge sheet of rusting steel structure to slip, just as it was breaking the surface, and plummet 15,000 feet to the seabed. Undefeated, in August 1998 RMS Titanic returned for another attempt and this time succeeded in safely landing their catch. The salvors claim that this sheet of metal has been raised for the purpose of further laboratory analysis. Their opponents argue that it is just another publicity gimmick.

Like millions of others, I found the sight of the great shipwreck on the seabed awesome and mournful, and consider its discovery and the subsequent photography to have been a superb technological achievement. But I also think that the exhibition of recovered artefacts provided a different yet equally valid experience of what happened on that fateful day, and that it would have been a loss if either the extremists amongst the archaeological community or the holy place lobbyists had prevented such a public viewing taking place. The *Titanic* exhibition leaves one with many powerful images. London's National Maritime Museum was criticized for giving prominence to a leather Gladstone bag. Personally, I think their choice of this item was absolutely right. The bag had the initials RLB embossed on it. Inside was found a mysterious assortment of different currencies, including both Canadian and American, as well as a collection of jewellery that had at one time belonged to a number of different people. There was only one passenger on board with the initials RLB, and that was Richard Leonard Beckwith, a first-class passenger who escaped with his wife Sallie in Lifeboat No. 5. It is possible that he left his bag behind him. It also looks as if whoever held it last had been busy rifling the staterooms for whatever jewellery and money they could find. Such behaviour was not uncommon on a sinking ship. Alternatively, the bag might have belonged to the second class purser Reginald L. Barker. Whoever owned it, the Gladstone bag was in remarkably good condition and has been superbly restored. It conjures up perfectly so much of what the *Titanic* has stood for over the years: a reckless and desperate scramble for the comfort of wealth even when staring death in the face.

Note

In the autumn of 1998 the endless legal wrangling took a further curious turn. Independently of RMS Titanic, another corporation hired the Russian research ship *Keldysh* with its mini submersibles, the *Mirs*, to carry out sightseeing tours down to the wreck. RMS Titanic obtained an injunction to stop this happening, on the grounds that they and only they were the legitimate salvors in possession and so no one else had the right to go there. To the would-be tourist operators this claim to visual privacy and exclusivity seemed like an unreasonable extension of the concept of salvor in possession, and the trips went ahead regardless of the threat of consequential lawsuits.

ABOVE: *The painted cast-iron house flag and name plate from one of the* Titanic's *lifeboats. These fetched an astonishing $70,000 at an auction in New York in 1998.*

THE LUSITANIA
A DOUBLE LIFE

AT THE BEGINNING OF THE FIRST WORLD WAR, both the Allies (Britain, France and Russia) and the Central Powers (Germany, Austria, Hungary and Turkey) believed that naval supremacy would be a key factor in determining the outcome of the war. Britain and Germany had both built powerful new navies. The introduction by Britain's First Sea Lord, Admiral Jackie Fisher, of the Dreadnought class of battleship rendered all earlier warships obsolete, and the British Royal Navy was the larger and also the better prepared for war.

ABOVE: *Capt. William Turner was in his sixties when the* Lusitania *was sunk by a German U-boat. Despite his good record, Turner was blamed by the British High Command for the ship's sinking.*

The anticipated confrontation never materialized. Apart from two early actions in the South Atlantic – the second of which saw the German Pacific squadron destroyed off the Falkland Islands in December 1914 – there were few substantial encounters at sea until the Battle of Jutland in June 1916. For all the symbolic importance of battleships, their usefulness was largely compromised by exposure to the new hazards of submarines, aeroplanes and mines. Both before and after Jutland, apart from occasional engagements on Britain's east coast, Germany's High Seas Fleet was kept contained in its North Sea bases.

It was the submarine, previously regarded merely as an auxiliary weapon, that was about to become the most significant warship of all. In February 1915, Germany announced a blockade, declaring the waters around the British Isles a war zone. Merchant ships entering them would be sunk by submarines – if necessary without warning. A new era of naval warfare had begun. Britain responded by seizing cargoes bound for German ports, while the US government issued a warning that Germany would be held responsible for any American ships sunk and lives lost. It was in this context that on 7 May 1915, the 762-foot long, 30,396-ton Cunard liner *Lusitania*, sailing from New York and bound for Liverpool with nearly 2,000 passengers and crew, was sunk by a German U-boat about 12 miles off the south coast of Ireland. 1,195 lives were lost.

OPPOSITE: *In the years before the First World War the British company Cunard faced fierce competition for the transatlantic passenger trade. Its response was to build the* Lusitania *and the* Mauretania.

The sinking of the *Lusitania* has passed into legend as a brutal German war crime that galvanized public opinion, ushering the United States into the First World War. As with

RIGHT: *The* Lusitania *leaving New York harbour surrounded by tugs.*

most historical events that become legend, the truth is not quite that simple; it must be remembered that the *Lusitania* was no normal passenger liner and that the United States did not enter the war until almost two years after the sinking. The *Lusitania*, however, has also achieved another kind of celebrity status. For most of this century, many have believed that the ship was carrying treasure – soon after the war a rumour began to circulate about how the sunken hull contained a fortune in gold bars. This speculation was no doubt intensified by the almost paranoid official secrecy around the ship's sinking. A series of unauthorized and often clandestine salvage attempts took place at frequent intervals from the 1920s to the 1980s. As it happens, research in Bank of England archives, in files that have only relatively recently been made available to the public, has effectively disproved the existence of gold. It is still possible, however, that the *Lusitania* was carrying valuable art works.

The *Lusitania*, a privately owned Cunard liner, was the fastest and finest ship of its day and undertook its maiden voyage in September 1907. The ship afforded its first-class passengers the ultimate in luxury travel. The domed dining saloon, furnished in sumptuous Louis XVI style, was the embodiment of the gracious Edwardian living to which the well-heeled passengers were accustomed. Such opulence came at a price for those who wished to travel in such luxury – a one-way first-class ticket cost $4,000, equivalent to some $200,000 today. Even the third-class passengers enjoyed a standard of food and accommodation that transatlantic voyagers of one hundred years earlier could hardly have dreamed possible.

Most of the *Lusitania*'s 1,255 passengers were unaware, however, that the ship had been conceived as a warship as well as a liner. It had been built with the assistance of a massive £2.6 million loan from the British Admiralty – in return the Admiralty had stipulated that

LEFT: *The pillars in the*
Lusitania's *splendid dining room*
were painted white and gold; the
balcony floor, also seen here, was
used for informal music and
after-dinner coffee.

67

the design allow the *Lusitania* to be converted into an armed merchant cruiser in the event of war. It had, for instance, longitudinal compartments for the stowage of coal, a standard Admiralty requirement, but one which may well have contributed to its rapid sinking. In 1913, as the likelihood of war with Germany increased, the *Lusitania* was drydocked and fitted with revolving gun placements. These were kept carefully concealed below decks but could be brought into action in the space of a few minutes.

When the war started, the prevailing Cruiser Convention stated that when a blockading warship confronted a merchant marine ship, the warship was required to identify itself. Should the ships prove to be on opposite sides, the captain of the merchant ship would be given the opportunity to disembark his passengers into the lifeboats, and the ship would be seized or sunk. The purpose was to minimize loss of civilian life, and for the opening months of the war the Convention was observed. The sinking of the *Lusitania* was to change all this when it was torpedoed without warning. While the *Lusitania* was not the first merchant ship to be sunk in this peremptory manner, it was the first to result in such a catastrophic loss of life. The *Lusitania* went down in under 20 minutes. While the loss provoked outrage, it was not well known that Winston Churchill, First Lord of the Admiralty, had effectively ordered all merchant marine captains to ignore the Cruiser Convention, thus forcing the Germans to open fire before disembarkation could take place. He had also instructed merchant captains to camouflage their ships and fly the American flag; Churchill's reasoning was that the German U-boats would sooner or later mistake an American merchant ship for a British one and attack it, and that the United States would be dragged into the war as a consequence.

Immediately following the sinking, there was widespread speculation about the exact nature of the cargo the *Lusitania* was carrying on her final and fatal voyage. US customs regulations did not permit the export of munitions by merchant ship to any of the warring

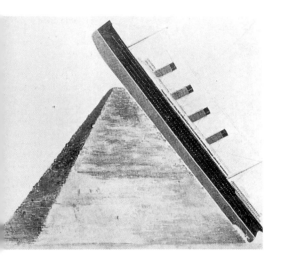

BELOW: *The colossal scale of the latest liners fascinated the Edwardians. The* Lusitania *was the largest ship of its day, the top of its funnel standing at a height of 155 feet and its length from stern to stern 785 feet. The* Titanic, *however, soon overtook it in size.*

CUNARD LINE

Lusitania
Mauretan

European nations. To do so would not only expose civilians to an unwarranted risk but also endanger US neutrality. Despite these regulations, the British managed to obtain large quantities of contraband cargo, largely thanks to their numerous sympathizers in influential positions in New York. Therefore, it is almost certain that, unknown to the passengers sipping cocktails in the *Lusitania*'s elegant lounge, large quantities of lethal explosives were secreted in the holds. The British Admiralty has consistently denied the presence of explosives on the ship, and the official manifest makes no mention of them. Shells are referred to, but through a quirk in the US customs regulations, shells could be exported provided that they were 'non-explosive in bulk', as the shells on the *Lusitania* were described. A close examination of the manifest reveals certain anomalies that point to an elaborate subterfuge. There is, for instance, mention of $150,000 worth of furs shipped by Alfred Fraser, who is now known to have been a clandestine operative who worked for the British. The supposed furs were shipped from Rheaboat and Hopewell, two American towns not known for their activities in connection with the fur trade but both of which

ABOVE: *The* Lusitania *at full steam was the swiftest ship of its day and soon captured the coveted Blue Riband award for the fastest transatlantic crossing.*

69

possessed Dupont factories, which manufactured gun cotton, a highly unstable explosive that the British badly needed for sea-mining operations. The furs were allegedly shipped to Babcock & Co. in Liverpool, a firm which has no history of dealing in furs and whose records show no imports for 1915. Dupont, however, do have records that refer to the shipment of 600 tons of gun cotton to the Cunard wharf in New York on 27 April – just a few days before the *Lusitania* left port.

There are other questions concerning the loss of the *Lusitania* that the British Admiralty has never properly addressed. In the days immediately before the *Lusitania*'s last voyage there was plenty of talk about whether or not the Germans might try to sink it, and the Germans even published a warning in the American press to the effect that all ships entering British waters were in peril. Despite the potential dangers, the Admiralty took no measures to provide any defence for the incoming *Lusitania*. Indeed, the one ship of any significance that patrolled the waters off southern Ireland, HMS *Juno*, was ordered back into Queenstown just hours before the *Lusitania* was due to arrive in the danger zone.

The submarine *U–20*, commanded by Kapitanleutnant Walter Schweiger, slipped out of Emden, Germany's westernmost North Sea port, on 30 April 1915. It travelled around the north coast of Scotland and down the west coast of Ireland, a back-door approach to British shipping lanes that had been used for centuries by Britain's enemies. Wireless messages from the *U–20* and the *U–30*, which had preceded the *U–20*, to German naval headquarters were intercepted and deciphered by British intelligence, and the Admiralty was well aware that this U-boat menace was heading for the waters off southern Ireland and Cornwall. By 6 May, the U-boats had sunk nine ships between them.

At 1.20 p.m. on Friday, 7 May, Schweiger saw smoke from the funnels of an approaching liner at a distance of about 14 miles. The huge ship on the horizon was correctly identified as the *Lusitania*. At 2.10 p.m. Schweiger fired a single torpedo at a range of 700 metres. The captain's log records how it struck the *Lusitania* just behind the bridge. Schweiger did not, however, expect to see a second explosion that occurred shortly after the torpedo hit, followed by the rapid plunging of the *Lusitania* beneath the waves.

The *Lusitania* sank in only 18 minutes. The crew made a valiant effort to launch the lifeboats, but the ship developed a severe starboard list that hampered their efforts to lower lifeboats on the port side. The davits did not work, the ropes stuck, the restraining chains became fouled and the uncontrollable boats smashed against the ship's side as fast as they

ABOVE AND RIGHT: *Kapitan-Leutnant Walter Schweiger, captain of the submarine U-20 (right) which sank the* Lusitania. *Schweiger went on record as only firing one torpedo, but most of those on board the* Lusitania *heard two distinct explosions.*

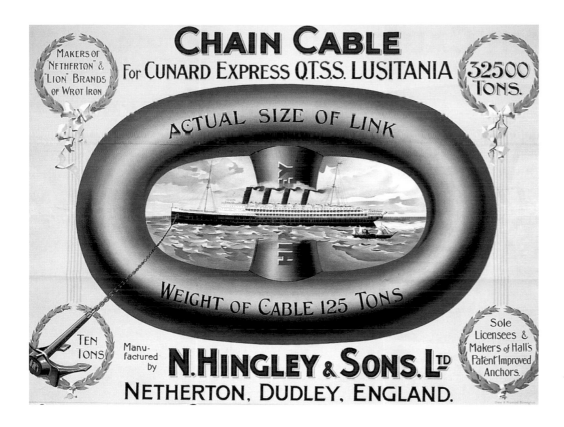

were lowered. Several boats crashed into the waiting passengers, killing and injuring many. Another boat, full to capacity with women and children, tipped up and swung vertically so that everyone within was thrown into the sea. In the ensuing chaos, an order came through that no more boats were to be loaded. An impetuous American, Isaac Lehmann, promptly drew his gun and ordered the officer in charge to start loading the disputed boat again. The officer did not argue and loading and lowering was resumed. The result was yet another lifeboat smashed to pieces. The boats on the starboard side did not fare much better. They tended to swing out too far from the ship, and even when they reached the water safely they were in extreme danger from falling debris. Of the 48 lifeboats, only six made it into Queenstown.

Most of the survivors were picked up by the flotilla of small boats that came out of Kinsale and Queenstown to assist in the rescue. One of the lucky survivors was Margaret Mackworth. 'I suddenly felt the water about me and was terrified less I should be caught in something and held under,' she later recalled. 'I went right under a long way and when I came to the surface, I swallowed a lot of water before I remembered to close my mouth tight. I was half unconscious but I managed to seize a [life] boat that I saw in front of me and cling to it . . . After being in the water some time, I became unconscious, and the next thing I remember is lying on the deck of the Bluebell with a sailor bending over me . . . I was in the water two and one half hours, half of that time unconscious.' A more dramatic description of the scene of devastation was provided by a passenger on the ship *Missanbie*, which passed through the area of the sinking 24 hours later. 'My God, it has happened . . . Lifeboats. One with a pair of boots and a hat within. Collapsible boats.

RIGHT: *A dramatic poster illustrates how the British government exploited the sinking of the Lusitania as war propaganda.*

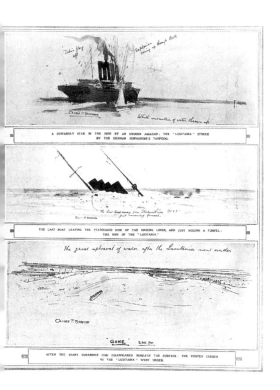

ABOVE: *Sketches by Oliver Bernard, an artist who survived the* Lusitania *disaster, shows the ship's sinking.*

Some with sides not up. An oar. Whale boats keel upwards. A body with lifebelt slipping off at neck. Now a bald head bobs up not twenty feet away ghastly in the sunshine. The water almost motionless. The silence. The shrieking of that silence.' A rather more terse comment was provided by another survivor named Dr Page. 'Don't ask me about it,' he said, 'I wouldn't talk for a guinea a word.' Out of 1,959 people on board, there were 764 survivors. The most famous of the 124 Americans who perished, the multimillionaire Alfred Vanderbilt, made no effort to save himself and apparently spent his final moments fastening life-jackets to children. His body was never recovered despite his family's offer of a £1,000 reward. As so often with disasters, extraordinary generosity was displayed by people from all walks of life.

The immediate reaction of Winston Churchill and Sir John Fisher at the Admiralty and Captain Richard Webb, Director of the Trade Division of the Admiralty at the Board of Trade was to pin the blame for the disaster on the luckless Captain Turner, who survived the sinking, on the grounds that he had recklessly disobeyed orders. All three men censured him in the severest terms. Webb wrote a memorandum describing Turner as 'not a fool but a knave', and Churchill considered that the 'Admiralty case against the Captain should be pressed before Lord Mersey by a skilful counsel . . . we shall pursue the Captain without check.' What order Captain Turner is supposed to have disobeyed is not at all clear. Approaching southern Ireland he received two telegrams. It is true that the first instructed him to remain in mid Channel, about 20 miles off the coast, and that when the *Lusitania* was sunk she was in fact only 12 miles off the coast. But the telegram ignored the fact that it had been very foggy in the Atlantic for two days prior to the sinking and that, like all good seamen, Turner was anxious to make a landfall to establish his precise position. The subsequent telegram contradicted the former and stated that a submarine was operating 20 miles off Coningbeg Light. It is difficult not to draw the conclusion that the venom Churchill and his associates directed at Captain Turner was an instinctive defensive reaction to the catastrophe. Equally, if any awkward questions were to arise, it was useful for the Admiralty to have a scapegoat. Neither Fisher nor Churchill remained in office long after the sinking. Fisher resigned as First Sea Lord within two weeks and Churchill was replaced soon after by A. J. Balfour.

The *Lusitania* was sunk in approximately 300 feet of water. The bow hit the seabed while the stern of the ship was still protruding high into the air. With such a notorious ship lying in relatively shallow water, it was inevitable that sooner or later an attempt would be made to salvage the wreck, especially with press speculation on the millions of pounds of gold bullion reputedly held on board fuelling the would-be salvors' dreams. The first attempt to salvage the *Lusitania* was made in 1923 by the grandly named British Semper Paratus Salvage Company, headed by a Count Landi, who claimed that there was £3 million of gold in the purser's safe. He was followed by a succession of other hopefuls, including Captain Benjamin Leavitt and Simon Lake. Amazingly, none of these expeditions even succeeded in locating the massive hulk of the *Lusitania*, let alone salvaging it. The ship was finally located in October 1935 by one of the first echo-sounders, deployed by the Tritonia Corporation of Scotland. The company had linked up with the Manchester engineer Peress, who had developed a diving suit strong enough to withstand the pressure of the sea at 300 feet. On 27 October 1935 diver Jim Jarrett became the first man to descend to the wreck of the *Lusitania*. The first big shock for the

ABOVE: *The* Lusitania *was equipped with forty-eight lifeboats, but only six made it safely to shore. The sudden precipitous list that followed the torpedoing made launching the boats both difficult and dangerous.*

salvage company was just how dark it was at this relatively shallow depth. Apart from work on the *Egypt* by Italian company Sorima in 1932, there had been very little salvage at this depth of water. The next few years were spent in developing lighting systems and concluding contracts with interested film companies. Then in 1938 the British government banned all further operations owing to the impending war.

After the Second World War the *Lusitania* was used by the Royal Navy for target practice; the depth charges that were dropped on the rotting liner further damaged the hull. Unexploded depth charges still litter the site, and make salvage work particularly hazardous. In June 1948, an Admiralty ship, the *Reclaim*, moored over the *Lusitania* and sent down Royal Navy divers. The motive for this descent remains a secret. In the 1950s the salvage company Risdon Beazley Ltd moored over the wreck on a number of occasions. Their interest was the substantial quantities of copper and brass that the *Lusitania* was known to have carried, but no recoveries were made. In 1960, in conjunction with the BBC, the American diver John Light descended to the wreck using scuba gear, resulting in the film *50 Fathoms Deep*, one of the earliest underwater films. By the end of the 1970s, however, despite these various explorations, very few valuables had been recovered from the impressive liner. What expedition after expedition had come to realize was that there was a considerable difference between putting a diver on a wreck and supplying that diver with sufficient power and time to enable any significant recoveries.

In the early 1980s the American company Oceaneering, experts in the maintenance and supervision of offshore oil installations, were contracted by a new consortium led by Welshman John Pierce. Using saturation diving techniques, and with the back-up of powerful grabs operated from the surface, this was the best-equipped expedition to date. A number of trophies were successfully retrieved from the *Lusitania*, including 6,000 silver-plated teaspoons, a box of gold watch cases, 172 brass clocks, an assortment of plates and dishes, portholes, fuses, some empty picture frames, and three of the four huge bronze propellors. Alas, no gold bullion was discovered. Since the Oceaneering salvage, as so often happens where shipwrecks are concerned, various parties involved have ended up in court in an attempt to establish ownership of the recovered artefacts. The Department of Transport laid claim to the recovered items, arguing that as the original ownership was unclear, title passed automatically to the Crown as a Droit of Admiralty. Mr Justice Sheen rejected this argument, stating that as the *Lusitania* lay in international waters it was beyond the jurisdiction of the Crown, and because ownership could not be proved, the salvors acquired title as 'salvors in possession'. More recently an American, Greg Beamis, claimed that the artefacts belonged to him because he had acquired the rights to the *Lusitania*'s hull, fixtures and fittings from Cunard. However, while some of the recovered artefacts fell into this category of ship's fixtures and fittings, it would not include any items that were originally carried as cargo, as Cunard would not have been the original owner of such items.

As a result of all these occurrences, the question arises as to whether there ever was anything on the *Lusitania* worth salvaging. The likelihood of a large quantity of British government-owned gold bullion being on board is minimal. In 1915 the United Kingdom was busily shipping gold to America to pay for arms purchases; it rarely, if ever, moved in the opposite direction. In his fascinating book on the subject of the *Lusitania* sinking, Colin Simpson makes a very good case for there being a considerable quantity of gold

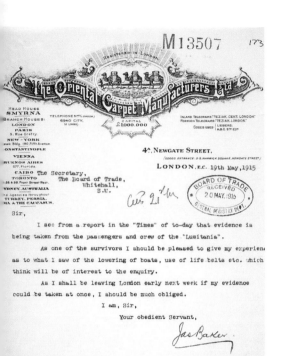

ABOVE: *Passengers wishing to give evidence to the Board of Trade inquiry were required to submit written 'proofs' of their evidence. 135 passengers submitted proofs.*

sovereigns and other valuables in the purser's safe. His view is that most of the first-class passengers would have carried £40–50 worth of gold sovereigns in loose change for their day-to-day purchases – purchases that would not be paid for until the end of the voyage. As there were 291 first-class passengers on that final voyage, it is clear that this 'loose change' could add up to a considerable quantity of sovereigns. In addition, a number of passengers would have deposited their jewellery in a safe deposit within the purser's cabin. It is known, for instance, that there was an insurance claim for one pearl necklace valued at $100,000. Unfortunately, the two Oceaneering expeditions in the early 1980s failed to penetrate to the area of the ship where the purser's safe was kept, owing to the enormous quantity of collapsed wreckage in the vicinity.

Perhaps the most fascinating story relating to the *Lusitania* does not involve gold or jewellery at all, but art treasures. Simpson claims that Sir Hugh Lane, director of the National Gallery in Ireland, had a number of valuable paintings on board, including works by Rubens, Titian and Monet. Until recently, it was considered that such paintings would inevitably have been destroyed by seawater, and Oceaneering's discovery of empty picture frames would appear to confirm this. However, the manifest in the Customs House, New York, shows only one package of paintings insured for $2,312 – hardly the value of a group of old masters. It is quite possible that the empty frames relate to this package, though the Lane paintings may not have appeared on the manifest at all, as they would have been shipped as part of his personal luggage. Speculation has been fuelled and appetites whetted by Simpson's recent claim that these alleged rare works were sealed in special zinc containers in order to protect them from the seawater. The Irish government took the story seriously enough to place a preservation order on the site in February 1995, banning any further dives. Quite how this ban can be reconciled with the fact that a British court ruled that the wreck lay in international waters is unclear.

There is one further mystery that has still not been satisfactorily explained. This concerns the second explosion that almost all observers of the original catastrophe record as having witnessed. Until recently, it had been widely assumed that this secondary explosion was caused by the explosives that had been illicitly carried in the *Lusitania*'s cargo holds. In 1993 Ballard carried out the most detailed film examination of the wreck that has yet been achieved. His conclusion was that the second explosion was probably caused by the original torpedo igniting coal dust. He ruled out the explosives theory arguing that the *Lusitania*'s magazine was too far away from the place where the torpedo struck and the bulkhead in between the two places was still intact.

According to Simpson, the spot where the torpedo struck was not used as a coal bunker on the *Lusitania*'s final voyage, even though it is described as such on the plans. This is because this space had been converted into extra cargo carrying capacity. This seems quite logical. It is known that the *Lusitania* was running at reduced speeds on her final voyage in order to conserve coal, and there was a desperate need to increase cargo capacity on inward bound shipping at the time. This again opens up the possibility that explosive material was present either within or just above the forward coal bunker where the torpedo struck and somewhat qualifies Ballard's conclusions. Until the secret files on the *Lusitania* are finally opened, the exact truth is unlikely to be known.

ABOVE: *One of the propellors from the* Lusitania *that can be found at the National Merseyside Maritime Museum in Liverpool.*

BELOW: *Leavitt was one of many would-be salvors who attempted to regain the 'treasure' of the* Lusitania. *Here, we see his 'all-metal diving suit for deep waters'.*

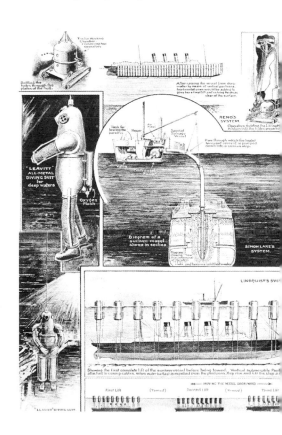

THE TUBANTIA
THE KAISER'S BUTTER

ABOVE: *Kaiser Wilhelm II Emperor of Germany was the personal inspiration behind the rapid expansion of the German Kriegsmarine in the building of the new super class of battleship known as the Dreadnoughts.*

WHEN THE FIRST WORLD WAR BROKE OUT THE *Tubantia* was the latest and most luxurious liner belonging to the proud Koninklijke Holländsche Lloyd shipping line of Amsterdam. Built in Glasgow, it was 560 feet long, with a gross tonnage of 14,053 tons, and had been launched on 15 November 1913 from the Linthouse stocks of the famous Clydeside shipbuilding firm of Alexander Stephen & Sons Ltd. The *Tubantia* was destined by its owners for the rapidly growing passenger business between Europe and South America.

It had cost £300,000 to build and, like most liners of this period, it had been constructed to resemble a first-class floating hotel, with opulent staterooms and beautifully fitted *cabines des luxes*. The verandah cafe on the promenade deck, with its elegant cane furniture and Art Nouveau decorated glass, was particularly favoured by the ladies as a place to gather for tea, while the more sumptuous virtues of the first class smoking room were designed to appeal to the male sex. Although the *Tubantia* was redolent of the affluence and self-confidence of an age that would shortly come to a brutal end, it would be a mistake to regard the ship as in any way backward-looking or outdated. Quite the contrary. The *Tubantia* was designed and built almost as a celebration of that miraculous new source of power – electricity. For some years electricity had been used on board ships for lighting and ventilation purposes, but on the *Tubantia* it was deployed in every conceivable context. There were electric radiators in the cabins; there were electric dishwashers for the crockery and cutlery, electric washing machines, ironing machines and potato peeling machines; even the boot-polishers, the cigar-lighters and the equestrian exercisers were worked by electricity. Most resplendently of all, between the two funnels was hung a giant illuminated sign spelling out the name Tubantia, which could be easily seen a long way off on the darkest of nights. This last novel electrical feature is of critical and somewhat mysterious significance when one comes to consider the liner's ultimate fate.

OPPOSITE: *A German U-boat poster from the First World War. The U-boats inflicted crippling losses on British merchant shipping. What was most surprising is that the convoy system used to counter these losses was not introduced by the Admiralty until 1917.*

77

ABOVE: *The verandah cafe on the promenade deck of the Tubantia. However, on the ship's last voyage there were hardly any passengers on board – a direct effect of the war.*

On Wednesday, 15 March 1916 the *Tubantia* left Amsterdam on its regular run to Buenos Aires in Argentina. Holland was neutral at this time and her ships were permitted to sail the seas without fear of attack. When four miles east-north-east of the North Hinder Lightship, some 50 miles off the Dutch coast, the *Tubantia* suddenly experienced a violent explosion on its starboard side, amidships, and rapidly began to sink. The first wireless operator managed to get a signal to Scheveningen before abandoning ship. It said simply: 'Tubantia torpedoed and lost. Am now leaving ship with Captain. Do not worry.' Fortunately, although the liner had capacity for 1,520 passengers, it was only carrying 87 at the time. Clearly the war had had a serious effect on passenger traffic. The crew of 294, together with the passengers, all managed to reach the safety of three other steamers, the *Breda*, the *Krakatau* and *La Campine*, who came to the rescue.

There followed a furious war of words in the press as to where the responsibility lay. The British claimed that it was a torpedo from a German submarine that had caused the explosion. The Germans countered that it was a British mine. At the inquiry which followed, most of the Dutch crewmen questioned said they thought a torpedo struck the ship, whereupon the German press argued that it must have been a torpedo from a British submarine. Meanwhile various theories were considered as to why the Germans would have wished to sink the neutral *Tubantia*, particularly as there were nineteen

German passengers on board at the time. The sinking could have been the result of incompetence, but it is difficult to imagine how the *Tubantia*, particularly given its position and its illuminated name sign, could have been mistaken for enemy shipping. One explanation put forward was that the liner was carrying a large quantity of valuable German securities. There was a desperate need to support failing German credit in South America. The theory was that if the English had searched the *Tubantia*, as they doubtless would, and discovered the securities, they would have been confiscated as contraband cargo. The only way the Germans could be absolutely sure of getting their securities to South America was to sink them, in which case they could have them reissued in South America. It may have sounded far-fetched, but it was the only plausible explanation for the sinking – if it was accepted that the *Tubantia* had been sunk deliberately by the Germans.

Some interesting evidence surfaced unexpectedly regarding the vexed issue of who was responsible for the sinking. Two lifeboats from the *Tubantia* were picked up by a passing Dutch steamer and taken to Rotterdam. In one of them fragments of bronze metal were found, which may have come from a German torpedo tube air chamber. Only the Germans used bronze in their torpedo tubes, which were manufactured exclusively by the Schwartzkopf Company. The liner's owners, Koninklijke Hollandsche Lloyd, then decided to send divers down to examine the wreck. Their examination concluded that the hole in the ship's side had definitely been made by a torpedo. In the face of this new evidence the German government was prepared to accept responsibility, and in May 1916 it offered the Dutch company £300,000 in compensation for the loss of the ship. The Dutch refused, on the grounds that the ship was now worth far more than this. The Germans then offered to transfer one of the largest vessels of the Hamburg-Amerika line to the Dutch. For whatever reason, this offer too was not accepted. The question of compensation dragged on after the war. An International Committee of Inquiry concluded in February 1922 that the German government was not officially obliged to compensate the Dutch company, because it had never been conclusively established whether the torpedo that sank the *Tubantia* had been deliberately aimed or was simply a stray one adrift. Nevertheless, the German government did settle the claim, which had reached a total of £830,000.

This might well have been the end of the *Tubantia* story, but for the fact that within days of the conclusion of the inquiry a well-financed British-based salvage company headed by Major Sydney Vincent Sippe DSO, in conjunction with French shipowners, sent divers down to the wreck to try to retrieve the cargo of gold, worth £2 million at that time. The belief was that this gold was in the form of two million pre-war twenty-mark German coins and was being sent by the Kaiser to South America. (If that was the case, of course, the sinking was almost certainly accidental.) What brought this top-secret salvage expedition to the world's attention was that in July 1923 Count Landi's firm also started work on the *Tubantia*. Major Sippe promptly went to the courts to seek an injunction and began an action for damages. The trial that followed turned out to be a landmark in British salvage law. The court decided in favour of Major Sippe on the grounds that he was the salvor in possession of the wreck, having located it first, and because he had already commenced operations, which had not been concluded. The ingenious argument of Count Landi's lawyers – that Major Sippe could not be described as salvor in possession until he was physically in possession of the desired valuable cargo,

ABOVE: *This 'iron man' diving suit proved too cumbersome for practical use, something that became apparent to Captain C. Wilson (right), who led two or three expeditions in search of the* Tubantia's *gold in the 1930s.*

namely the gold – held no sway with the judge. Count Landi was forbidden to go near the wreck while Major Sippe continued with his salvage attempt.

Major Sippe might have won the legal battle for the *Tubantia*'s gold, but the battle on the ocean floor proved more intractable. His divers had managed to penetrate into the liner's fourth cargo hold, where the gold was believed to have been stowed in casks described on the manifest as butter. Removing the vast quantities of other miscellaneous cargo, however, was not easy. It involved burrowing deep into the *Tubantia*'s hull, which created the danger of six huge decks above collapsing downwards as the supporting cargo was removed. In addition there were strong currents in the area, reducing working time to the few hours of slack water each day. During 1923 only 200 diving hours were achieved, and during 1924 just 191 hours – out of these hours one-third of the time was spent on the ascent and descent. By the end of 1924 Major Sippe had spent nearly £100,000 on the project, a colossal sum of money at 1924 values. At the beginning of the 1925 season Major Sippe decided to hire the famous Royal Navy diver Captain Damant, who had recently masterminded the salvage of the *Laurentic* gold, to inspect the wreck and give his professional opinion as to the chances of success.

Captain Damant's report is a very professional and incisive document. He made a total of five separate dives on the wreck. Numbers 2 and 3 holds were both blown out and empty. He did not get the opportunity to examine No. 1 hold but concentrated his efforts, as instructed, on No. 4. He described his experience in the following terms:

> It is possible to reach the cargo in No. 4 hold by crawling aft under certain overhanging plates and through a moderate sized aperture, and I have done so in company with Clear [one of Sippe's divers] and afterwards a second time alone. One finds oneself resting on soft mud through which can be felt various items of cargo; towards the fore part of the hold is undisturbed cargo rising above the mud.
>
> The space is constricted and the darkness absolute, for the movements of one's body fill the water with suspended mud through which no light, however powerful, could shine effectively. Thus, it is impossible for divers to accomplish useful work there. The roof of the hold is torn and probably quite unstable.

Damant's report cannot have been encouraging news for the salvage team. He praised the team of six divers for their work and said that they had achieved as much as could reasonably be expected of them during the previous two years. His conclusion, however, was that it was impossible to continue to remove cargo through the hole that had been cut in the ship's side because as the cargo was removed the six decks above would simply collapse downwards, as these decks had already parted from the longitudinal sections of the hull. This would make the approach that had been followed for the last two years by Major Sippe both self-defeating and dangerous. Captain Damant's advice was that the six overhanging decks needed to be removed first and then the cargo could be removed without fear of the entire structure collapsing downwards. He estimated that this would take a minimum of three years' further work, and he was not sure that the present ship being deployed by the salvors had the necessary lifting power to remove the overhanging sections of deck, even after they

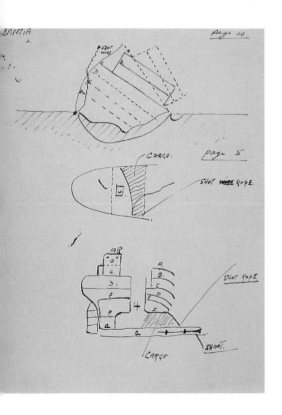

ABOVE: *Captain Damant's drawings of the condition of the* Tubantia *as it lay on the seabed in 1925 after two years of diving work. His report suggested that a minimum of three years further work would be required to penetrate that area of the ship where it was thought the treasure was contained.*

had been blasted to pieces. Major Sippe read the report and abandoned operations. He now had neither the finance nor the will to continue.

During my own researches into the *Tubantia* cargo I came across a manifest that had come to light in a Paris archive. It made interesting reading. On its final voyage the *Tubantia* had been carrying a standard mixed general cargo consisting largely of items such as 2,000 crates of Dutch gin or 18,550 empty basket-covered demijohns. It was a relatively light cargo, which explains why most of the holds had been found empty. Interestingly, there were ten crates of butter listed, but there was nothing to indicate that the butter was really crates of gold. This was hardly surprising. The British Admiralty was also in the habit of sending gold by ship during wartime and describing it on the manifest in such exotic terms as boxes of nails. However, it would have been quite impossible to fit the quantity of gold mentioned by Sippe in just ten crates. It didn't look very positive. But tucked away on a back page was a rather more exciting entry. It was a very definite reference to a large quantity of cut diamonds having been shipped, a prize that had eluded Major Sippe and which presumably still lies somewhere amid the *Tubantia* wreckage.

ABOVE: *The* Tubantia *moored at Montevideo in 1915. The electric lights with the ship's name can be seen suspended between the funnels.*

HMS HAMPSHIRE
LORD KITCHENER'S LAST MISSION

IN EARLY JUNE 1916 THE FIRST WORLD WAR was two years old and its outcome highly uncertain. On the Western Front the British and German armies faced each other, deadlocked, in their trenches (the massive British offensive on the Somme being just a month away), while further south the French were suffering fearful losses in their heroic defence of Verdun. In the East the Russians had just launched a major new offensive against Austria on a 200-mile front. How much longer Russia would sustain the fight on the Eastern Front was becoming a major source of anxiety to her allies, however, as Tsar Nicholas II's hold on power was already weakening in the face of the Bolshevik threat.

In London, meanwhile, the mood was one of near paranoia. Intrigue and suspicion were rife. Unrest in Ireland and the knowledge that the Nationalists were negotiating, if not colluding, with the Germans had led to rumours not just of German spies listening in every tavern and Turkish bath house but also of Irish saboteurs undermining the war effort. It was against this feverish background that, on 5 June, Britain's Secretary of State for War, Lord Kitchener of Khartoum, set out on a highly secretive military mission to Russia, probably with the aim of stiffening the Tsar's resolve and offering him support in maintaining the Anglo-Russian alliance.

To reach St Petersburg, Kitchener was to sail by warship through the dangerous waters to the north of Scotland and along the coast of Norway, well inside the Arctic Circle, then south past the Kola Peninsula of Russia and through the White Sea to the port of Archangel. A few days previously, on 31 May, the only major naval engagement of the war had been fought, when the British and German fleets met at the Battle of Jutland. This was an unexpected engagement, and proved indecisive, as both commanders exercised great caution. Nevertheless, the battle ended with the loss of three British battleships and one German. The news of the British losses was greeted with dismay at home, but the Battle of Jutland was not a total disaster, since the naval status quo was unaffected, and thereafter the

ABOVE: *The first salvage attempt on the* Hampshire *in the 1930s was carried out clandestinely. It later emerged that Sir Basil Zaharoff (above), the infamous arms dealer, was behind it.*

OPPOSITE: *Lord Kitchener, who is portrayed in this famous recruiting poster, was popular with the nation, but was seen as a liability by certain members of the War Cabinet, including Lloyd George.*

ABOVE: *The* Hampshire *was an armoured cruiser that had only just returned from the Battle of Jutland, when it was detailed to carry Lord Kitchener on an urgent mission to Russia.*

blockade of Germany's fleet in its North Sea bases was successfully maintained until the end of the war. A far greater shock to the nation, perhaps the most traumatic news of the war to date, was the announcement on 6 June that the cruiser HMS *Hampshire* had been sunk off the coast of the Orkney Islands and that Lord Kitchener had drowned.

To the British public Kitchener was not just some elderly politician but a great general, the conqueror of the Sudan, the avenger of General Gordon of Khartoum, the scourge of the Boers and a unique symbol of British imperial power. It was Kitchener's stern face and pointing finger in the famous 'Your Country Needs You' poster that had persuaded over a million young men to volunteer in the early months of the war. This enthusiasm for Kitchener was not shared in government circles, however, where his opposition to conscription and his autocratic ways had made him deeply unpopular. By 1916 his Cabinet colleagues, notably David Lloyd George (who would replace Asquith as prime minister by the end of the year), regarded the sixty-five-year-old Kitchener as a hopelessly outmoded and ineffectual leader and, in anticipation of sacking him, had discreetly stripped him of much of his influence. They were only too pleased when he was out of the country. Indeed, on the very evening of Kitchener's departure for Russia, Walter Hines Page, the US ambassador in London, recorded in his dispatch, with uncanny foresight, 'There is [in England] a hope and a feeling that he [Kitchener] may not come back.' It is perhaps not altogether surprising that the fanciful rumours which followed his death stretched not only to Irish sabotage but even to treachery in high places.

Although there now seems little doubt that what sank the *Hampshire* was not sabotage, but a mine, and that what brought ship and mine into contact was not treachery, but incompetence, the suspicions were to linger. An air of mystery continued to surround both the *Hampshire*'s loss and the exact nature of Kitchener's mission. Some years later the speculation extended to what else, apart from a national icon, the ship was carrying when it sank. For many there was reason to believe that its cargo may have included a large consignment of gold.

Lord Kitchener left London from King's Cross station on the evening of Sunday, 4 June in the company of a small group of officials and servants. He was bound for Scapa Flow, in the Orkneys, the war base of the Grand Fleet, to which it had recently returned after the Battle of Jutland. He travelled by train overnight to Thurso, in the extreme north of Scotland, and crossed to Scapa Flow the following morning on the destroyer *Royal Oak*. He had lunch with Admiral Sir John Jellicoe, Commander-in-Chief of the Grand Fleet, aboard the latter's flagship the *Iron Duke* and then transferred to the cruiser HMS *Hampshire*, which had been designated some days before to make the voyage to Archangel. Already a fierce gale was blowing from the northeast. It was suggested to Kitchener that he might delay his voyage for twenty-four hours, but he refused to contemplate any delay. It was then that the British naval authorities made the first of a series of fatal blunders. In view of the gale they decided to re-route the *Hampshire* up the west coast of Orkney rather than up the east coast, which was the more usual route for warships. The reasoning was that the *Hampshire* would be able

LEFT: *One of the very last photographs of Kitchener taken on 5 June 1916, it shows him the day before his death at Scapa Flow on board the* Iron Duke, *the flagship of the battle fleet.*

to make better speed up the west coast which was on the lee side of the storm, and therefore be safer from attack by enemy submarine. But the decision was based on meteorological ignorance. The *Hampshire* had hardly put to sea before the storm swung round from northeast to northwest, as was common with this kind of cyclone.

The *Hampshire*, with a top speed of twenty-two knots, was still able to make eighteen knots even in the adverse weather conditions. The two destroyers, *Unity* and *Victor*, that had been assigned to escort her, however, quickly fell behind. The *Hampshire* reduced its speed to 15 knots and headed in closer to land. But the destroyers continued to drop back. At 6.30 p.m. Captain Herbert Savill of the *Hampshire* signalled to the destroyers to return to port. If they could not keep up, their continuing was senseless. It was a fateful decision.

At approximately 7.40 p.m. the *Hampshire* was about one and a half miles offshore between Marwick Head and the Brough of Birsay on the very northwest corner of the mainland of Orkney. This is one of the bleakest and most remote spots in the entire British Isles and even though it was summertime, it was still a bitterly cold grey evening. Suddenly and disturbingly, above the screaming of the gale, a loud explosion was heard from below amidships, in the vicinity of the boiler room. The ship immediately took on a sharp list to starboard. The electric lights went out. Hundreds of men found themselves trapped below deck. Many of the firemen and stokers were severely burned with scalding water. Others were injured by flying debris. Within twenty minutes the *Hampshire* had gone down bows

BELOW: *A contemporary artist's impression of the sinking of the* Hampshire. *It went down in less than twenty minutes in extremely cold water. There were only twelve survivors out of the 662 people on board.*

first. The appalling weather and the speed of the sinking had made it impossible to get off any boats, though an unsuccessful attempt was made to launch the Captain's galley. The only chance of survival was to cling to a Carley life-raft. Three of these were successfully launched but they were grossly overcrowded, about 70 men grimly hanging on to each raft. One by one, as it got dark, most of these men dropped off. Of the 662 people on board the *Hampshire* only twelve survived. None of these survivors was among the seven members of Kitchener's mission. According to those who survived, Kitchener was last seen standing calmly on the bridge deck in the company of Captain Savill, making no apparent effort to save himself. A fortune-teller had once told him that he would die by water. The roll-call of fatalities made it one of the worst naval disasters of the war.

No distress signal was transmitted by wireless from the sinking ship; not even a rocket was fired. Such omissions can only be explained as a result of the almost total paralysis that overtook the *Hampshire* from the moment of the explosion. But an islander called Joe Angus, a gunner in the Orkney Territorial Forces, noticed a cruiser in distress from his look-out at Birsay. He saw evidence of an explosion aft of the bridge. He immediately informed his corporal and urgent telegrams were dispatched to naval headquarters at Longhope. There was some confusion on the part of the observers about whether or not the ship was a cruiser or a battlecruiser, and the first telegraphic message did not include the information that the *Hampshire* had sunk. This, together with a certain pedantic concern for correct detail on the part of the senior officer at Longhope, Vice-Admiral Sir F.E. Brock, caused a delay in sending rescue craft until 9.45 p.m. There was also long-lasting bitterness among the islanders, over the fact that the naval authorities forbade them to launch the island's own lifeboat to assist in the rescue. The Navy also issued instructions that all the islanders remain indoors away from the cliffs in the vicinity of the disaster. The reason for this high-handed and insensitive behaviour on the part of the Navy no doubt had something to do with establishing proper security for Kitchener and the members of his mission in the event of their being rescued. Certainly there were fears at the time among the naval authorities that the island had been infiltrated by Irish and German saboteurs. But the effect of the ban was counter-productive, in that those who were lucky enough to reach the shore alive were deprived of help in scaling the cliffs. This belated obsession with security thus probably only served to increase the death toll.

The reaction of the British nation to the death of Kitchener was one of stunned disbelief. Kitchener, more than any other single man, was identified as the leader of the British war effort. It was a terrible psychological blow, even though there were some high up in government circles and the armed forces who were secretly relieved by his demise. A sizeable proportion of the population simply refused to believe that Kitchener was really dead. Rumours immediately began to proliferate about how he had been seen leaving the sinking ship in a dinghy or how a soldier in uniform had been seen coming ashore. The fact that Kitchener's body was never recovered lent credence to the rumours. A tendency to mythologize rapidly overtook events and there was a strong belief among some of the more credulous sections of the population that Kitchener would one day return to lead his men again. Others accepted Kitchener's death but looked around for someone to blame. The Irish were the obvious suspects, particularly because the *Hampshire* had been for a refit in Belfast a few months before it sank. Wild theories were elaborated about how time bombs had been fitted to the ship or stowaways were secreted somewhere deep in the ship's holds.

ABOVE: *Stoker Walter Farnden was one of the few who made it to land and survived his ordeal. The disaster was made worse by the British security forces on Orkney stopping the local people from offering assistance to those sailors that reached the bottom of the cliffs.*

ABOVE: *Many theories were propounded as to the cause of the* Hampshire's *sinking. However, the most likely explanation is that it fell victim to a magnetic mine, like the one illustrated, placed by U-75 on the West side of Orkney just a few days before the sinking.*

OPPOSITE: *The front page of the* Daily Chronicle *on 7 June 1916. The British nation was deeply shocked by news of Kitchener's death and a sizeable proportion simply refused to believe in it.*

The idea of sabotage was later fuelled by the publication of a number of books in Germany after the end of the war. Written by acknowledged German spies, they all personally claimed credit for the sinking. *The Man who Killed Kitchener* by Fritz Duquesne was one example. *One Against England* by Ernst Carl was another. Neither book has much credibility, but they all helped to keep the issue of the *Hampshire* alive, as well as to reinforce a general public unease that something rather murky and scandalous had taken place, about which the authorities were being less than frank.

The pressure became so intense that in 1926, ten years after the sinking, the government was forced to issue a White Paper, revealing the findings of an internal inquiry. The intention was to lay the entire *Hampshire* controversy to rest. Certain matters that had caused disquiet were cleared up. The issue of HMS *Laurel*, for instance, was explained. HMS *Laurel* had been listed in the government's own data as having sunk on 2 June 1916 in approximately the same position as the *Hampshire*. The obvious question was why, in view of this sinking only three days before the *Hampshire* sailed, the cruiser was routed through the same area without its being carefully swept for mines beforehand. The banal answer was that the listing was a printing error. HMS *Laurel* did not sink on 2 June at all, but on 22 June. The government was less successful, however, in its attempt to explain away the presence of mines off Marwick Head. It argued that up until 5 June the western Orkney route had been free of mines, and therefore the presence of them on 5 June had to be the result of a mistake on the part of the German minelayer *U-75* rather than evidence of British naval complacency. It was not a convincing argument.

The White Paper failed altogether to deal with the two most serious criticisms that could be levelled against the authorities. First, there had been a serious lack of security concerning Kitchener's voyage. His impending mission had been openly discussed in most of the capitals of Europe from late May onwards, and it is almost certain that German intelligence would have picked up on it. Secondly, there was confusion regarding mine clearance in the area where the *Hampshire* went down (the details of which only fully emerged in 1959 with the publication of Donald McCormick's excellent book on the subject, entitled *Kitchener's Death*). On 26 May 1916, ten days before the *Hampshire* left, a German deciphering officer at the Neumünster listening station near Kiel picked up a coded message from a British destroyer to the Admiralty, stating that the route to the west of the Orkneys had been cleared of mines and was now safe for transit. The message was repeated three times. From this the Germans concluded that this route must have been designated for the passage of an important ship and included the area in their next minelaying sortie – previously they had ignored this route, used only by small unimportant merchant ships. On 28 May the *U-75*, under Commander Kurt Beitzen, was dispatched to lay mines on the west side of Orkney, which he successfully accomplished. The extraordinary thing about this episode is not only the woeful lapse in security, but that there is no record in British naval files of any such signal ever having been made from a British destroyer to the Admiralty. Furthermore there is no record that this western route was swept free of mines on 26 May, and the decision to use it for the *Hampshire* was only taken at the last minute. It can only be concluded that the signal intercepted by the German listening station was a rogue signal sent out by Naval Intelligence Division under Admiral Hall deliberately to mislead the Germans. Admiral Hall was fond of such cat-and-mouse games with the enemy. It seems that in the aftermath of the Battle of Jutland, which

The Daily Chronicle

No. 16,911. LONDON, WEDNESDAY, JUNE 7, 1916. ONE HALFPENNY.

TRAGIC LOSS OF LORD KITCHENER AND STAFF.

Extra Late Edition.

LORD KITCHENER DROWNED.

LOST WITH HIS STAFF ON H.M.S. HAMPSHIRE.

ON MISSION TO RUSSIA

WARSHIP TORPEDOED OR MINED OFF THE ORKNEYS.

PRESS BUREAU, 1.40 p.m.; June 6.

The Secretary of the Admiralty announces that the following telegram has been received from the Commander-in-Chief of the Grand Fleet at 10.30 (British Summer Time) this morning:—

I have to report, with deep regret, that his Majesty's ship Hampshire (Captain Herbert J. Savill, R.N.), with Lord Kitchener and his Staff on board, was sunk last night about 8 p.m., to the west of the Orkneys, either by a mine or torpedo.

Four boats were seen by observers on shore to leave the ship.

The wind was N.N.W., and heavy seas were running.

Patrol vessels and destroyers at once proceeded to the spot, and a party was sent along the coast to search, but only some bodies and a capsized boat have been found up to the present.

As the whole shore has been searched from the seaward, I greatly fear that there is little hope of there being any survivors.

No report has yet been received from the search party on shore.

H.M.S. Hampshire was on her way to Russia.

3.55 p.m.

The Secretary, War Office, notifies:—

With reference to the announcement of the loss of H.M.S. Hampshire, that the special party consisted of

LORD KITCHENER,
Lt.-Colonel O. A. FitzGerald, C.M.G. (Personal Military Secretary),
Brigadier-General W. Ellershaw,
Second Lieutenant R. D. Macpherson (8th Cameron Highlanders),
Mr. H. J. O'Beirne, C.V.O., C.B., (of the Foreign Office),
Sir H. F. Donaldson, K.C.B., and
Mr. L. S. Robertson (of the Ministry of Munitions).

Mr. L. C. Rix, shorthand clerk, Detective MacLaughlin, of Scotland Yard, and the following personal servants: Henry Surguy, — Shields, Walter Gurney and Driver D. C. Brown, R.H.A., were also attached to the party.

6.30 p.m.

Lord Kitchener, on the invitation of his Imperial Majesty, had left England on a visit to Russia. The Secretary of State was accompanied by Mr. O'Beirne, Sir Frederick Donaldson and Brigadier-General Ellershaw, and at the request of H.M. Government was to have taken the opportunity of discussing important military and financial questions.

KING GEORGE'S MESSAGE TO THE ARMY.

By his Majesty's command the following Order has been issued to the Army:—

The King has learned with profound regret of the disaster by which the Secretary of State for War has lost his life while proceeding on a special mission to the Emperor of Russia.

Field-Marshal Lord Kitchener gave 45 years of distinguished service to the State, and it is largely due to his administrative genius and unwearying energy that the country has been able to create and place in the field the Armies which are to-day upholding the traditional glories of our Empire.

Lord Kitchener will be mourned by the Army as a great soldier who, under conditions of unexampled difficulty, rendered supreme and devoted service both to the Army and the State.

His Majesty the King commands that officers of the Army shall wear mourning with their uniform on the melancholy occasion of the death of the late Field-Marshal Right Hon. H. H. Earl Kitchener of Khartoum, K.G., K.P., G.C.B., O.M., G.C.S.I., G.C.M.G., G.C.I.E., Colonel Commandant Royal Engineers, Colonel Irish Guards, Secretary of State for War—for a period of one week, commencing June 7, 1916.

Officers are to wear crepe on the left arm of the uniform and of the greatcoat.

WAR MINISTER AT WORK AND AT EASE.

HIS DISCIPLINARY REFORM IN THE WAR OFFICE.

"HUMAN AND LOVABLE."

By One Who Knew Him.

One did not need to be near Kitchener to know him as he was known by a nation. But if a nation can mourn him as a great soldier and a great servant we, who were among the rarely favoured circle of his intimates, have to lament in him a loss that we can hardly realise. To some of us, at least, he was the greatest man we knew.

Like all great men, he had a public life and a private life. Men who sometimes judged him austere by his deeds were often strangely overcome to discover him afterwards generous, even boyish, in his affections and his manner. Most people, even people comparatively well informed, loved to speak and write of him as of a perfect but passionless machine. The word was quite just, and quite true—until you saw and heard him laugh. Then you realised, with a shock, that the extraordinary machine called Kitchener was the highest type of machine—an extraordinary man, and a man, moreover, very human and lovable in his unofficial moments.

"Cold" and "austere" are adjectives that have been worked to death about him, but none who knew him well and saw him at his work and at his ease could ever accept them as characteristic. Cold and austere he was, of course, on occasions. He could be cold and even terrible to a man who shirked his duty. He was often austere in the face of frivolity. But if there was one quality in him that the world outside, friendly or hostile, knew and appreciated least, it was, perhaps, that of his really buoyant and exquisite humour. He laughed easily and heartily; his whole face lighting and his appearance changing as if miraculously. When he returned from Egypt in 1898, and was entertained by a crowd of admiring but frankly curious Savages at the Club in Adelphi-terrace, his reputation as a soldier had preceded him, but not the reputation of his humour. That came as a final, a most surprising discovery.

ORIENTAL POLITENESS.

It was the humour in him that I first remarked, one memorable day in the Libyan Desert over 30 years ago. It was this humour, in company with his marvellous knowledge of racial characteristics (and his skill in languages), that enabled him to deal with and overcome the resentment, the jealousy, and the egotism of petty rulers. Then there was his unfailing charm of manner, his courtesy, his almost Oriental politeness and discretion. In Egypt he was often to be seen sitting in his garden, receiving sheik after sheik, native official after official, and always with the most attentive patience, the most genial warmth.

The same personal charm was seen during his regime at the War Office, where he had to receive innumerable visitors. He was never, as has been very commonly supposed, an inaccessible Minister. Every distinguished foreigner coming to London desired above all things to see Kitchener, and all went away surprised and delighted with his kindly manner and his courteous speech. Even those whose requests were refused went away unaggrieved, certain that their case had been fairly considered, justly weighed, and decided without fear or favour.

"K."

At the War Office his presence was like a great spiritual broom. It swept clean. Only "K.," as his friends and subordinates alike called him, could have accomplished the disciplinary revolution that enabled that cumbrous department to support a burden suddenly multiplied a hundredfold. For the first 14 months of the war "K." made the War Office his home. He worked there, lunched and dined there, and often slept there. His personal tastes and habits were simple, but not affectedly so. He was singularly free from fads, though he was fastidious as any naval commander on the point of cleanliness.

Of recreations, in the ordinary sense, he had few or none. One remembers the mild ripple of interest that passed through the public mind when Kitchener began to learn golf. One had never associated him—it is typical of the appeal he made to popular imagination—with a game like golf, or with any game at all but that of soldiering.

WAR LORD AND HIS CRITICS.

If he had a weakness at all, it was a weakness for old china and old furniture, the latter of the English school. He knew nothing of French china, and nothing of pictures, though he would occasionally admit he liked a certain work. But the collecting of china and furniture amounted in him to a passion. His fine house at Broome Park, in Kent, was filled with them; and filled, too, with excellent judgment.

It is impossible that such a finely sensitive character as Kitchener's could have borne without pain the ingratitude and the injustice of his recent critics. But he certainly was

(Continued on Page 6.)

LORD KITCHENER.

Born June 24, 1850.—Died June 5, 1916. [Elliott & Fry.

No more in soldier fashion will he greet
With lifted hand the gazer in the street.
O friends, our chief state-oracle is mute:
Mourn for the man of long-enduring blood,
The statesman-warrior, moderate, resolute,
Whole in himself, a common good.
Mourn for the man of amplest influence,
Yet clearest of ambitious crime,
Our greatest yet with least pretence,
Great in council and great in war,
Foremost captain of his time,
Rich in saving common-sense,
And, as the greatest only are,
In his simplicity sublime.

TENNYSON'S "ODE" (1852).

NEW COMMANDER AT ROSYTH.

SIR F. T. HAMILTON SUCCEEDS SIR ROBERT LOWRY.

It is officially announced that the King has approved the appointment of Vice-Admiral Sir Frederick T. Hamilton, K.C.B., C.V.O., to be Commander-in-Chief at Rosyth, in succession to Admiral Sir Robert Lowry; and of Acting Vice-Admiral the Hon. Sir Somerset Arthur Gough-Calthorpe, K.C.B., C.V.O., to be a Lord Commissioner of the Admiralty, in succession to Vice-Admiral Sir Frederick Hamilton.

THE LOST CRUISER.

H.M.S. Hampshire was an armoured cruiser of the County class, of 10,850 tons, built at Elswick, and completed in 1905. The total estimated cost of the ship, including guns, was £856,527. Her principal armament consisted of four 7.5-inch guns, six 6-inch guns, and twenty 3-pounders. She carried a complement of 655 men.

ST. PAUL'S MEMORIAL SERVICE.

A memorial service for Lord Kitchener will be held in St. Paul's Cathedral. No date has yet been fixed, but the Dean and Chapter are in communication with the authorities with regard to the service.

STOP PRESS NEWS.

RECEPTION OF THE NEWS IN LONDON.

LOWERING THE FLAG AT THE WAR OFFICE.

The scene in the streets when the evening papers appeared with the first public notification of the disaster was an unforgettable one. There was no demonstration—no gathering of any crowd, even before the War Office; but what impressed one was the deep, poignant emotion aroused by the news, the sudden hush, as it were, which this tragic passing away of the great soldier brought about, and which seemed for a moment almost to arrest the busy life of the great city.

Strangers in the streets and on the buses shared each other's papers. At the newspaper stands eager customers tore the papers from the hands of newsvendors, who were unable to distribute quickly enough the sheets for which there was such a demand, and in several cases many times the value was paid by purchasers. Occupants of cars and buses, suddenly catching sight of the black-lettered posters, stopped the vehicles and alighted to buy papers.

Only on one other occasion since the war broke out has any news so gripped the public mind, and seemed so completely to stay for a time the roaring tide of the streets. The first occasion was last Friday, when the first Admiralty announcement of the North Sea battle was made. Then, as was the case yesterday, the dominant impression of the streets was of straggling lines of people intent upon one thing alone, the brief statement in the "stop press" of the papers.

Outside Charing Cross two soldiers, each wearing the South African riband, silently showed a paper to two girls who excitedly inquired "Is it true?" Neither spoke a word, but in the eyes of each were tears more eloquent than any spoken requiem.

In Whitehall an inkling of the sad news had been obtained before the official statement was issued, when attention was attracted by the big Union Jack which suddenly fluttered to the head of the tall mast over the War Office and then slowly fell to half-mast. The only flag on any of the Government buildings, its loneliness seemed to enhance the sadness of the message it conveyed.

STORMING OF VAUX.
(BY ONE WHO FOUGHT.)

TWENTY THREE ATTACKS IN EIGHTEEN HOURS.

OFFICER'S STORY OF FURIOUS HAND-TO-HAND FIGHTING.

From "The Daily Chronicle" Special Correspondent, G. H. Perris.

PARIS, June 6.

German attacks on the Vaux position continued yesterday and last night, but without any success. A wounded French officer, who fell on the glacis of the fort on Sunday evening during one of the assaults by a brigade of the German 23rd Reserve Corps, says that on Friday and Saturday the French soldiers on the north-west of the fort repelled 17 attacks and made six counter-attacks, and this after a bombardment of 26 hours and against a plentiful use of flame projectors and poison gas.

His own and another regiment bore the onslaught of a division and a half. "The enemy have suffered frightful losses. Our 75's made a veritable massacre, a butchery.

"On Saturday morning two German regiments were advancing against the western moat of the fort and were caught under the fire of the batteries.

GREY LINE VANISHED.

"Five minutes after fire was opened, the grey line of the assailants had simply disappeared. There were not even corpses left—only dispersed on every side were fragments of what had lately been animate.

"The struggle in the northern moat was the most desperate I have seen. Line after line was sent forward. The men fought with knife, dagger and revolver.

"Two of our soldiers who had lost all their arms were using their helmets as bludgeons. An Oberleutnant went down before them with his skull smashed in. We fought like this for 18 hours, new reinforcements being brought up on both sides. Never perhaps have the Germans made so extensive a use of flaming liquid. Streams of fire were poured into our lines, some part of which had to be evacuated; but these were afterwards retaken by counter-attack.

"There were sundry gallant episodes. A captain atrociously burned in the face and neck was in his own expression 'Done for'; but, forgetting his sufferings, he returned to take command of his company. A sergeant at the height of an attack threw himself upon one of the men carrying a flame projector, and, turning the pump round, he directed it upon the Boches, many of whom were burned."

G. H. PERRIS.

BOMBARDING VAUX FORT.

FOILED ENEMY RESORTS TO BIG GUN FIRE.

PARIS, Tuesday Afternoon.

Official.—East of the Meuse two German attacks delivered last night against our positions between Vaux and Damloup completely failed. No change is reported in the situation at the fort of Vaux, which the enemy is bombarding with continued violence.—Reuter.

Tuesday Night.

North of Verdun no infantry action was reported in the course of the day. Artillery fighting, however, continued with the same violence in the region of Vaux and Damloup.

Chief-of-Battalion Raynal, who is defending the Vaux Fort, has been appointed a Commander of the Legion of Honour.—Reuter.

AMSTERDAM, Tuesday.

The communiqué issued in Berlin to-day says: East of the Meuse, after a renewed and very severe artillery preparation, the enemy four times attacked the position of the brave East Prussians on the Fumin ridge (north-west corner of Vaux Hill) without any serious success. The co-operation of our artillery curtain fire and machine-gun and infantry fire inflicted especially heavy losses on the enemy.—Reuter.

FIGHT ON BAGDAD ROAD.

BLOWS AT TURKS BY RUSSIANS FROM PERSIAN BORDER.

To-day's communiqué says: Beyond Erzerum, in the direction of Baiburt and Erzingan, the Turks supported by artillery took the offensive in several sectors of our front, but were everywhere repulsed.

On Saturday we dealt a blow at the Turks near Khanikin, 86 miles to the north-east of Bagdad.—Reuter.

From Tiflis, in Transcaucasia, on Saturday last M. Barbi reported (according to an Exchange telegram) the "new and glorious victory" of the Russians near Rowandiz, 250 miles N. of Bagdad. The entire Turkish division was smashed and fled in panic, pursued by the Russians. A Turkish regiment that had come from the Gallipoli Peninsula was completely annihilated. Included in the booty taken by the Russians were heavy guns and machine guns.

LAST DAY OF GROUP SYSTEM.

The group system closes, except for previously rejected men and for those who hereafter attain the age of 18, at midnight to-night.

BATTLE AGAINST 700,000.

FAR-REACHING EFFECTS OF RUSSIA'S BLOW.

25,000 PRISONERS: THREE STRONG LINES BROKEN.

HINDENBURG TAKES CHARGE.

[It is officially announced in Petrograd (said Reuter last evening) that on the 250 miles front from the Pripet to the Rumanian frontier the Russians continued to develop the success already reported. Up to the present the number of prisoners taken has been increased to 480 officers and more than 25,000 men, while 27 guns and more than 50 machine-guns have been captured.]

From "The Daily Chronicle" Special Correspondent, Harold Williams.

PETROGRAD, June 6.

News of the beginning of General Brussiloff's offensive on the south-western front was greeted in the Duma yesterday with ringing cheers, and the general feeling is one of hopeful anticipation.

Few details are yet to hand of the actual progress made, but the fact that the first day was successful, and that unusually large numbers of prisoners were taken gives ground for great confidence.

The moment chosen was singularly opportune. The Central Powers had thrown all the emphasis of their offensive to the West. The Germans engaged at Verdun had left their section of the Russian front heavily fortified, and were, with their allies, boasting that, with the help of their artillery and machine-guns, they would be able to hold the Russians behind their forests of barbed wire.

ONLY TWO GERMAN DIVISIONS.

The Austrians were engaged on the Italian campaign, and had left on the Russian south-western front forces not exceeding 700,000 men, supported by not more than two German divisions.

The long spell of warm weather had dried up the roads, and the Russians had not now to contend with those serious transport difficulties that hampered their advance in December.

Just south of the Pripet the Russian line runs along the western edge of the Polesie marshes; so that their advance brings them out into the open country of Volhynia. Meanwhile, the swamps behind them have, during the winter, been made passable by the construction of a remarkable network of timber roadways.

The whole technical organisation of General Brussiloff's armies has made amazing progress, the men are in splendid form, and the accumulation of energy is such that for some time past the whole front has been restlessly waiting for the command to advance.

There are no data at present for an estimate of the possible extent of the advance; but that it will relieve pressure on the Italian front is certain; while its ultimate effect may be to dilute the intensity of the German effort at Verdun.

In any case the summer operations are crystallising into exceedingly interesting formations.

HAROLD WILLIAMS.

RUSSIA RE-ARMED.

BERLIN SHOCKED: HINDENBURG AS AUSTRO-GERMAN LEADER

The correspondent of the Berlin "Tageblatt" at the Eastern Front telegraphs that the Russian artillery fire over the whole front has been very pronounced. It is supposed that they are equipped with new guns and large quantities of ammunition, because the fire has been of a most violent character. — Exchange (Copenhagen.)

A report from Bucharest states that the battle in Galicia (Tarnopol region) has been disastrous for the Austrians, whose lines were broken at several points.—Wireless Press.

Russia's offensive has produced a shattering effect in Berlin (says an Exchange Amsterdam wire). Troops are being rushed from Serbia to Galicia. Hindenburg is personally commanding the German-Austrian operations. He is said to have declared that "this time the Russians are in great earnest." No reinforcements have been sent from Germany to the Austrians.

Marcel Hutin, in the "Echo de Paris," reports that north-west and west of Tarnopol, in front of Zepenoff Olyka, the great Russian advance through three strongly fortified Austrian lines has yielded more than 15,000 prisoners, and the number is growing. "The Russian offensive is the result of co-ordination on the part of the Allies."—Exchange telegram.

Fighting in the flooded areas of the Pinsk marshes has been done in small boats. Small rowing-boats used by the Russians each hold four or five combatants, besides the oarsmen. The Germans have been using similar boats. The floods are rapidly subsiding.—Wireless Press.

took place on 31 May, this crucial piece of counter-intelligence games playing was not communicated to Admiral Jellicoe, and that the latter, in complete ignorance and because of the freak weather, then inadvertently directed the *Hampshire* into the trap that British Naval Intelligence had instigated as a diversionary tactic. This was incompetence on a grand scale.

The White Paper did not put an end to the *Hampshire* scandal. But the next time the infamous cruiser hit the headlines of the world's press it was in a different context entirely. An article in the *Berliner Illustrierte Zeitung* in 1933 carried a report referring to the salvage of £10,000 in gold bars from the *Hampshire*'s strong-room. Suddenly HMS *Hampshire* had been transformed from *cause célèbre* into a treasure ship. The British and American press picked up on the story and soon the furore of interest was such that the Admiralty was once again obliged to issue a statement. It claimed that it knew nothing of the salvage, but that HMS *Hampshire* remained the property of HM Government and could not be touched without the permission of HM Government. It then further confused matters by denying that it had ever made any statement on the subject at all.

Some light was thrown on the mystery of the *Hampshire* treasure with the publication of a book called *Unlocking Adventure* by Charles Courtney in the early 1950s. Courtney described in some detail a highly secretive salvage attempt on HMS *Hampshire* in 1933 by a group of divers working off a ship called *KSR* out of Kiel under a Captain Brandt. According to Courtney, £60,000 worth of gold had been recovered when the salvage was aborted by a serious accident that resulted in one diver being killed and two others being taken to hospital. Courtney claimed that there was in total £2 million worth of gold on board the *Hampshire*, and that the main purpose of Kitchener's mission had been to provide the Tsar with this financial support. There are aspects of Courtney's description which suggest a certain amount of romantic embellishment, particularly concerning the miraculously preserved dead bodies he claimed to have encountered within the hull of the *Hampshire*. It is questionable whether or not any diving operation could possibly have taken place, in view of the fierce currents that run in the area of Marwick Head. Even today, with all the improvements in diving technology, it would still be a difficult and complex operation. However, Courtney does provide a wealth of circumstantial detail, much of which has the ring of truth. For example, the presence of a strange ship in the vicinity of Marwick Head during long periods of the summer of 1933 was corroborated by local observers on the island itself. Perhaps the most interesting aspect of Courtney's account, however, is not the graphic description he provides of diving inside the wreck but the detail he gives about the group of international financiers who backed the operation. This group included both the German industrialist Krupp and the notorious arms dealer Basil Zaharoff.

The mention of Zaharoff supports the contention that certain aspects of Courtney's account were most probably true, if not his version of the actual diving operation. First, Zaharoff had an acknowledged interest in salvage and had already been part of a syndicate that had financed the highly successful recovery of gold from the *Egypt* in 1931, in a depth of about 350 feet – very similar to the depth at which the *Hampshire* lay. Secondly, Zaharoff's secretary went on record as stating that Zaharoff frequently talked about the gold that he believed was on the *Hampshire*. Thirdly, and most interestingly of all, Zaharoff and Lloyd George were extremely close in 1916, with Zaharoff carrying out a number of quasi-diplomatic missions that were too delicate or too nefarious to entrust to the usual channels.

If anyone was in a good position to know what was on the *Hampshire* when it sailed, it would have been Zaharoff. He was the kind of man who made it his business to know such things.

The problem with the *Hampshire* gold theory is that the government, the Bank of England and the Admiralty have all consistently denied any knowledge of gold being on board. This is not quite the same thing as saying that there is no gold. It could also be explained as typical secrecy on the part of a government anxious not to have outsiders attempting to plunder the wreck, but unwilling to sponsor a salvage itself both because of its status as a war grave and because of the intrinsic difficulties involved. Still, there are aspects of the gold theory that do not add up. If Kitchener's mission had been partly involved with the transport of a massive quantity of gold, one would expect him to have been accompanied by senior Bank of England employees. The only civil servants who went on the mission were from the Ministry of Munitions, which ties in with the official explanation of the mission as being concerned with logistical support for the Russian war effort. More damning still for the gold enthusiasts is the evidence provided by cabinet papers inside the Public Record Office. There one can indeed find references to the transit of £10 million worth of gold involving Russia during the first half of 1916. However, the gold was being sent by Russia from Vladivostok to Canada for the credit of the British government as a payment for arms supplies from Britain, and not in the other direction. It would seem perverse if not inconceivable that at the same time as Russia was sending gold to Canada to credit the British account held there, Britain was sending gold to Russia.

But there are some wrecks which never cease to tease the imagination, and the *Hampshire* can be considered one of these. As recently as the 1980s, the ship was back in the news again. A new consortium, including a German-based underwater film-maker, was accused by the Ministry of Defence of illicitly removing items from the wreck. This highly secretive operation failed to throw any public light on the presence or otherwise of gold, but it did confirm that the damage to the *Hampshire*'s hull was more consistent with the explosion of a mine then an internal explosion caused by a saboteur's bomb.

One possible theory that has never been fully explored is that if there was gold on the *Hampshire*, it was not British gold at all, but privately owned Russian gold, held by the Romanov family in Britain, gold that was suddenly required in Russia in 1916 because of the state of emergency in which the Romanovs found themselves. One thing is certain. The *Hampshire* continues to exert an enduring fascination over treasure-hunters and shipwreck enthusiasts.

LEFT: *The cap band for Midshipman E. E. Fellowes who was lost on the* Hampshire. *The severe weather meant that it was impossible to launch any lifeboats and so the only chance of survival was to cling to a liferaft.*

52, LEADENHALL STREET,

LONDON, E.C.3.

10th March, 1925

F. W. Emler Esq.,
    Board of Trade
        Finance Department,
            Great George Street,
                S. W.

Dear Mr.Emler,

GOLD AT HAITI:

      I am in receipt of your letter and enclose
cheque herewith for £7. 2. 3. for cost of cables.

      The matter of recovery is in an interesting
position.   I am satisfied that the gold is or was at
Haiti, but unfortunately one of the gentlemen who knew
where it was and seemed able to obtain recovery, was found
dead in the streets of New York and the Map shewing the
position of the gold is apparently missing.   I have
had a long communication from my Agent in New York and
all I can say is that the letter itself was worth the
cost of the cables.   It reads more like one of Louis
Stevenson's romances.

          Yours sincerely,

THE APPAM
TREASURE ISLAND

On 3 September 1924 Sir Esme Howard, His Majesty's Ambassador at the British Embassy in Manchester, Massachusetts, received a telegram from George R. Mayo of the Friars Club in New York. Mr Mayo claimed that he had information concerning the whereabouts of a large quantity of British gold seized by a German ship during the First World War. He was prepared to divulge the location for a big percentage. He cited Judge Mackenzie Moss, Assistant Secretary to the Treasury, as a personal reference.

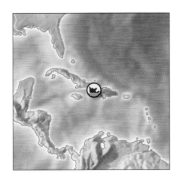

Sir Esme Howard took the telegram seriously. He promptly contacted His Majesty's Consul-General in New York and asked him to interview George Mayo. Together with a colleague, a Mr Cherry, Mayo presented himself at the British Consulate and provided further intriguing details. The gold consisted of £365,000 in British sovereigns. It had been deposited somewhere in Haiti. The present German government did not know of its whereabouts, but certain friends of the former Kaiser were in possession of the relevant details. Mayo and Cherry stressed that there was considerable urgency in the matter because a former German naval officer was already in Haiti making enquiries, in an endeavour to recover the gold. In return for their efforts Mayo and Cherry wanted 33 per cent of the proceeds.

Sir Esme decided to refer the gold story to the Right Honourable Ramsay MacDonald MP, the future British Prime Minister, then at the Treasury. He referred the matter to the Board of Trade, where a Mr Hipwood was finally given responsibility to investigate further. The first step was to establish whether there was any evidence of a loss of British gold during the war. Mr Hipwood put the matter succinctly in his minutes of 14 October 1924: 'The British Government could only take part in a treasure hunt of this kind if they were pretty confident that the treasure would turn out to be their property.' The Cargoes Miscellaneous Office could throw no light on the matter, nor could the Bank of England, nor the Admiralty. Sir Norman Hill of War Risk Insurance was consulted, but he also came up with nothing. Hipwood then contacted a specialist in marine insurance matters at the insurers,

ABOVE: *Count Nikolaus Burggraf und Graf zu Dohna-Schlodien is photographed on the bridge of the German raider ship Möwe. He was a highly effective commander who treated his prisoners in a civilized manner.*

OPPOSITE: *W. Hargreaves was an expert on marine insurance matters and was asked to investigate the Haiti gold story by the Board of Trade.*

C.T. Bowring, Mr Hargreaves, who posted a notice of the supposed loss at Lloyds of London and asked for any underwriters involved to come forward. Nobody responded. It was beginning to look as if the two Americans' story was nothing but a wild fabrication. Hargreaves sent Hipwood a note. 'After making many enquiries I cannot trace any Underwriter who paid a loss on gold in vessels captured or sunk by Germans.' The trail had gone cold.

One of the many surprising aspects of this story is that such a large loss of gold from a British ship should have been forgotten about so completely, not only by the insurance world but also by the relevant authorities including the Admiralty and the Bank of England. As it turned out, the Mayo/Cherry story was not a complete fabrication. It was only when a man who had been a passenger on a ship called the *Appam* heard about the rumoured loss of gold and came forward that the facts began to be clarified. This man worked in one of the big banks in the City of London. He had been a passenger on the Elder Dempster ship *Appam* in 1916 when she had been captured by the German cruiser *Möwe*, and he remembered hearing that a large quantity of gold had been removed from her holds. Once the name of the ship had been established it was relatively simple to trace the underwriters involved.

Negotiations with Mayo and Cherry suddenly returned to the top of the agenda. The Treasury were consulted, and the Foreign Office were asked to send the necessary cables, using a Foreign Office code. The Consul in New York was instructed by telegram to conclude negotiations with Mayo and Cherry, agreeing if necessary to their terms of 33 per cent of the total gold recovered.

The *Möwe* (whose name means seagull) was one of a second generation of German navy surface raiders developed during the latter part of 1915. At this stage of the war Germany did not yet have sufficient numbers of submarines to disrupt British trade on a major scale and surface raiders were used to supplement the U-boat threat. The *Möwe* was a converted cargo ship, the *Pongo* which had carried bananas from Togoland, the former German colony in West Africa. Nondescript in appearance, the *Möwe* was equipped with five carefully concealed and powerfully destructive 15cm guns, supplemented by four torpedo tubes. It was also capable of changing its silhouette at will by means of a fake funnel and a false superstructure. Moreover, it had the advantage over previous raiders of being comparatively economical on fuel and therefore able to remain at sea much longer without the service of supply boats. It was commanded by a humane and unflappable Prussian count whose full title was Nikolaus Burggraf und Graf zu Dohna-Schlodien.

The *Möwe* slipped out of the German port of Kiel in December 1915 for its first cruise, making a wide sweep north of Scotland and west of Ireland and then tracking south. Count Dohna-Schlodien largely ignored all ships with two or more funnels on the basis that these were most likely to be passenger ships. The problem with chasing passenger ships was that often they were too fast for him to catch, and if he was lucky enough to overhaul and sink one, there was then the problem of what to do with the passengers – this was still a period when war at sea was conducted along relatively honourable lines, and Count Dohna-Schlodien did not believe in simply abandoning his victims to take their chances in lifeboats. The Count's ideal target was the slow tramping cargo ship that was straggling across the ocean by itself. He claimed his first victim on 11 January 1916 around 150 miles west of Finisterre, in northwest Spain. Here he stopped the steamer *Farringford*, which was carrying a cargo of 4,700 tons of copper, and sank it, the crew having first been taken on board the *Möwe*. In the days that followed, a succession of British cargo ships met a similar fate.

It was also on 11 January that the screw steamer *Appam* left Dakar in West Africa for Liverpool. The *Appam* was a large cargo/passenger ship of 7,781 gross tons, 425 feet long, built by Harland and Wolff for the British & African Steam Navigation Company. She had forty German prisoners of war on board, captured from German territories in West Africa. At around 12.30 on 15 January, in clear weather, Captain Harrison of the *Appam* noticed smoke on the horizon. By 3.00 p.m., at which time the *Appam* was approaching Madeira, the mystery vessel was identified as a tramp steamer in bad need of a fresh coat of paint. As the two ships closed, the anonymous tramp steamer suddenly swung across the *Appam*'s bows and signalled for the larger vessel to stop. Captain Harrison, thinking that the other vessel was in some kind of distress, ordered the radio officer to send a signal. The signal was jammed and the *Möwe* immediately disclosed its true identity, revealed its guns and fired a shot across the *Appam*'s bows. Captain Harrison surrendered, but not before he had thrown overboard all the ship's papers and code-books. The *Appam* was armed with a single twelve-pounder gun at its stern, but in order to preserve the lives of his passengers Captain Harrison decided not to deploy it.

The *Appam* was a most fortunate capture for Count Dohna-Schlodien at this point in his cruise. The ample accommodation available meant that he was able to transfer the numerous captured British crew members that he had with him on the already overcrowded *Möwe*. As a most unexpected bonus, a large quantity of gold was discovered in the *Appam*'s strong-room. Sixteen heavy boxes were subsequently transferred to the *Möwe*, of which fourteen contained gold bars and the other two flasks of gold dust. Count Dohna-Schlodien was later to estimate that the largest of the bars weighed sixty pounds and that the total value of the gold was in excess of one million German marks. Mayo and Cherry's information concerning both the

ABOVE: *The* Möwe *was capable of disguising its appearance by means of a fake funnel and a false superstructure. This photograph shows the ship in the 1920s in its third incarnation, the* Greenbrier.

total value and the nature of the gold, however, was not consistent with these findings and raises doubts as to whether the *Appam* cargo was the one they were talking about.

Leutnant Hans Berg was put in charge of the *Appam* with a prize crew. After two more days sailing in a southwesterly direction and two more captures, the Count ordered Berg to take the *Appam* into the US port of Newport News, Virginia. The *Möwe*, meanwhile, continued on its destructive course south and west towards the Caribbean. The two ships parted company, never to meet again.

The British Consul in New York, Sir K. Armstrong, under instructions from London, reopened negotiations with Mayo and Cherry. Further facts were emerging. Cherry had originally obtained his information about the stolen gold hidden in Haiti from a German named Armgaard Karl Graves. The previous year Graves, under the assumed name of Paul K. Granett, had become a naturalized citizen of Haiti and had obtained a concession for oil and mineral research on an area of land where the gold was supposedly hidden. Further research by the Consul-General revealed that Graves had been a German spy during the war, and since the end of the war had written a book about his experiences. Graves had

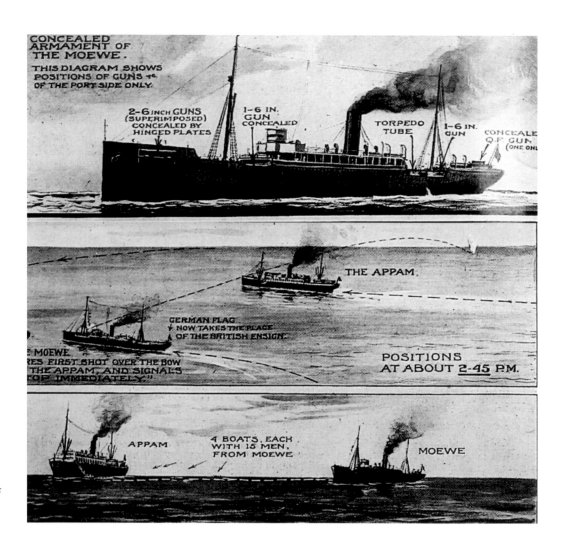

RIGHT: *This line drawing illustrates how beneath the* Möwe's *innocent appearance it carried a quantity of powerful weaponry.*

also obtained an advance of $15,000 from Cherry for the purposes of assisting in the hunt for the gold. This helped explain why Cherry and Mayo were now so desperate to get the British authorities involved under a new deal which they hoped would forestall Graves' attempt to double-cross them. The Consulate requested their representative in Port au Prince to start making discreet enquiries as to the whereabouts of Karl Graves.

Negotiations with Mayo and Cherry dragged on. The authorities fussed about whether it was legally correct for them to promise a percentage of the gold to the two Americans when the gold might belong to the German government under the laws of war or even to the Haiti government as treasure trove. Then, in March of the following year, there was an unexpected development. Mr Hargreaves, of the insurers C.T. Bowring, described the new situation succinctly in his letter to the Board of Trade of 10 March: 'I am satisfied that the gold is or was at Haiti, but unfortunately one of the gentlemen who knew where it was and seemed able to obtain recovery, was found dead in the streets of New York and the map showing the position of the gold is apparently missing.' The letter does not state whether the victim was Mayo or Cherry, but the British government's involvement in the search for the missing gold ended with this incident.

Hargreaves was astute and respected in the world of London insurance throughout the war and during the 1920s. It is therefore difficult to explain his continued belief that there was gold buried in Haiti, particularly after he had been made fully aware of the dubious role played by Karl Graves in the proceedings. Unfortunately, there were a number of letters and telegrams concerning the affair that are not in the Public Record Office archives, but which might have thrown further light on the entire murky business had they survived. Whatever gold was or was not buried on the island, it is now clear that it did not come from the *Appam*. The *Möwe* never went near Haiti, as is made clear from the track chart of its movements based on German naval records. What is more, Count Dohna-Schlodien handed over every last penny of the captured *Appam* gold to the German Reichsbank. As a reward for his achievement and honesty he was presented by the Kaiser with one empty wooden gold box.

THE LAURENTIC
DAMANT'S BIG HAUL

I N JANUARY 1917 LIEUTENANT-COMMANDER G.C.C. DAMANT, as he was known at the time, was summoned to an urgent meeting at the Admiralty with a grim-faced Director of Naval Ordnance and was told that he was about to be provided with highly confidential information. Damant had been selected because he already had a reputation as an experienced and efficient navy diver who had successfully carried out a number of difficult and dangerous operations. Even more important, his honesty and integrity were without question. The Director then divulged that a few days earlier the White Star liner *Laurentic* had been sunk off Lough Swilly, in the far north of Ireland, and, rather more to the purpose of the present meeting, it had been carrying 35 tons of gold ingots stowed in its second-class baggage room, valued at the time at a staggering £5 million – today worth in excess of £250 million. Damant was asked what he thought the chances were of a successful salvage, bearing in mind that the *Laurentic* was lying in twenty-three fathoms of water in a very exposed position and that the gold was locked deep in the holds of the huge liner. Damant, a laconic, practical man, not given to bluff and bluster, replied that he thought it was possible, given appropriate resources. He was promised that everything he needed would be made available. Little did he realize at that point that he was starting on a seven-year salvage epic that was to set a new world record for quantity of gold recovered, and one which stands to this day.

The 14,892-ton liner *Laurentic* had been built by the famous Belfast shipbuilders Harland and Wolff in 1908 for the White Star Line's transatlantic crossings. At the outbreak of the First World War it was requisitioned for troop carrying and a year later was converted into an auxiliary armed cruiser. It was in this last manifestation that it set out from Liverpool on 23 January 1917, under the command of Captain Reginald Norton, *en route* to Halifax, in Canada. The main purpose of the voyage was the delivery of £5 million of gold, to be used to pay for munitions. By this stage of the war Allied shipping losses were reaching their peak. The *Laurentic* called in to Lough Swilly for a brief stop and left again on 25 January.

OPPOSITE: *At the outbreak of the war the* Laurentic *was converted from a luxury liner to an auxiliary armed cruiser used for troop carrying.*

ABOVE: *Nearly half the 722 men on board were lost when the* Laurentic *ran into a minefield just north of Malin head. The minefield had been laid just a few days before by the German submarine* U-80.

An hour after departure, as it rounded Malin Head, the luckless ship ran into a minefield laid a few days previously by the German submarine *U–80*. Two explosions were heard in quick succession, and within forty-five minutes the ship was down. Accounts vary greatly as to the number of lives lost, but of the 722 men on board almost half were either drowned or died of exposure in the bitterly cold January weather.

The wreck was quickly located and found to be lying on its port side, with the decks at such a precipitous angle that it was impossible to walk on them. At this depth the heavy swell of the surface sea also caused strong horizontal surges of water below, so that the divers were in constant danger of being swept off their feet and carried away. The only means of negotiating the ship was to cling tightly to the top starboard rail some 60 feet above the seabed and edge one's way along it. It was a strange combination of diving and mountaineeering. An added danger was from the heavy wooden blocks, used for lowering the ship's lifeboats, which were now hanging loose from the ship's davits and swinging wildly around in the subsurface currents, threatening instant concussion to any diver unlucky enough to make contact.

Damant's salvage ship was moored above the wreck, using a four-point mooring system. It was essential that the salvage ship should be held as tightly as possible, because any untoward movement could cause stress on the diver's air line or increase the chance of it snagging on an overhang of fractured steel. Damant had been issued with structural plans of the *Laurentic* and calculated that the shortest route to the second-class baggage room, where the gold was stowed, was through a watertight door in the hull of the ship, known as the entry port, situated about half-way down the ship's side. Using charges of gun cotton, the enormous steel doors were blasted open and hoisted to the surface on wires. Inside these outer doors was a barred iron gate that had to be blasted off. It was then a matter of clearing away the miscellaneous packing-cases blocking the passageway that led on a downward slope to the strong-room. Once the strong-room door was reached, diver E.C. Miller forced it open using a hammer and chisel. Having got it open, he literally fell into a room full of boxes of gold. The boxes were quite small, about twelve inches square and six inches deep, but each one weighed 140 pounds, making them extremely awkward to handle. Each box contained six gold bars and each gold bar was approximately 9 inches by 3 inches by 1.5 inches. Miller managed to get one box out that evening and three more the following morning. The operation so far had taken just two weeks, despite poor weather conditions. Damant confidently expected that the entire £5 million would be brought to the surface within another month. What he did not take into account was the ferocity of the sea off Malin Head in more extreme weather conditions.

Miller had just brought up his fourth box when the wind changed direction and a northerly gale started blowing, bringing diving operations to a halt. During the next week wreckage began coming ashore from the ship, which indicated that the hull was breaking up – it was an inauspicious sign. When the divers returned to the wreck the entry port, which had previously been 62 feet below the surface, was now 103 feet below. The entire ship had collapsed downwards through 40 feet. The passageway that Miller had formerly negotiated standing up had now been squeezed down to a height of just 18 inches.

Successful salvors require two qualities above all others: patience and persistence. By means of carefully calculated explosions, Damant began blasting his way back through the crushed ship to where he knew the strong-room had once been. It was a tunnelling operation requiring constant shoring up of the structure overhead to prevent the weight of

LEFT: *The* HMS Laurentic *at anchor in Porto Grande, in its guise as an armed merchant cruiser.*

ABOVE: *The top illustration shows diver Light blown up feet first while working on the wreck of the* Laurentic. *This was likely to happen if the air pumped down to the diver was at a greater pressure than the surrounding water. The illustration below shows one of Captain Damant's divers digging down for gold.*

the upper decks crushing downwards a second time. Meanwhile the colossal liner was still settling on the seabed, with frequent shudderings and the groaning of tearing metal. The diver was dependent on his air line to breathe, and if it snagged he faced immediate drowning. Damant's was an immensely hazardous salvage operation. The strong-room was eventually reached a second time – but it was empty. The floor had been ripped open and the gold had fallen through into the tangled bowels of the ship.

Damant decided that he could not risk tunnelling downwards any further. Instead he now determined to remove the entire superstructure of the ship that was lying above where the strong-room had once been, creating a kind of bowl. It was slow, painstaking work. Each plate of steel had to be loosened by explosions of gun cotton and then hoisted out of the way to the surface. This method too was not without its perils. On one occasion diver Blachford was crawling under a plate of steel, already partially hoisted on a wire from the salvage ship. He was trying to place another charge of gun cotton where the plate was still attached to the wreck in order to free it. Suddenly, the wire gave way and the steel plate came crashing down, trapping Blachford beneath it. He immediately used his underwater telephone to communicate with those on the surface ship, asking calmly for more air to be pumped down. The air pressure was increased as requested, and another diver called Light was instructed to go and see what was wrong. Blachford's strained voice continued to be heard asking for more air. Damant was reluctant to turn the pressure up too strongly for fear that the diver's suit would explode and he would immediately drown. On the other hand it was possible that the suit had already torn and that Blachford needed the increased air pressure to keep back the encroaching water. It was not possible to communicate with Blachford, and Damant decided against turning the air pressure up any higher. Fortunately, Light reached Blachford with great speed, secured another wire to the steel plate and got it winched off Blachford's trapped body. Blachford had been calling for more air because he felt the weight of the plate was crushing his chest. He was lucky to get back to the surface with nothing more than a few bruises.

The precariousness of the wreck's structure was not the only threat to a diver's safety. The German U-boats were still laying mines in the area, and when the minesweepers detonated a mine within a radius of five miles the divers down below were likely to receive a violent shock. Despite the obvious hazards, however, the work continued through two long months. It was akin to picking through a giant scrapheap – as well as metal, there was enormous quantities of lumber, ship's furnishings, bedding and food supplies to work through. It all had to be put in giant buckets and hoisted to the surface. It was Miller again who first found gold, this time in the shape of ten loose bars. This gave the divers a new focus for their activities, and by enlarging the hole around where these first bars had been found they soon discovered more. By September 1917 £800,000 worth of gold had been brought up, but this still left £4,200,000 worth of gold somewhere in the debris. The weather deteriorated and operations were suspended until the following spring. As the spring of 1918 arrived, however, Damant and his team of expert divers were required elsewhere on what Damant teasingly described as even more exciting work. Because of this interruption it was not until the spring of 1919 that he returned to the *Laurentic*, this time with an improved salvage ship called the *Racer*. To Damant's surprise the wreck was still in much the same state as it had been when they left it nearly two years before, and within a few weeks bars of gold were again being brought to the surface. As the season wore on the

BELOW: *The top drawing shows the state of the* Laurentic *was in when divers first found it on the seabed in 1917. The bottom drawing shows how the decks had collapsed onto one another and the steel plates of the hull had buckled by the time the divers abandoned operations in 1924.*

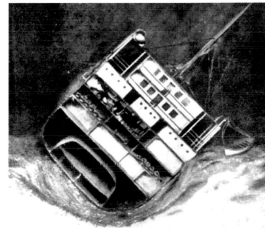

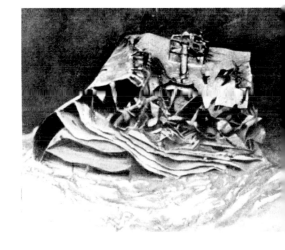

rate of recovery began to slacken. There was also a renewed threat from the overhanging superstructure on either side, which rose high above the hole that had been excavated and was beginning to lean inwards over the divers like two slowly collapsing skyscrapers. By the year end only a further £470,000 had been salvaged.

By the spring of 1920 the entire subterranean landscape had changed yet again. The leaning towers had finally collapsed, covering the previous year's excavations with thousands of tons of debris, including beds, chairs, porcelain, baths, planking, pipes and all manner of the ship's fittings and furniture. To make matters worse, sand and stone were now also being washed inside the hull of the ship, so that as fast as the divers dug by day, their work was likely to be filled up again overnight. Pumps and grabs were deployed from the surface ship to try to remove some of the overburden, but they were found to be ineffectual, partly because of the problem of keeping the salvage ship still enough on its moorings and partly because of the varied nature of the items they were dealing with. In the end the entire job was done by hand, with divers picking over the rubbish until their fingers bled. They were issued with protective diving gloves, but none of the divers wore them because the thickness of the material made it impossible to feel the subtle smoothness of a gold bar when occasionally one came to hand.

For two entire summer seasons, 1920 and 1921, only a small flow of gold bars came to the surface. The main bulk of the gold was still out of reach. Searching through the debris pile was an arduous and relentless business. Frequently, as soon as the divers excavated a hole, the sea would wash sand and gravel back into the ship, obliterating weeks of work in a single night. It was during this period that Damant's leadership qualities were at their most vital. He had always exercised great care to ensure that if his divers worked harder on the bottom than usual, lifting a steel plate or digging out a gold bar, then the decompression time was increased to compensate. He now instituted a system of short 30-minute sessions on the seabed during which the divers worked flat out shovelling sand. The quantity of sand that each diver shifted was hoisted to the surface, carefully weighed and dumped out of the way. By this means a friendly competition was set up between the divers, which helped to relieve the mind-numbing tedium of their work on the bottom as well as to increase productivity. At the same time Damant was always careful to ensure that safety regulations were observed. A second dive was not allowed for four hours after completion of the first, and the period on the bottom was shortened to 25 minutes. He was very aware that the harder a diver worked, the more time he required to spend on decompression, which is why he kept the working sessions so short. Also the danger of 'bends' was always greater on the second dive. The *Racer* was equipped with a recompression chamber on board to help divers who did suffer from attacks of the 'bends'. The *Laurentic* project was remarkable not least because at the end of the seven-year salvage operation none of the divers had suffered a serious accident. But during 1920 and 1921 only fifty more gold bars were recovered in total.

Sometimes the sea reveals as well as conceals. When the divers returned for the 1922 season, two feet of silt had been washed away and a number of gold bars could be seen sticking out of the sand. That year proved to be the best so far, with 895 more bars being recovered. Many of them were twisted and crushed completely out of their original shape as a result of the grinding they had suffered between the massive steel plates of the collapsing ship. Almost all evidence of the original wooden boxes had disappeared. Most of the bars were discovered 18–24 inches beneath the sand. The compacted sand itself was loosened by means of water from a high-pressure hose.

The 1923 season was better still, bringing a haul of 1,255 gold ingots to the surface. By the end of the season the divers had cleared right down to the steel hull of the ship on the lower port side. Some of the gold, however, had worked through rents and gaps in the hull and so lay below the ship and out of reach. The entire port hull section was now cut up over an area of 2,000 square feet and the metal slabs removed. In 1924 another 129 bars were recovered. The salvage operation had now recovered a total of 3,186 bars out of an original total of 3,211. After seven long years, with 25 bars still unaccounted for, the Admiralty decided to terminate proceedings. The salvage team as a whole, which included the divers, received as a bonus a total 0.125 per cent of the gold recovered, to be shared between them. The diver who brought up £45,000 worth of gold in one day was awarded an especially generous tin of cigarettes.

It was inevitable that with twenty-five bars of gold still remaining other salvors would sooner or later turn their attention to the *Laurentic*. In 1931 the Malet Salvage Syndicate visited the site and recovered a further five bars. In 1953 Risdon Beazley Marine Ltd also carried out an operation, but without any success. Since then there have been a number of further attempts, but no more bars have come to light. Treasure ships invariably keep something back for themselves. The attraction of the *Laurentic* for future treasure hunters may well be enhanced, however, by recently obtained evidence that when it sank it was also carrying, in addition to the gold bullion, £60,000 in ship's money, most probably in the form of sovereigns, which was never accounted for. That quantity, which is much more than was usually carried for contingency use, would today be worth in excess of £5 million. But where would it have been stowed?

ABOVE: *A brass porthole from the* Laurentic *corroded and twisted but still recognisably a porthole.*

PILOT BOAT NO.19

DARK DAYS

ON 3 SEPTEMBER 1939, FOLLOWING ADOLF HITLER'S invasion of Poland, Britain and France declared war on Germany and the Second World War began. Shortly afterwards the first British troops were crossing the Channel to bolster the defences against the threatened invasion by the Germans, but only in northern France, as Holland and Belgium had repeatedly emphasized their neutrality. For the next few months, during what became known as the 'phoney war', the armies on either side made no aggressive move – this was until April 1940, when Germany suddenly invaded Norway and Denmark.

At sea, however, it was a different story. As early as 17 September 1939 the British aircraft carrier *Courageous* was torpedoed and sunk by a German submarine off the coast of Ireland, an ominous reminder of the stranglehold imposed by the U-boats in the previous war. By November, Allied shipping losses had been greatly increased by the introduction of a new weapon, the magnetic mine, which was lethally effective against any iron-hulled ship passing over it. A month later, following the retrieval and dismantling of a magnetic mine, the British were able to develop a countermeasure: it was possible to protect a ship's hull by wrapping a demagnetizing coil around it. Known as 'degaussing', this became a vital part of a ship's defences.

On the morning of 10 May 1940 German ground forces under General Fedor von Bock made a lightning attack across the Belgian and Dutch frontiers, with devastating results. The attack on the ground was backed up by massive aerial support and the dropping of thousands of German parachute troops. For months the governments of Holland and Belgium, against all the evidence, had stubbornly refused to believe that Hitler would ever invade. It was for this reason that neither country had co-operated with Britain and France in any serious defensive contingency planning. They were worried that co-operation might compromise their neutrality. In the event, when the invasion came they were ill prepared

Above: *The crisis of May 1940, with German troops marching into Holland and Belgium, led to Winston Churchill being appointed as Prime Minister of Britain and taking overall responsibility for the future conduct of the war.*

and hopelessly outmatched. At about 7.00 a.m. both governments appealed to Britain and France for help, but it was already too late. It was at 4.30 p.m. on the same day that the British Prime Minister, Neville Chamberlain resigned in favour of a national coalition government led by Winston Churchill.

The German plan was to convince the Allies that it was the 1914 scenario all over again – an outflanking invasion of France via the Low Countries. Within forty-eight hours Holland and Belgium had been virtually overrun, and French and British forces were drawn northwards to stem the tide. Meanwhile, further south, seven Panzer divisions with 1,800 tanks forged their way through the hills of the Ardennes, across the River Meuse and into the heartland of France. By 21 May the Germans had reached the Channel near Abbeville, the Allied forces in the north were cut off, and only the 'miracle' of the Dunkirk evacuation prevented total disaster. For the Allies these were probably the darkest days of the war.

As the first news of the German invasion reached Britain early on 10 May, orders were issued for immediate sorties across the North Sea to destroy key strategic installations along the Dutch and Belgian coastline before they fell into German hands and could be used against the Allies. Among those contacted was Lt.-Commander John Younghusband, in command of the destroyer HMS *Wild Swan*, then at Dover. He was ordered to embark Special Party B and stores and make for the Hook of Holland as fast as possible.

Special Party B was a small contingent of highly trained men, under the leadership of Commander J.A.C. Hill, an expert in demolition. Their assignment was to destroy installations such as oil depots, airfields, sea defences and bridges. The *Wild Swan* arrived off the port of the Hook at 4.30 p.m. Younghusband knew from various signals received earlier that day that magnetic mines had recently been dropped in the entrance to Hook harbour, but he still needed to get in and land his party and their equipment. Luckily he spotted a Dutch pilot boat in the vicinity and with the assistance of the Dutch pilot, who claimed to know where the mines were placed, they made a dramatic entry at 20 knots on the wrong side of the channel marker buoys. Younghusband afterwards described this manoeuvre in his official report as 'somewhat hair-raising'. Meanwhile a large squadron of German bombers were attacking overhead.

The port of the Hook was still at this point held by the Dutch, and the British ship was greeted by a loud cheer as it berthed at the quayside. The feelings of the locals, however, quickly became more ambivalent when they discovered the real purpose of the *Wild Swan*'s desperate sortie through the minefield. The local Dutch commander came on board and interviewed Commander Hill. He was not happy with the idea of having his harbour demolished. He hadn't given up hope of stemming the German advance, even while German paratroopers were falling out of the sky in ever increasing numbers. Commander Hill mollified the Dutchman by assuring him that it was only intended to set the demolition fuses in place. They would not be triggered until the Dutch command gave instructions. In any case the Hook was not the main target of Hill's demolition squad. Far more important strategically were the huge port of Rotterdam and its airfield at Waalhaven. However, the transport that Hill had been promised did not materialize and he was left without any obvious method of reaching Rotterdam. German troops were everywhere, many of the streets were blocked or under heavy gunfire, and the civil administration was in chaos. In the absence of transport Hill decided to commandeer *Pilot Boat No. 19*. He was half-way through loading his explosives when, at 6.31 p.m., an urgent naval cipher came through to the *Wild Swan* from the British Admiralty. It read as follows:

> Dutch foreign minister states that there is a large amount of gold at Rotterdam. Estimated weight 36 tons. It is essential to get gold away tonight. Make all arrangements in co-operation with local authorities. Gold to be loaded in merchant ships or *Wild Swan* as convenient.

Younghusband and Hill held an immediate crisis meeting to decide how to carry out these new and unexpected instructions. After careful consideration it was decided that Hill would take the pilot boat and attempt to bring back the gold to the Hook, where it could be transferred on to HMS *Wild Swan* for shipment across the North Sea to England. It was felt that the pilot boat had the better chance of getting through to Rotterdam, approximately 20 miles inland. There was little or no possibility of the *Wild Swan* itself being able to penetrate up the narrow waterway, where it would have been an easy target for the German planes. The pilot boat would be a less tempting one. The only problem was that it had no degaussing equipment and was thus particularly vulnerable to magnetic mines.

While the German invasion had taken the Dutch military forces completely by surprise, the bankers in Rotterdam proved to be somewhat better prepared. Since the beginning of the year over fifty million guilders had already been transferred to New York. Far more than that amount still remained in the vaults of the Netherlands Bank, but at least it was all packed and ready for evacuation.

Hill took three of his men with him and left for Rotterdam at 8:15 p.m., 10 May. Arriving in Rotterdam around midnight, he discovered that the southern and eastern parts of the town were already controlled by German troops. To make matters more confusing, many of these German troops were disguised as Dutch troops and even, according to some

reports, as women. The evacuation of the gold was clearly going to be an extremely hazardous business. On more than one occasion, making his way from the dockside to the Netherlands Bank, Hill was arrested by the Dutch authorities, only to be released again when they discovered who he was. Eventually, with the assistance of Dutch marines, the gold was loaded into three vans and brought safely through the narrow back streets of Rotterdam to the dockside of Lekhaven, where *Pilot Boat No. 19* was still waiting. The 200 heavy boxes, each containing four ingots, were then manhandled from the vans into the limited stowage space of the small boat. The only place for such a quantity of gold was on deck. Commander Hill then set off once again in the early hours of the morning up the narrow and perilous waterway for the Hook of Holland.

Younghusband was meanwhile having a busy night of it. Soon after Hill's departure a Dutch naval and military mission arrived under Major-General J.W. van Borschot, requesting safe passage to England. This small group of senior Dutch officers were tired and hungry, having set out from The Hague at 5 a.m. They said they were originally to have flown from The Hague in a small plane, but the plane was commandeered by senior members of the Dutch government, leaving them no alternative but to try to find their way to a port and a friendly ship. Younghusband arranged for them to be fed.

German planes continued to fly low overhead, dropping bombs. The gunners on the *Wild Swan* returned fire but to little effect. Younghusband was somewhat puzzled, after a while, as to why his ship remained unscathed by the heavy aerial bombardment. Then it occurred to him that as long as they remained moored close to the wharves they were probably relatively safe. It was not in German interests to destroy a port which they hoped soon to be making good use of themselves. Their targets were rather Dutch gun emplacements and military installations. German paratroopers were, however, continuing to descend from the skies with the assistance of night-time flares. There was a danger that the *Wild Swan* might be boarded by enemy troops, which were becoming very numerous along the right bank of the river. To help avert such an attack, Younghusband ordered the moorings to be loosened and the ship to be edged twenty feet or so away from the dockside.

At 2.15 a.m. Younghusband received a message from British Naval Command requesting him to get in touch with the Consul-General in Rotterdam, who was to direct all British and Norwegian shipping to depart immediately as the situation was deteriorating. Younghusband got through on the telephone and relayed the message. There was no news from the Consul-General as to the whereabouts or progress of Commander Hill. However, in a later phone call the harbour-master of Rotterdam told Younghusband that *Pilot Boat No. 19* was at that moment loading.

At around dawn on 11 May the destroyers *Wyvern*, *Hyperion* and *Havock* arrived with more demolition parties to support those that were already working. By now the pilot boat was overdue, and on the *Wild Swan* they were beginning to worry about what had happened to it. Their worst fears were confirmed at 7.45 a.m., when Younghusband was informed by the Dutch authorities that on its return journey along the waterway the pilot boat had hit a magnetic mine off the eastern end of Rozenburg Island. Commander Hill and his three assistants had all been killed instantly. Of the 22 Dutch crew only three survived, all seriously injured.

Shortly before dawn on 12 May the *Wild Swan* was ordered to leave the harbour and patrol along the Dutch coast between the Hook and Ymuiden. On passing through the narrow harbour entrance the ship was attacked by a German plane diving almost vertically out of the sky and dropping four bombs, all of which only missed their target by distances of thirty to fifty feet. Turning sharply in a desperate effort to swerve away from the attack, the *Wild Swan* grounded briefly, which caused the ship considerable damage and what Younghusband later termed 'condenseritis'. However, this did not prevent the destroyer from lending invaluable assistance later that same day when the Dutch troopship *Princess Juliana* was heavily bombed off the Hook. The *Wild Swan* went alongside and took off 30 men trapped in the bows of the sinking ship shortly before it went down and then picked up another ten out of the water.

There are conflicting accounts of what happened to the gold that sank off the eastern end of Rozenburg Island. According to some authorities the Germans discovered its whereabouts and salvaged part of it during the war, leaving the Dutch salvage company Smit Tak to pick up the rest when hostilities ended. Enquiries with Smit Tak themselves, however, suggest a somewhat different scenario. The initial reaction of their senior management was one of amazement that anyone outside a small circle of senior Dutch and British officials should know anything about the lost gold. On being pressed, however, they confirmed that they had carried out a highly secretive salvage operation as almost their first job after the war. According to this source the Germans had not recovered anything, having been completely unaware of the fortune in gold that sat in shallow water right under their noses throughout hostilities. Perhaps the more interesting question is not who picked up the lost ingots, but how many still remain in the mud.

THE EMPRESS OF BRITAIN

CATHEDRAL ON THE SEA FLOOR

ONE OF THE MOST HAUNTING TREASURE MYSTERIES of the Second World War centres on the sad fate of the giant liner *Empress of Britain*. In 1995 a multimillion dollar operation, financed by private investors, was carried out in conditions of the utmost secrecy on the upturned hull lying on the seabed some sixty miles off the wild northwest coast of Ireland. Its purpose was to salvage the gold bullion that the investors believed the Empress had been carrying when it was bombed, torpedoed and finally sunk in October 1940. A highly respected Aberdeen-based company, that spends most of its time on lucrative North Sea oil-related contracts, was chartered in to carry out the operation. It was conducted in a quick and professional manner, using the latest in saturation diving techniques from a ship dynamically positioned over the site. A neat hole was cut through the external steel plates of the hull in order to gain access to the bullion room. Once inside, the divers discovered that the raging fire, started by the bombing, had gutted almost the entire wreck. Just a silent shell remained, like a huge empty dome rising from the seabed. To stand inside this ravaged cathedral, which was lit up by their powerful headlamp torches, was an awesome and sombre experience.

As it happened, the bullion room, a reinforced chamber towards the bow of the ship, the position of which could be precisely identified from the plans, had escaped the worst of the fire and was still surprisingly intact, albeit upside down. The floor, formerly the ceiling, was covered in a thick layer of silt. To the disappointment of the salvors, however, there was no gold. What they did find, unexpectedly, was the skeleton of a man. It was well known that forty-nine unfortunate men, women and children had lost their lives during the original disaster, but most of these had leapt from the burning ship and drowned. Why would anyone have been in the bullion room, a place of top security, during the ship's last perilous moments? It made no obvious sense. The salvage team held a short service of commemoration for the unidentified corpse and aborted the project.

ABOVE: *Captain Charles Howard Sapsworth CVO had been hoping to dock his ship in Liverpool one day ahead of schedule when the* Empress *came under aerial attack.*

OPPOSITE: *The* Empress of Britain *was built by the Clyde shipbuilders John Brown & Co for the Canadian Pacific Railway Company to cater for the rapidly expanding luxury world cruise market.*

ABOVE: *A cut away of the
Empress which shows the location
of the tennis court just to the stern
of the aft funnel, where Mrs Joan
Stephenson and her friend Mrs
Wallace had their morning game
as well as the specie room directly
below the bridge but seven decks
down.*

The *Empress of Britain* had been constructed in Scotland in 1931 by the Clyde shipbuilders John Brown & Co. for the giant Canadian Pacific Railway Company. It was not the biggest ship in the world, but at 42,348 tons and with a length of 733 feet it was impressively large. The designers' brief had been to create a ship capacious enough to give its clientele that feeling of being in a floating palace, but slim enough to squeeze through the Suez and Panama canals. The latter was an important consideration because the *Empress* had been built specifically to cater for the rapidly expanding luxury world cruise market. In this role it was a great success and the name *Empress of Britain* soon became synonymous with riches and privilege. The ship had all the extravagance of a Hollywood film set, with its Turkish baths and cinemas, soda fountains and knickerbocker bars, tennis and squash courts and swimming pools. All this was to change rapidly when war broke out. On 24 November 1939 the *Empress* was requisitioned, painted battleship grey, and reborn as a sombre utilitarian troopship. It was a sudden and dramatic reincarnation.

On 6 August 1940 the *Empress of Britain* left Liverpool for Suez, via Cape Town in South Africa. It was a thankfully uneventful voyage. On 23 September the liner began its return journey from Suez. There were over one thousand passengers on board – mainly

servicemen returning on leave or being redeployed, as well as wives, who were being evacuated from the deteriorating situation in the Middle East. Some of the passengers disembarked at Durban and Cape Town. There were 647 people on board including crew, for the final leg of the journey from Cape Town to Liverpool.

Britain had learnt the lesson of the First World War with regard to the defensive importance of travelling in convoy. Ships such as the *Empress* were still permitted to sail by themselves, however, because of their superior speed. The *Empress* was capable of 24 knots, and could easily outdistance any predatory U-boat. Unfortunately, the same invulnerability did not apply to aerial attack.

By 26 October the *Empress* was cruising up the west coast of Ireland and almost safely home after a round trip in excess of 20,000 miles. It was not due to dock in Liverpool until the 28 October, but Captain Sapsworth CVO had made such good speed that he was considering trying to arrive at high tide on the 27 October. Most of the passengers had relished the voyage on a ship whose luxurious appointments might well have been beyond their means in peacetime. Mrs Joan Stephenson and her friend Mrs Wallace were just preparing for their usual morning game of tennis on the superb court situated towards the aft of the open-air Sports Deck. Lord and Lady Yarborough were lingering over breakfast. Mrs Rona Trotter was packing away some of her personal items ready for disembarkation in the next day or so. Major George Trotter was strolling along the First Class Promenade Deck taking the air. It was a cloudy morning with a slight easterly wind. Few of these apparently carefree passengers can have been entirely unaware of the fact that the ship, while certainly on its final stretch, was also entering the most dangerous phase of the voyage. It was after all the home waters that were infested by U-boats and overflown by German bombers.

Oberleutnant Bernard Jope had taken off from Bordeaux at 4.00 a.m. that same morning in a Focke-Wulf C 200 Condor with a crew of six. The plane had a top speed of 180 mph, could stay in the air for fifteen hours without refuelling and was carrying six 250 kg bombs, a highly destructive payload. It was Jope's first operational flight as a commander. He was 26 years old.

It was Able Seaman Petch who was the first to spot a plane on the port quarter, at a distance of some 3–4,000 yards. He pointed it out to Chief Petty Officer Jevans. At first it was assumed that the plane was probably friendly, most likely sent by Coastal Command

BELOW: *The six members of the crew of the Focke-Wulf plane that bombed the* Empress *including their commander Oberleutnant Bernhard Jope.*

114

to provide air cover for the incoming liner. When the plane wheeled to approach the stern of the ship and all four of its engines became visible, however, it was immediately obvious that it was an enemy bomber. Within seconds a bomb had hit the *Empress* amidships, wreaking huge damage. The ship's gunners returned fire, but to little effect. The time was 9.20 a.m. The wireless room sent an SOS giving the position of attack as 55.08° North, 10.46° West. Mrs Wallace lay dead, face down on the tennis court, still clutching her racket. Fire broke out and began to spread rapidly.

Bernard Jope swung his plane round and came back for a second run. The ship was already partially obscured by a dense black cloud, and this time his bombs missed. He turned and came back for a third time, on this occasion approaching the bow of the ship, strafing the bridge with cannon shot before dropping his final lethal bombs. He scored a second hit. He then headed back to German-occupied France, touching down at Brest with one engine damaged by the liner's guns.

The *Empress* was in chaos, with sirens sounding continually and everyone running in different directions in a desperate effort to escape the raging fires. There was no obvious place of safety. There was very little order, little discipline and a total breakdown of communication between different parts of the ship. And yet, despite this appalling nightmare, numerous individuals were to behave with quite extraordinary heroism during the next eight harrowing hours.

The situation on board the *Empress* might not have been so dire if the fire hoses had been working, but the bombing had fractured the water mains and so, as hose after hose was manhandled into position and switched on, nothing but a desultory trickle of water came out. By 9.50 a.m. the entire centre section of the ship was ablaze and Captain Sapsworth, still on the bridge, gave the order to abandon ship. The klaxon wailed continuously. The lights went out and everyone who was below deck, where many were still sheltering from the bombs, was plunged into darkness.

The order to abandon ship was easier to give than it was to carry out. The problem was that most of the passengers were driven by the intensity of the heat either to the very fore of the ship or right to the aft. While the lifeboats were all situated along the central part of the ship where the fire was at its most violent. In addition, the *Empress* was still moving through the water at considerable speed. The Captain had got a message down to the engine-room instructing the Chief Engineer to switch the engines off and get his men out. Nevertheless, 40,000 tons of impetus takes a lot of stopping. So even if a lifeboat was successfully lowered to the water, it immediately dragged on its ropes and had to be cut free to avoid upsetting, whereupon it would promptly disappear behind the stern and be of no use to those left aboard. A further hazard was that the fire kept burning the ropes themselves, with the result that a boat would suddenly tumble through the air or those climbing down a rope towards a boat already launched would find themselves hurtling into the water.

Despite the appalling circumstances a number of boats were successfully launched, but contained few people and lost contact with the burning ship once they hit the water. The crowds, clustered together in an ever decreasing space, watched helplessly as one lifeboat after another receded into the distance. In these circumstances, the two lifeboats equipped with engines should have been of critical assistance, because they should have had the power not only to manoeuvre back towards the ship themselves but also to tow

ABOVE: *A view of the* Empress *still burning, taken shortly before nightfall – all the crew and passengers had been taken off.*

other lifeboats back to where they could be of some use. Sadly, while both motorboats were successfully launched, neither of the engines worked. Still worse, one of the boats was so poorly maintained that three planks in the bottom of it had immediately sprung and it quickly began to fill with water. The occupants, including Able Seaman Petch, bailed for all they were worth. At around noon another boat approached with Captain Sapsworth in command. Those in Petch's rapidly sinking boat asked to be transferred, but the Captain explained that his boat was already too crowded. He agreed, however, to the transfer of those who had been injured. Shortly afterwards the motorboat overturned. Some of the previous occupants, including Petch, came to the surface and were able to cling on to the upturned craft. Many, however, never made it back up. At around 1.30 p.m. a friendly Sunderland flying boat flew over those who were still hanging grimly on and dropped a rubber dinghy. It landed some distance away. Able Seaman Pullen decided he would swim for it, but he was more exhausted than he had realized and was unable to reach it. Swimming back, he began to flounder. If it had not been for Able Seaman Hipwell letting go of his own precarious hold and swimming to his friend's assistance, Pullen would certainly have drowned. As it was, Hipwell was able to drag him back to the upturned lifeboat, where they hung on together for another four hours before they were finally picked up.

The Captain and the Chief Officer, together with four other officers, had all escaped in the same boat. It was not one of the very first boats to be launched, but these men certainly left the ship while the majority of the passengers were still trapped on it. It is arguable that in the circumstances they had no choice but to get into the nearest boat or else be burned alive. This is the conclusion that the subsequent Court of Inquiry reached, and it would be most unfair to criticize these men for behaving as they did in the truly terrifying situation in which they found themselves. Still, the early departure of most of the ship's officers does emphasize the heroism of those who stayed behind to help the many passengers who were still trapped.

One such man was Dr Delorme. He worked away in the operating theatre on C Deck, tending to those who had been injured in the bombing raid with no thought to his own safety. He did not leave the ship until after two o'clock in the afternoon, several hours after the Captain's departure, and then only after he had seen that all the stretcher cases he had been in charge of had been safely lowered into a lifeboat that the Bosun and Petty Officer Hitchener had finally managed to row back to the ship's side. In his sterling efforts he was ably assisted by Fifth Officer Bonwick. Another hero was Engineer Jimmy England. He successfully made five separate journeys down into the labyrinth of the ship to drag five injured and collapsed people up to the operating theatre. He never returned from his sixth journey, and yet he received no posthumous award and was not mentioned in dispatches.

Lieutenant-Commander Garrett and Chief Petty Officer Frederick Ransome were also notably selfless in their conduct. Both men stayed with the 300 or so passengers trapped in the tiny forecastle area during the long hours when there appeared to be little or no hope of salvation, the only prospect being either a forty-foot jump into icy water or being burned alive. Several of the passengers later testified to the courageous way in which these two men had kept up the morale and discipline of those who had been left behind. Garrett was the last to leave the ship. He had had a number of earlier opportunities of saving

ABOVE: *Survivors from the* Empress *in one of the ship's lifeboats. Around 300 passengers were trapped in the forecastle area on the burning ship for over six hours before an unnamed sailor managed to get the motor on one of the lifeboats working and the disembarkation of the remaining passengers could be completed.*

himself, which he declined to take. He twice made the journey from the main body of the ship to the foredeck and back, once by traversing underneath the raging fire along the blacked-out C Deck, and once by scaling the precipitous bridge itself. The first journey was conducted in order to lead a large number of people who were lost in the darkness to the relative safety and fresh air of the foredeck. The second journey was made in a vain attempt to try to reach one of the boats that was still hanging from its davits. During this latter desperate sortie Garrett was accompanied by Ransome. They failed to reach the boat, but Ransome did discover the prone body of Mrs Willis on the Promenade Deck and carried her to the temporary safety of the foredeck, where she later recovered consciousness and from where eventually she was to be rescued. But the arrival of a rescue boat for those in the bow of the ship was still some way off. In this desperate situation Ransome and Able Seaman Giles offered to try to swim to one of the empty boats that could still be seen bobbing around in the distance, with a view to rowing it back to the bow of the ship and taking off at least some of the stranded passengers. It was a desperate solution but both men were good swimmers. Unfortunately, they were quite incapable of making the distance against a heavy swell. After a while they gave up and took to just floating. They were lucky to be fished out of the water, still alive, some hours later, by the Captain's boat.

It was around two o'clock when No. 4 boat under the charge of Petty Officer Hitchener finally made it back to the bow of the *Empress*. Even then only a small proportion of the passengers could be taken off. It was a tribute to Lieutenant-Commander Garrett's strong discipline that there was an orderly disembarkation and not a mad rush. It was at this belated hour that an engineer with some elementary knowledge of engines was transferred to the one remaining but still non-functioning motorboat under Lieutenant-Commander Harry Baker. This unnamed mechanical genius succeeded, where all previous attempts had failed, in getting the stubborn engine to sputter into life. This was the critical breakthrough. With a working engine Baker quickly collected two more lifeboats and towed them to the bow of the *Empress*. By 4.30 the last of the passengers from the foredeck had been safely taken off. It was just then that the destroyers *Echo* and *Burza*, alerted by the SOS of some seven hours before, appeared on the horizon.

At the time that the *Empress of Britain* had originally been bombed, two troopships escorted by four warships were *en route* to Greenock, in Scotland, and were also off the west coast of Ireland in a position about 100 miles southwest of the *Empress*. At 10.30 a.m. the Flag Officer at Greenock, who had previously received the liner's SOS, ordered two of the destroyers from this convoy to go and investigate what had happened and to offer assistance. The destroyers *Echo* and *Burza* were promptly detached and routed at top speed to the position given by the *Empress*. The liner was not difficult to find. The column of black smoke from the fire could be seen at a distance of 60 miles. But even at top speed it was still six hours before the destroyers arrived. The last of the passengers having already been taken off, the destroyers set about picking up survivors from the small boats as well as those still swimming in the water and clinging to debris. Among the latter were Petch and his companions. However, twelve of the original twenty or so had by then given up the struggle. Three trawlers arrived at around 5.50 p.m. and they also assisted with the

BELOW: *A boarding party approach the still burning* Empress *in order to take it in tow on the morning of Sunday 27 October 1940.*

rescue. An hour later two more destroyers, *Broke* and *Sardonyx*, arrived. They had been ordered out of the port of Londonderry to go to the scene of the disaster. By this time it was almost dark, but the fire was still raging on the *Empress*, lighting up the surrounding sea, a gruesome but also a spectacular sight. The sick and the wounded were tended to as best they could be on the various rescue ships, Dr Delorme continuing to offer his tireless services wherever they could be of use.

Echo and *Burza* returned to port, as did the three trawlers. *Broke* and *Sardonyx* guarded the hulk of the *Empress* through the night, awaiting the arrival of the tugs *Marauder* and *Thames*. As the fires on the *Empress* were already dying down and there was no sign that it had taken on any water, it was decided to attempt to tow the burning ship into port. The tugs arrived at dawn the next day. A boarding party of seventeen men under Sub-Lieutenant Letty climbed up on to the forepart of the hull at 9.30 a.m. to attach the huge hawsers for the tow. Fires were still burning, parts of the steel decks were twisted and buckled, all the superb woodwork was charred and smouldering and a strong acrid choking smell hung everywhere. The hawsers were quickly attached, a quantity of personal effects and money were collected and the boarding party left by 10.50.

The tow began at the painfully slow speed of four to five knots, making the convoy a sitting target for U-boats. The destroyers swept around the *Empress* to try to safeguard it. Later that morning another German Focke-Wulf Condor was spotted, but it did not attack. Then a report came in that a British Coastal Command plane had spotted a U-boat some fifty miles to the south of the *Empress* and heading north.

Commander Hans Jenisch of the submarine *U-32* had followed the momentous events of the 26th via a series of signals from Berlin, but he had not approached the scene of the action, on the assumption that the *Empress* was finished. The following morning, however, he received a further signal to the effect that the *Empress* was still afloat and being towed. He caught up with the convoy later that same day, submerged, and continued to trail them through the night, picking up their propellor noise on his hydrophones. At some time after midnight the U-boat slipped through the destroyers' protective screen and shortly before 2.00 a.m. fired three torpedoes. The first failed to function, the second missed its target, while the third struck amidships. The U-boat remained in the vicinity observing developments. Interestingly, Hans Jenisch states that during this period he observed lights moving about on the *Empress* – which is odd, because at this time no one was supposed to be on board. Nine minutes later the *Empress of Britain* heeled over on her port side and sank. Fortunately the two tugs were able to slip their hawsers in time, or they would have been dragged down too, like tiny cockleshells attached to a huge stone.

That might well have been the end of the tragic story of the *Empress of Britain*. It was not many years, however, before there was talk of a shipment of gold having been on the *Empress* when it sank. The circumstantial evidence for such a shipment having been made is very strong. South Africa was a major gold producer. The British authorities were desperate to ship as much gold as possible to North America during 1940 to support the nation's ailing credit lines. The preferred route was from Cape Town to Sydney, Australia, and then to Ottawa via the Pacific. The problem with this route was that by the autumn of 1940 the gold was becoming uselessly stockpiled in Sydney, as there was not enough suitable shipping available for the onward voyage to Ottawa. The temptation to sidestep

ABOVE: *A close-up of the boarding party under the command of Sub Lieutenant Angus Letty (later promoted to Captain). Note the flame resistant headgear being worn.*

ABOVE: *The German submarine
U-32 under the command of
Hans Jenisch fired three torpedoes
at the* Empress. *The first failed
to function, the second missed
its target but the third
struck amidships.*

OPPOSITE: *A picture of the
Cathay Smoking Lounge of the
doomed ship, designed by Edmund
Dulac, whose fantasy book
illustrations from that period
are now collectors' items.*

the log-jam by putting South African gold on the *Empress of Britain*, which was sailing direct to the UK, would have been considerable. The *Empress*, with its superior speed, was also exactly the type of ship favoured by the Admiralty and the Bank of England for the purpose of shipping gold.

The stories about gold were given considerable credence by an article that appeared in the *Daily Mail* of 8 January 1949. This gave a detailed account of how there was to be a salvage attempt on the *Empress* in the summer of that year to try to recover gold that was valued at the time at £4 million. Divers were to be used in conjunction with an early style decompression chamber. The item was not picked up by any other newspapers and there were no follow-up reports. It would be easy to dismiss the entire piece as nothing more than journalistic fantasy. The report certainly was erroneous in several important respects. It referred, for instance, to the *Empress* lying in 180 feet of water on its starboard side. It is now known that it lies upside down in 500 feet of water. However, it is odd that such a detailed item should have appeared, seemingly out of thin air.

Formal enquiries made to the various authorities that might have been involved with any gold shipment were characteristically unproductive. The Bank of England and the Admiralty neither denied nor confirmed that gold had been on board. Official statements of known cargo amounted to 300 tons of sugar, valued at £5,000, and naval stores. But it is well known that during wartime official statements of cargo where gold is involved rarely reveal the truth. The following excerpt from a report dated 15/01/1944, abstracted from file ADM 116/5484 in the Public Record Office, sums up the prevailing system. 'South Africa. Shipments of bullion in transports and merchant ships have been arranged in the past with nominal documentation only and secrecy has been regarded as paramount. Skeleton papers have been prepared and consignments have been described as "War Stores", masters giving receipts accordingly.' Under such circumstances of official deception it is not surprising that it afterwards becomes very difficult to unravel the truth about the ships that carried gold.

The stories of huge quantities of bullion having been on board continued to circulate in treasure-hunting circles. Then, in March 1985, a member of the Shipping Policy Unit of the Department of Transport wrote a very revealing letter to a would-be salvor. In the letter it was clearly stated that the *Empress of Britain* had indeed carried gold but that the gold had already been recovered. The letter specifically referred to two files, War Risk Insurance file 935 and War Risk Insurance file 938. It also added in a footnote that both files had been destroyed. There is no reason to doubt the authenticity of this information. However, it raises as many questions as it answers. If the gold on the *Empress of Britain* was salvaged, when exactly did this salvage take place?

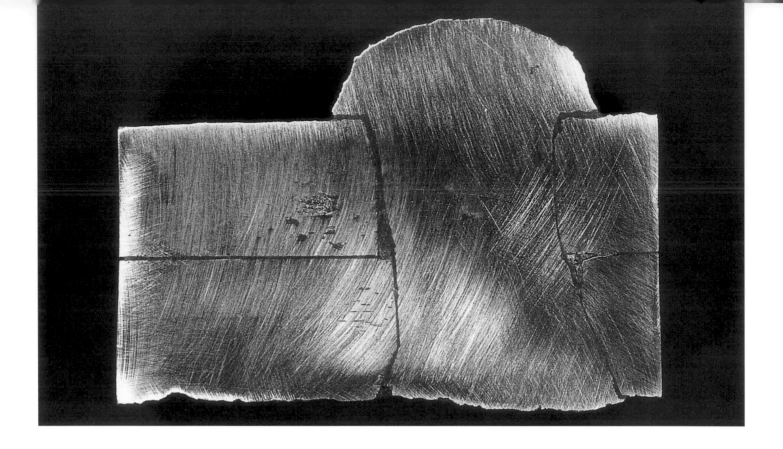

ABOVE: *A polished section of one of the* Empress' *rivets – one of over three million such rivets that were originally put in place by hand.*

One possibility is that there was indeed a salvage effort shortly after the war, as reported by the *Daily Mail*. But if this was so, why was it felt necessary to keep the project so quiet? And how was it carried out? It was impossible at the time for divers to go down to a depth anything like 500 feet. Grabbing operations from the surface had taken place at those depths, but to grab into a huge upturned hull would have been quite impossible. Furthermore, those who took part in the expedition of 1995 said there was no evidence of any previous salvage attempt having taken place from outside the ship's hull.

LEFT AND OPPOSITE PAGE: *Terry Playle, Chairman of Designaztec Limited, confirmed that his company recovered the ship's bell and anchor whilst diving on the* Empress of Britain *during October 1998.*

An alternative explanation is that the gold was removed during the tow. Officially, Sub-Lieutenant Letty's men were on board for only just over an hour. That would hardly have given enough time to remove a large stack of ingots from a bullion room seven decks down on a ship that was still red hot and full of choking smoke. However, perhaps some of the boarding party were left on board the *Empress* for the specific purpose of disembarking the gold. This might explain the lights seen by Commander Jenisch when his torpedo hit. It could also explain the skeleton trapped inside the bullion room when the ship sank.

It is just possible that the victim in the bullion room was someone who had been in this part of the ship when the bombing took place. But it seems unlikely. After all, what would he have been doing there? It could perhaps have been a piece of opportunistic thievery during a moment of crisis, but the more probable explanation is that the body was that of someone who had been participating in a salvage attempt. Whether this happened during the tow or after the war is impossible to say definitively. But perhaps the most intriguing question of all is why the War Risk Insurance Office considered it necessary to destroy their files on the subject.

THE EDINBURGH
ARCTIC CONVOY

THE CONVOY SYSTEM, in which merchant ships sail in groups under the protection of escorting warships, has been used to good effect for centuries. In the First World War this principle was ignored by the Allied Forces, at huge cost in lives and shipping, until as late as 1917. No such mistake was made in the Second World War, when the convoy system was used from the outset. Losses were still very high in the early years, largely because of a shortage of naval vessels, but were greatly reduced, at least on the North Atlantic routes, once the supply of escorts was increased.

Following the entry of Soviet Russia into the war on the side of the Allies in June 1941, a new and even more perilous route had been opened up. Groups of thirty or more merchant ships would be assembled in Scotland or Iceland and sail in convoy eastwards across the Arctic Ocean to the northern Soviet ports of Murmansk and Archangel. They carried vital supplies of tanks and planes, tin and aluminium and other raw materials to enable the beleaguered Russians to sustain their fight on the Eastern Front. In part payment for this aid, much of which was supplied on credit, the Russians would ship back consignments of gold to Britain.

Even the words, Arctic convoy, are enough to chill the blood. Certainly the voyage between Britain and Soviet Russia during the Second World War has to be considered as one of the grimmest experiences in the history of naval warfare. The constant and intense threat of attack from U-boats, aircraft and German surface ships, while traversing waters that were virtually controlled by the enemy, was deeply unnerving. Over two-thirds of the ships in one convoy, PQ17, were lost through enemy action, in what was one of the most terrible naval debacles of the war. But it was the bitterly hostile weather conditions within the Arctic Circle that gave the voyage its peculiarly treacherous quality. So much ice would form over a ship's superstructure that it was in real danger of becoming top-heavy if the ice was not constantly chipped off and cleared. Steam jets were used to keep the guns clear, but as fast as the ice was melted an even tougher new layer would form. Meanwhile there was always the knowledge that if you ended up in the water, your life expectancy was no more than a few minutes.

ABOVE: *Captain Hugh Faulkner (left) with Rear Admiral Stuart Bonham-Carter on board* HMS Edinburgh. *Captain Faulkner was the only ship's Captain who took part in the battle that followed who did not receive a DSO, despite being recommended for it by Bonham-Carter.*

OPPOSITE: *On board* HMS Edinburgh *inside the Arctic circle showing a heavily iced-up ship and gun. The ice had to be constantly chipped away and cleared to prevent the ship from becoming top heavy.*

ABOVE: *The Russian convoy was one of the most dangerous of missions. It was, however, essential to the war effort that Russia was kept supplied with strategic metals and armaments. This painting by the war artist Charles Pears shows the amazing effect of the Northern Lights.*

On 29 April 1942, HMS *Edinburgh* left Murmansk, escorting convoy PQ11 on the return voyage to Britain. The *Edinburgh* was a 10,000-ton cruiser class warship built at Wallsend-on-Tyne in northeast England. It was 613 feet long, had a top speed of 32.5 knots and was armed with a formidable array of twelve six-inch and twelve four-inch guns, as well as four Walrus type aircraft. There were 850 men on board, including nearly thirty naval personnel who were being shipped back to Britain suffering from gangrenous frost-bite and who were described in official documents as 'cot cases'. There was also a handful of passengers, mainly Czech and Polish officials. As the largest and most powerful of the escorting warships, the *Edinburgh* was the flagship for Rear-Admiral Stuart Bonham-Carter – the overall commander of the convoy. The *Edinburgh* itself was under the command of Captain Hugh Faulkner, who was the only captain to be involved in the subsequent battle who did not receive a DSO, much to Bonham-Carter's personal chagrin, although Faulkner was 'mentioned in despatches'. The allocation of awards often appeared to be quite arbitrary to those most closely involved in the events themselves.

Shortly before departure the *Edinburgh* received ninety-three small wooden boxes. Each box was supplied with two lead seals. The boxes were loaded by means of a crane on the dockside and stowed in a bomb room situated on the starboard side of the ship, beneath the bridge and deep inside the hull. The contents of the boxes were supposed to be kept a strict secret, but as one of them fell during loading and broke open on deck, it was soon common knowledge among the crew that the *Edinburgh* was carrying gold. She was in fact carrying 465 bars of it, packed five to a box, and each bar weighing approximately twenty-eight pounds. The total value of the gold was £1,547,080 insured one-third in London and two-thirds in Moscow. The total weight was approximately five and a half tons.

German aerial surveillance had already observed convoy QP11 forming in Murmansk, and at 11.20 a.m. on the second day out, 30 April, the submarine *U-456*, under the command of Kapitanleutnant Max Teichert, sighted the cruiser. At this point the *Edinburgh* was some fifteen miles ahead of the rest of the convoy, attempting to establish

the limit of the ice-field. The U-boat stalked the cruiser for nearly five hours before the opportune moment arrived for firing its torpedos. The first torpedo struck the *Edinburgh* on the starboard side close to the bomb room. The main switchboard room was quickly flooded, as were a number of associated rooms. Almost immediately a second torpedo hit the stern of the ship. The entire aft section broke off and sank, together with the steering gear. There was considerable further flooding and the *Edinburgh* took on a sharp list. However, the water ingress was contained by the closing of the watertight doors and the battening down of hatches, and within half an hour the list was corrected by the flooding of other compartments with seawater. A third torpedo fired by the U-boat missed its target.

A number of men who were in the areas where the torpedos hit were killed outright by the impact. Others were less fortunate. They found themselves deep down in the ship with no available exit route. One particularly sad death was that of Neville Holt, a 17-year-old ordinary seaman, who was trapped in the telegraph room. He was in voice contact with the bridge but had no means of escape. Water had already encroached on to other decks above him. An officer on the bridge talked to him until he no longer received any replies.

As soon as the rest of the convoy was aware of what had occurred, destroyers *Foresight* and *Forester*, together with the Russian destroyers *Gremyaschi* and *Sokrushitelni*, rushed to the stricken cruiser to provide cover. The bulk of the convoy, meanwhile, now under the command of HMS *Bulldog*, continued *en route* for Britain. The only hope for the disabled

ABOVE: HMS Edinburgh *photographed in Scapa Flow on the 28 October 1941. Edinburgh was a cruiser class warship with a crew of over 800 men and a top speed of 32.5 knots. A sister ship, HMS Belfast, has been preserved as a museum on the River Thames, close to London Bridge*

Edinburgh was to limp back to Murmansk. The ship's engines were still functioning and, after the initial few moments of shock and chaos, order had been restored. The problem was that the *Edinburgh* could no longer sail in a straight line. The lack of steering gear meant that it just went round and round in circles like a helpless drunk. HMS *Foresight* took the *Edinburgh* in tow, but it was not powerful enough to correct the waywardness of the much heavier cruiser. A more successful solution proved to be for the *Edinburgh* to take the *Foresight* in tow, using the destroyer as a kind of makeshift rudder. By this means the *Edinburgh* was able to make progress but still only at a painfully slow three or four knots. Murmansk, 250 miles away, would take the best part of four days to reach, and meanwhile the damaged cruiser would be virtually a sitting target for any marauding U-boat.

The Germans had certainly not forgotten about the limping British battleship. Max Teichert had radioed back details of his recent confrontation with the *Edinburgh* to the German naval base at Kirkenes, in Norway, and three German destroyers, the *Hermann Schoemann*, the *Z24* and the *Z25*, were now heading at top speed towards the *Edinburgh*'s position. First they attacked the remains of convoy QP11, which was by this time heading as fast as possible towards the safety of Iceland. The German ships were supported by aircraft, but even so the attack was relatively brief and ineffective. One convoy straggler was hit and sunk, but the Russian crew were safely taken off by a British trawler. The convoy dispersed and the German destroyers did not give chase. They were clearly more interested in intercepting the *Edinburgh* before it could get back to a Russian port.

Early on 1 May the Russian destroyers *Sokrushitelni* and *Gremyaschi*, still providing the damaged and slowly moving *Edinburgh* with protective cover, signalled to Rear-Admiral Bonham-Carter that they were running short of fuel and would have to return immediately to Murmansk. They promised to return as soon as possible. This meant that the *Edinburgh* could

RIGHT: *As the war progressed convoys were provided with air cover as well as naval protection. The system of travelling in convoy went back many centuries and was extremely effective in reducing losses even though individual captains of merchant ships often complained about how it slowed them down.*

LEFT: *This photograph shows the moment of impact as the torpedo fired by* HMS Foresight *strikes* HMS Edinburgh. *Rear Admiral Bonham-Carter was later to be criticized for abandoning ship prematurely, but he robustly defended his decision as having been taken in the best interests of his men.*

no longer afford to use HMS *Foresight* as a rudder because both of the remaining destroyers were needed to provide protection. This further hampered progress. On the evening of 1 May the minesweepers *Hussar*, *Harrier*, *Gossamer* and *Niger*, together with a Russian tug and escort vessel *Rubin*, joined the stricken *Edinburgh* and its two faithful destroyers, still desperately trying to reach the safety of the Kola Inlet but making painfully slow progress. The minesweepers had been sent out from Murmansk to assist when news first arrived there of the *Edinburgh*'s plight, and though they fought valiantly in the forthcoming battle they were not really a substitute for the two Russian destroyers that had still not reappeared.

The German fleet caught up with its quarry early on the morning of 2 May. A fierce battle ensued, during which the crippled *Edinburgh*, despite its lack of manoeuvrability, still managed to sink the largest of the German destroyers, the *Hermann Schoemann*. Shortly afterwards the *Edinburgh* was itself hit by a third torpedo fired from the *Z24*. It struck on the port side beneath the bridge almost opposite to where the first torpedo had struck. The *Edinburgh* took on a sharp list to port and Rear-Admiral Bonham-Carter was most concerned that his ship might turn turtle. He immediately ordered its abandonment. The minesweepers *Harrier* and *Gossamer* came alongside, and 800 men, including about 50 sick and seriously injured on stretchers, were lowered into the small ships. But still the *Edinburgh* did not sink and continued to linger on in the gloom of an Arctic evening. On the horizon the German destroyers still lurked, possibly preparing to renew the attack. Some of Bonham-Carter's men suggested that the *Edinburgh* should be reboarded and a further attempt made to sail it into port. Bonham-Carter rejected the advice and instead instructed the *Foresight* to fire yet another torpedo into the cruiser at a range of 1,500 yards. This was the end for the *Edinburgh*. It promptly sank by the stern and slid beneath the water, bows upright. The watching seamen solemnly toasted their undefeated ship. In the subsequent inquiry Bonham-Carter received some criticism for abandoning the *Edinburgh* when he did, but he stoutly defended his action, asserting that in similar circumstances he would do exactly the same again. It is difficult not to agree with him. Ships do not sink according to a pre-agreed time-scale and it was impossible to predict how suddenly the *Edinburgh* might or might not go down.

Morale on board the *Edinburgh* had remained extraordinarily high throughout the three days of hostilities in extremely adverse conditions. The interesting victualling report written on 5 May 1942 makes it clear that the men were allowed constant access to hot food, sausages and bacon, sausage rolls and 'tiddy oggies', as well as drinks – tea, coffee and cocoa – as and when they wanted them, a concession that was apparently not abused and must have been most welcome with temperatures well below freezing. It is also interesting to

ABOVE: *A badly crippled* HMS Edinburgh *photographed from* HMS Gossamer *shortly before sinking. It is difficult to believe that a ship in this state could have made it back safely to Murmansk.*

note that nowhere in any of the official papers concerning the battle is there any mention of the gold in the bomb room that was lost, though there is reference to the ship sinking with 160 sausage rolls still on board, 'much to the chagrin of the victualling staff'.

The actions of the minesweepers, each equipped with only a single small gun but repeatedly attacking the German destroyers head on, were singled out for praise in subsequent reports. Indeed German naval documents make it clear that the German ships mistook the minesweepers for destroyers, and that this was part of the reason why they did not press home their advantage in the early stages of the battle. Less complimentary words were reserved for the Russian ships *Sokrushitelni* and *Gremyaschi*. It was generally considered in British circles that their failure to turn up again had more to do with May Day celebrations in Murmansk than difficulties with refuelling.

It might have been sausage rolls and not gold bars that were in the thoughts of the sailors as they watched the *Edinburgh* go down, but the gold was not altogether forgotten. My father, Thomas Pickford, came to hear about it in the early 1950s, and after some years of research he approached the Treasury. In 1954, the British government gave the company he worked with, Risdon Beazley Ltd, formal permission to carry out salvage operations. However, the project was never going to be easy. The depth of water was formidable and the size of the ship was very large. The volume of gold, although extremely valuable, was very small – one of the problems with gold salvage. All these factors counted against it. Risdon Beazley decided to concentrate on more attractive targets, particularly bulk copper and tin cargoes, in less politically sensitive waters, and the *Edinburgh* salvage was shelved for the time being.

In 1957 the *Edinburgh* site was designated a war grave, a factor that was to be of considerable consequence when it came to a number of different firms competing for the contract in the early 1980s. The British government's attitude to war graves has always been at best peculiarly confused, and at worst hypocritical. For some unexplained reasons only warships lost during enemy action are designated as war graves, even though many more British citizens have lost their lives on merchant ships than HM ships during war. Also, war grave or not, this has not stopped HM ships being salvaged with government approval if it has been considered expedient.

In the late 1970s a former North Sea oil rig worker named Keith Jessop, who had some knowledge of the *Edinburgh* project, interested a large Norwegian shipping company, Stolt Nielsen, in the idea of salvaging the gold. He maintained that there were ten tons of gold on the *Edinburgh*, not the five and a half tons referred to in government records. His reasoning was not altogether wild optimism. Most shipments of gold from Russia to Britain at this time involved ten tons of gold. More crucially, Admiral Golovko,who was in command of the Russian navy at Murmansk and responsible for loading Russian supplies, stated on record that ten tons of gold were put on the *Edinburgh*. Ten tons or five and a half tons – it made little difference to the Norwegians, who were eager to deploy the expensive ships and equipment that they had sitting idle during the oil recession. A search was mounted, but the *Edinburgh* was not found; nor were the other two targets that Jessop had mentioned. Both parties went their separate ways. However, despite this initial setback, the *Edinburgh*'s day as a salvage project had definitely arrived. Technologically the task was entirely feasible. And, despite the war graves issue, the goverment was keen to see a recovery of the gold carried out. Not only would it provide valuable revenue, but there was the possibility that if they did not enter into an agreement, the ship would be pirated, or the Russians might be tempted to go it alone.

OPPOSITE: *The first ingot to be recovered from the wreck of* HMS Edinburgh. *It was cast in Russia in 1937 and shows the communist government's identification marks.*

Nor was Jessop's enthusiasm diminished by his initial lack of success. After separating from Stolt Nielsen he managed to interest Rick Wharton and Malcolm Williams, two highly successful North Sea diving contractors who owned the North Sea Diving company Wharton Williams. Jessop's original concept and research was strengthened enormously by Wharton Williams technical expertise, financial strength and contacts. They in turn brought in Racal Decca, with their positioning and navigation expertise, and OSA, a shipping company that owned the state-of-the-art dynamically positioned dive support ship *Stephaniturm*. There were, however, two other rival companies also bidding for the *Edinburgh* contract. These were Risdon Beazley Ltd, with its long experience of salvage for governments around the world, and the Norwegian giant Stolt Nielsen.

In the event it was Keith Jessop's company, Jessop Marine Ltd, without any financial resources of its own, that won the contract. The salvors bid 'no cure–no pay' forty-five per cent of the proceeds for itself, fifty-five per cent for the British and Russian governments. The measure of the financial, organisational and operational input of Wharton Williams was reflected by their receiving 90% of the salvors' share. The state percentage was to be split two-thirds–one-third, with the Russians taking the lion's share. This split was in the same ratio as the original insurance of the gold by the two governments. The War Risk Insurance Office had underwritten £500,000 and the Russians £1 million of the original consignment. The award of the contract to Jessop Marine had the blessing of the Russians, who nevertheless reserved the right to have two observers on board throughout the recovery process.

In April 1981 the survey ship *Dammtor* left for the Barents Sea. After a ten-day search the wreck was found in the approximate position 72° North, 35° East. A Wharton Williams-owned Scorpio Remotely operated Vehicle (RoV) was used to take detailed film of the

BELOW: *A photograph taken at a depth of nearly 300 meters showing gold ingots stacked in the bomb room. If the torpedo which struck close by had damaged the bomb room then the ingots would probably have been impossible to recover.*

Keith Jessop with some of the first gold bars to be recovered, photographed on 15 September 1981. It was the realization of a dream that he had been struggling to achieve for many years.

wreck on the sea floor. The *Edinburgh* still looked to be in remarkably good condition considering all that it had been through. However, it was very unclear from the film whether the gold was still in the wreck and still recoverable. The bridge of the *Edinburgh* was missing and all the indications were that the ship had hit the bottom very hard stern first which may have resulted in the gold being flung into the shell stores towards the stern. Wharton Williams, who were financing the operation, spent three months of detailed engineering analysis during which time they also interviewed a number of survivors. They concluded that the risk of the gold having moved was a risk worth taking. Later that same year, on 30 August, the dive support ship *Stephaniturm* left the Scottish port of Peterhead to go to the wreck site with a team of handpicked deep-sea divers experienced in saturation techniques. They would be living in a special chamber for weeks at a time, breathing a mixture of helium and oxygen, working in shifts. All those involved, including the divers, were working on a 'no cure, no pay' basis, which meant that if the gold was not salvaged, they got nothing.

For two weeks the divers slowly cut their way into the hull of the *Edinburgh*. It was an extremely hazardous operation, particularly in view of the quantities of live ammunition that were left lying around. And there were times when faith in the project began to wane. The main worry was always that the bomb room might have been torn apart by the original torpedo explosion, in which case the gold would most probably have fallen through into some nether region of the giant hull and could take months if not years to find. Saturation diving was far too expensive to permit the operation to go on for much longer than one month. Then, on 15 September, diver John Rossier finally penetrated the bomb room, which proved to be still intact, and recovered the first bar of gold. By 7 October, 431 out of 465 bars had been recovered, worth in excess of £43 million, when salvage was suspended for that year owing to deteriorating weather. In 1986 Wharton Williams returned to the wreck using their dive-support vessel *Deepwater* and recovered all the remaining bars of gold. This made it not only the deepest salvage with divers but also an extremely rare 100% recovery.

The diving operation had been a triumph of meticulous planning and physical endurance. No divers had worked at such a depth before for so long a period of time. A number of them had developed bad ear infections, an occupational hazard of the business, and others had sustained bruised limbs or scalded feet from the hot water that circulated inside their suits to stop them from freezing to death in the sub-zero temperatures. But the sight of more and more gold bars piling up on the deck more than compensated for these minor discomforts.

For Keith Jessop the salvage of the *Edinburgh* gold was a tremendous personal achievement against all the odds. But, as so often in the treasure-hunting business, the success was not altogether unalloyed. After the salvage had been completed, an investigation into the circumstances under which the contract had been won led to Keith Jessop and an official at the Salvage Association, John Jackson, being tried at the Old Bailey on charges of conspiracy to defraud. At the trial, however, both Jackson and Jessop were acquitted of any wrongdoing. There was in fact at least one sound reason for the government preference for Jessop Marine over their better established rivals when awarding the contract. Jessop was committed to using divers and cutting gear, whereas Risdon Beazley still deployed what was known unflatteringly in the industry as a smash-and-grab technique. This involved blowing the ship open with explosives and then grabbing the cargo from the surface, the grab being controlled visually by a diver in a bell on the sea floor. It was considered, understandably, that the use of free divers was the method more appropriate to a war grave.

Only five and a half tons of gold was ever recovered from the *Edinburgh*. There are those, however, including Keith Jessop, who maintain that there are another four and a half tons still to be found.

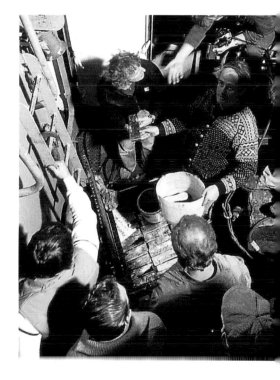

ABOVE: *John Clarke, who managed the project on behalf of the owners of the dive ship* Stephaniturm, *helps clean some of the gold bars.*

NAZI LOOT
ROMMEL'S GOLD

EUROPE IN THE LATE 1940S WAS AWASH with dubious characters who had extraordinary stories to tell about events they had witnessed during the war, and often murky personal histories to live down. In 1948 a young man calling himself Peter Fleig, a German Slovak in origin, walked into the French Consulate in Stuttgart, where he was then living, and requested a visa to visit Corsica for a diving holiday. Quite how the conversation developed is not known, but a suspicious consular official subjected Fleig to some rigorous cross-questioning and within 48 hours Fleig was on his way to Paris by train in the close company of the French *gendarmerie*. Further interviews took place, this time with Monsieur Richard, Minister and Plenipotentiary, Director of the Office of Wealth and Private Interests at the Ministry for Foreign Affairs. On 14 August 1948 Fleig was issued with an affidavit allowing him to visit Corsica. It was explained to Fleig that the mission he was now involved in was to be kept confidential. The Ministry of Finance made one million francs available for the trip, equivalent to £1 million today, a substantial amount of holiday spending money, though Fleig was given no control over the bank account. He was still in the company of the French police and he had to report to the Service des Renseignements Generaux de Bastia (the Bastia General Information Office), in Corsica.

Fleig's story was extraordinary. He had been born on 10 February 1919 at Romburg, in Czechoslovakia. Before the outbreak of war he was working as a diver at the port of La Spezia, in northern Italy. In 1942 he was conscripted into the German army to work as a diving specialist. In August 1943, three months after the surrender of all Axis forces in North Africa, and at a time when the Germans were being driven out of Sicily, he was summoned to a meeting with an SS officer named Dal and three other officers of the security service whose names he could not remember. He was required to accompany these officers in a small boat to the port of Bastia, in Corsica, then under German occupation. In the arsenal at Bastia he packed six crates with valuables and precious objects including gold

ABOVE: *Not long after his defeat in North Africa, Rommel plotted for the overthrow of Hitler. However, Hitler discovered the plot and Rommel committed suicide.*

OPPOSITE: *The Afrika Korps in the North African desert – it is the loot that the Afrika Korps were removing in their retreat that forms an integral part of Fleig's story.*

and silver coins, five church crosses ornamented with precious stones, engraved silver chalices and a quantity of paintings. He was told that these valuables were part of the loot of Rommel's retreating Afrika Korps. Some of the items had apparently been transferred to the arsenal from a convent, where Fleig also claimed to have been in attendance. The packing-cases were sealed and loaded on to a motorboat equipped with a small crane. The motorboat headed out of Bastia, turned south and deposited the packing-cases in the mouth of the Golo River at a depth of 150 feet. Fleig estimated that each packing case weighed 750 kilos. Before the cases were offloaded he dived to the sea bottom to check that it was suitable. Buoys were attached to the cases, a few metres above the seabed to make relocation easier. The officers then returned to La Spezia, where they were promptly arrested for dereliction of duty, courtmartialled and executed. Fleig himself, who had only been carrying out orders, was not sentenced but was instructed to try to recover the lost treasure. By then it was already too late, however, as the Allies had taken control of Corsica. Fleig was then conscripted into the Waffen SS and sent to fight on the Russian front.

When Fleig arrived in Corsica with his police escort in 1948 he was again subjected to intense cross-examination, with the assistance of interpreters because he spoke no French. Then the search for the submerged packing-cases began, with the technical assistance of a Monsieur Loebenburg, who owned a salvage company based in Bastia and had the requisite equipment. The search did not go well. Fleig seemed either unable or unwilling to identify the precise area where the packing-cases had been dumped. Loebenburg also noted that Fleig was not a very competent diver, perhaps because he was unfamiliar with French diving equipment. The search continued along a twelve-mile stretch of coastline for a month. Fleig's memory had suddenly become tantalizingly vague, and relations between Fleig and the authorities took a serious turn for the worse. Fleig had borrowed an expensive camera

RIGHT: *Wrecked shipping outside La Spezia harbour in northern Italy on the day after its capture by Allied troops. Renegade soldiers from Rommel's Afrika Korps were purportedly trying to evacuate stolen treasures through La Spezia shortly before the advancing allied army reached it.*

from Loebenburg. He pawned the camera to a third party for 3,000 francs. When Loebenburg asked for his camera back, Fleig was unable to produce it. He was arrested, tried and sentenced to two months in a Bastia prison. While in prison he sold his fellow inmates a series of treasure maps purporting to detail the exact position of the packing-cases. Each map was different. Shortly after his release he disappeared from the island. Fleig's credibility was shot to pieces.

In retrospect it is easy to cast doubt on Fleig's original story. Why, for instance, did the four SS officers return to La Spezia when they had clearly misappropriated German war booty? Also, Germans were not conscripted into the SS as Fleig claimed he had been. It was an elite position, not a punishment. A physical examination of Fleig carried out in Bastia revealed that he had the distinctive SS mark under his left armpit, which he had tried ineffectively to remove with cigarette burns. There were other confusing details. He claimed, for example, to have seen a sunken ship in Bastia harbour when he arrived at the beginning of September 1943, but it was known that there was no sunken ship in the harbour at that time. He was clearly a fantasist and a cheat.

The interesting question is not whether Fleig was an honest man – clearly he was not – but why the French authorities took his story seriously, to the tune of one million francs, and why they went on taking his story seriously even after his dishonesty was beyond doubt. For the French government did not abandon the search when Fleig fled. They continued to trawl the seabed in the area of the Golo River through 1949. And as late as November 1951 a top-level meeting was held in Bastia between Monsieur Ferrand, the local sub prefect, and Monsieur Berger, head of the Mission of the Ministry of Finance. The commander of the Corsican navy, the head of the Intelligence Service in Bastia, the director of Customs and one or two other experts were also in attendance. Their conclusion was that the business of Rommel's treasure still merited further investigation. There are only two possible explanations. Either governments are collectively as susceptible to the lure of treasure as any other gullible and greedy man in the street, or else the French authorities knew something that tied in with the Fleig story, something which predisposed them to believe it. It is this latter possibility that has helped keep the legend of Rommel's treasure alive and explains why the Golo estuary has witnessed a whole series of treasure hunts during the last forty years, most of them ill financed and ill equipped, but all of them driven by the hope that jewels beyond the dreams of avarice lay just behind the next lobster pot.

Among the more colourful of the treasure-hunters was the British aristocrat Lord Kilbracken, who joined the quest in the early 1960s. The account that he provides in his book, *Living Like a Lord*, is laced with scantily clad girls, glamorous white yachts and nefarious entrepreneurs, combined with a lot of hanging out in cafes drinking the local elixir. However, Kilbracken did, after some difficulty, track down Loebenburg, the man who had carried out the original search with Fleig as his guide. Loebenburg told Kilbracken that Fleig claimed to have seen a white light and a red light in line with each other when the launch carrying the treasure had moored in the Golo estuary and offloaded it. Loebenburg had deduced that the white light had to come from the only villa on the foreshore, while the red one was a beacon from an airfield about three miles inland. This gave a search area of about ten square miles, assuming Fleig's estimate to have been roughly correct, namely that he was two to three miles offshore when the treasure was dumped. Kilbracken was still more excited when a local fisherman, while trawling the bottom of the

RIGHT: *An Afrika Korps arm band.*

Golo estuary, caught a fishing buoy in his net. This obviously had to be one of the buoys that Fleig had tied to the packing-cases. However, the search that Kilbracken carried out was no more successful than previous efforts had been. It suffered from the usual twin bugbears of the treasure-hunting industry – poorly functioning equipment and terminally inadequate finance. The search was aborted almost as soon as it began.

By 1957 stories of Rommel's treasure had reached fever pitch in the European media. There was even a film, made in Germany, entitled *Rommel's Gold*. It was at this time that my father was asked to try to establish whether there was any truth to the rumours. He contacted a Norwegian colleague of his called Ditlef Lexow, who had good connections with senior officers of the German navy. Lexow tracked down a high-ranking member of Rommel's staff, who denied that any gold had been taken out of North Africa by German troops. However, this same officer provided the interesting information that the Bank of Rome had been evacuated of its contents in September 1943 and that Afrika Korps troops had been involved. It was decided to transfer the valuables northwards by sea because it was already becoming too dangerous to do so by land. He understood that the valuables were lost but did not know where. The contents of the bank had included money and jewels.

Pierre Bodenan, another of my father's colleagues who helped investigate the case, turned up some additional information. The war diary of the German navy shows that there was movement of motor launches at Civitavecchia on 15 September 1943. It also shows that Corsica was evacuated between 15 and 25 September and that there was a large convoy of German ships involved that came under heavy aerial attack. More recent investigations have even thrown some interesting new light on Peter Fleig. A lawyer called Herr Faller represented Fleig for approximately 20 years and during that time was involved with him in drawing up a number of contracts for the salvage of Rommel's treasure. As his lawyer, Faller was in a position to know Fleig better than most. According to Faller, Fleig's real name was Walter Kirner, a fact also supported by US intelligence records. He was born in 1923, not 1919. He never worked as a diver in La Spezia, and only learned to dive in Stuttgart after the war was over. He learned the story of the treasure from an SS officer while a prisoner of war. The part Fleig described himself as having played in the evacuation of the treasure was clearly pure fantasy. However, Fleig believed absolutely in the reality of the treasure itself.

A final piece of evidence perhaps suggests that there was after all some small kernel of truth to the Fleig/Kirner story. In the small town of Carrara, close to La Spezia, is the grave of a German officer called Dal – the name of the officer who Fleig always claimed had been in charge of the launch, and had subsequently been courtmartialled and executed.

THE FORT STIKINE
RAINING GOLD IN BOMBAY

IF THE *TITANIC* RANKS AS THE MOST GLAMOROUS of all treasure ships, the *Fort Stikine* was one of the more prosaic. It was a utilitarian product of the Lend-Lease system, under which the United States essentially allowed Britain to borrow war supplies on credit until after the war. Huge numbers of ships were supplied on this basis, the object being to maintain trade and keep war materials moving around the world at a time when German U-boats were destroying unprecedented tonnages of Allied shipping.

The *Fort Stikine* was one of 26 identical models, built in Canada with Lend-Lease funds, all 441 feet long and 57 feet across the beam, and all bearing names beginning with the prefix Fort. There was nothing fancy about its design. Fort Stikine was a solid, workmanlike merchant ship of 7,142 gross tons, capable of travelling at ten to eleven

LEFT: *This photograph shows the* Fort Stikine *in harbour. The* Fort Stikine *was one of twenty-six ships all given the prefix Fort. They were mundane cargo carriers built like the Liberty ships to keep the vital flow of goods moving around the world.*

knots and of carrying more than 7,000 tons of cargo in its holds. The ship was owned by the Ministry of Transport, managed by the Port Line and operated by the Bibby Line, a complicated arrangement but one that nevertheless seemed to work. The *Fort Stikine*'s first and only captain was Alexander Naismith. It was also his first and only command. Ship and man joined company in May 1942 and the lives of both ended on the same day, 14 April 1944.

The *Fort Stikine* steamed out of Birkenhead on a cold, foggy February morning in 1944, bound for Bombay in India, via Suez. For the present it was part of a large convoy heading initially north, around Ireland, and then south for the warmer waters of the Mediterranean Sea. The fog was so dense that in order to avoid collision the ships continually sounded their horns. It was a mournful procession. The *Stikine* sailed slightly apart from the others on one flank. The reason for this quarantining was that in addition to crates containing twelve Spitfire fighter planes, its cargo included 1,395 tons of explosives, of which 238 tons were of the highly sensitive category A type, stowed in the wings of its 'tween-decks. The *Stikine* was a floating bomb of horrendous proportions and the rest of the convoy had been instructed to keep its distance. The explosives were essential to the war effort in the Far East, and the *Stikine* was the only ship that was going the whole way. The others were all scheduled to peel off well before the Indian Ocean was reached.

Survivors of the *Stikine* disaster afterwards recalled that on the long voyage out the subject of the explosives was never discussed. The talk of the ship centred instead on another, rather more curious part of the *Stikine*'s cargo. In the upper half of No. 2 hold there was a specially constructed steel tank measuring five foot by four foot by four foot.

RIGHT: *The* Fort Stikine *travelled in convoy down the Irish Channel, across Biscay and into the Mediterranean but was kept at a distance from the rest of the fleet because of the explosives on board. After the Mediterranean it was routed by itself to Bombay.*

Inside the tank had been placed thirty-one wooden boxes, each containing four bars of gold. In 1944, this quantity of gold was worth in excess of £1 million. The use of such a vulnerable vessel as the *Stikine* for transit is evidence both of the dire shortage of more appropriate shipping and the urgency with which the gold was required. The lid of the tank had been padlocked and then welded on. But no amount of padlocking could prevent the presence of this gold becoming a subject of shipboard gossip. Soon fantasies involving hijacking and desert islands were a familiar source of distraction for the crew.

The first port of call for the *Stikine* was Suez, which was reached on 27 February. More coal was taken on board for the ship's bunkers. From Suez onwards the *Stikine* was well and truly on its own. The voyage down the Red Sea to Aden was relatively relaxing. The weather was warm and the numerous hazards of the Western Approaches and the Mediterranean were now well behind. Once they were past Aden, however, and sailing across the Arabian Sea to Karachi, there was again the lurking threat of German U-boats to contend with. Now that the *Stikine* no longer enjoyed the protection of the convoy, Captain Naismith adopted the Admiralty regulation zigzagging procedure, designed to make it more difficult for a U-boat to track the ship and target its torpedoes.

Karachi was reached safely on 30 March. Here the twelve crated Spitfires were unloaded, and in the vacated space the *Stikine* took on 8,700 bales of raw cotton, several thousand gallons of lubricating oil, sulphur, rice, resin, scrap iron and fish meal. It was a highly combustible cargo and sat uneasily with the thousands of tons of explosives that were already in the ship's holds. Captain Naismith and his senior officers were unhappy about the new cargo but they had no real choice but to accept it; during wartime, space was at a premium, and Bombay was only three days' sailing away. As a precaution Naismith increased the frequency of fire drills and the checking of all fire fighting equipment and anti-sabotage duty. As it happened, it was not the presence of the highly flammable cotton and oil that most upset the crew. It was the overwhelming stench of the fish meal.

The *Stikine* left Karachi on 9 April and arrived at Bombay on the 12th. It put into No. 1 berth, Victoria Dock. According to the regulations the *Stikine* should have flown a red flag to signify to other ships that it had explosives on board. However, captains were understandably reluctant to fly the red flag, feeling that it made their ships a particular target for both aerial attack and sabotage. The Independence Movement was gathering force in India at this time, and the threat of sabotage was a real and constant danger. Naismith chose not to fly the red flag. It was quite possibly a fatal error.

The presence of explosives on board meant that the *Stikine* was issued with a Certificate of Urgency for unloading, giving it priority over all other ships in dock at the time. It was not permitted to unload the special category A explosives directly on to the quayside, however, but only into lighters, none of which would be available for another twenty-four hours. It was to prove a critical loss of time. The dockworkers started on the oil drums and then, by popular request, the stinking fish meal was removed.

By midday on 14 April very few of the explosives had been landed. It was also about midday that the Chief Officer of the *Fort Crevier*, berthed opposite the *Fort Stikine*, first noticed smoke issuing from one of the *Stikine*'s ventilators. If the *Stikine* had been flying the red flag, perhaps he would have thought it worthwhile to inform someone on board of what he had seen. As it was he took no notice. At the subsequent inquiry it emerged that half a dozen other seamen on various ships around the port had also noticed the smoke

BELOW: *Profile and a cross-section of No 2 hold of the* Fort Stikine, *showing the stowage of cargo at the point that the fire was discovered, drawn by John Ennis.*

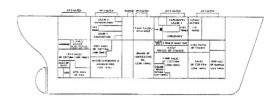

S.S. Fort Stikine: The cargo as it was disposed of the moment the fire was discovered.

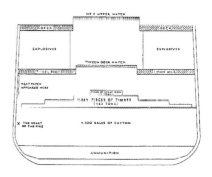

Cross-section of No 2 hold of the S.S. Fort Stikine, looking forward, showing the cargo that remained throughout the fire

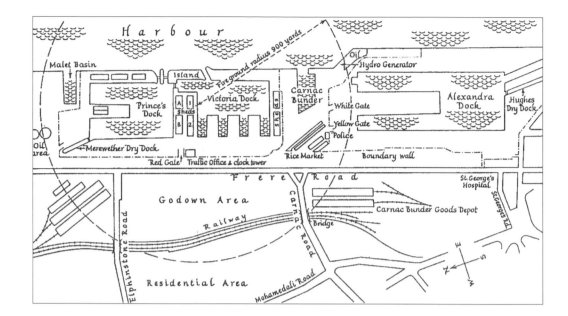

RIGHT: *Bombay Docks as they were in 1944 showing the area affected by fire within the circle, drawn by John Ennis.*

drifting from the *Stikine*. No one did anything. It was lunch hour, the docks were at a standstill and an atmosphere of tropical languor hung heavily in the air. Further valuable time was lost.

The stevedores returned to work around 1.45 p.m., and it was only then that those on board the *Stikine* itself noticed smoke coming from an area in No. 2 hold containing cotton bales. The cause was unclear. One possibility was that the raw cotton had been contaminated with oil, which would have made it a substance quite capable of spontaneous combustion. Alternatively, a lighted cigarette could have been dropped. Smoking was strictly prohibited, but the rule was not always followed. Then again, in the charged political atmosphere of Bombay in 1944, it is not impossible that the fire had been deliberately started. The ship's fire crew were alerted and three hoses of water were deployed into No. 2 hold in an attempt to douse the source of the smoke. At first it was considered that the fire was only a minor problem and it would be put out in a matter of minutes. No attempt was made to evacuate the ship or the dock workers. Everything continued as normal. In the previous five years there had been sixty fires on board ships within Bombay Docks, some carrying ammunition, and all had been successfully dealt with. After half an hour, however, with the smoke cloud stubbornly thickening, the Bombay city fire brigade were called in, under their chief, a Mr Norman Combs. Many more fire hoses were now being deployed from the quayside, but the fire still was not considered to be serious. Most of the crew continued to doze on their bunks, read or play cards. One or two came forwards and watched the fire brigade at work. At 2.30 p.m. Captain Oberst arrived on the scene. As the officer in charge of explosives at the docks he asked to see the ship's manifest. He was appalled by the combination of the fire in the cotton and the nature of the explosives that were being carried. He wanted the *Stikine* scuttled immediately. Captain Naismith was reluctant. It was his ship and, in any case, there was not enough water in the dock to submerge it.

At this point of impasse someone noticed that the bulkhead between Nos. 1 and 2 holds was getting very hot. In No. 1 hold there were a large number of detonators stowed against this bulkhead. It was vitally important to get them moved. Two extraordinarily brave fire officers, Mobarak Singh and Arthur Reynolds, volunteered to descend into No. 1 hold, by now also full of choking smoke, and shift the detonators away from the rapidly heating bulkhead. They accomplished their task before the ship went up. Reynolds, however, was to lose his life in the calamitous events that followed.

Colonel Sadler, a senior officer in the local army command, arrived on the scene. He was quite rightly worried about what would happen to the entire docks area if the *Stikine* exploded. He wanted the burning ship to steam out to sea. Again the discussion proved academic. The previous day a vital part of the ship's engine had been taken away for repairs, making it impossible for it to move under its own steam. Tugs were a possibility, but there were no tugs immediately available. And Combs, the fire chief, was opposed to moving the *Stikine* away from the quayside because that would mean he would no longer be able to deploy his fire engines. He was still of the opinion that given time he could bring the fire under control. Colonel Sadler reluctantly concurred. He was later to be killed trying to move one of the smaller boats in the dock away from the impending disaster.

It was now three o'clock. With stoical concentration the firemen, mostly Indians, continued to aim their hoses into No. 2 hold, even though by this time the deck was scorching hot on the the soles of their bare feet. So many millions of gallons of water had been pumped into the ship by now that it was beginning to take on a list. But the crew, war weary and insouciant, continued to idle away the afternoon while an ever-growing crowd of spectators lined the quayside. It was shortly after three that the paint on the outside of the ship began to bubble in one particular area. This was a clear sign that the fire inside the ship was getting worse. But for Combs it was also the first real indication of where the centre of the fire was. It had been impossible to see into the hold because of the density of the smoke. Also the firemen could only play their hoses into the centre of the lower hold because of the limited area of external access. Now, however, the seat of the fire had declared itself. It was in the aft port-side corner. It was hardly surprising that the water jets had failed to extinguish it. Combs immediately gave the order for a gas cutter to be fetched, so that an opening could be cut in the side of the ship and the fire attacked directly. The fire brigade had their own gas cutter, which was fetched from a nearby tender, but it could not be made to work. Another gas cutter had also been ordered from the nearby Mazagaon Docks, but a senior dock official, seeing the fire brigade had brought up their own gas cutter, phoned through to Mazagaon and cancelled the order. After a frustrating twenty minutes with the non-functioning gas cutter and a further loss of valuable time, the order to Mazagaon was put through again. When the men from Mazagaon finally drove through the dock gates less than an hour later they were all killed instantly before they could even get out of their car.

While Combs struggled unsuccessfully to get the gas cutter to work, the firemen on deck continued to play their hoses into the hold. Hoses and feet had to be protected with wooden duckboards from the now scorching steel of the deck. It was a heroically brave effort, yet it proved counterproductive. The effect of the water inside the lower hold was to raise the level of the burning cotton which floated on the surface of the water until it was just below the 'tween-decks where the explosives were stowed. At about 3.45 p.m. huge flames began to leap out of the hatchway. Within minutes the flames had reached the height

ABOVE: *A tower of smoke resulting from the explosion of the Fort Stikine. The explosion was so powerful that entire ships were lifted out of the water and deposited on dry land.*

of the ship's mast. Naismith finally gave the order to abandon ship. It was immediately evident to everyone that the *Stikine* was doomed. The crowd began surging away from the quayside towards the dock gates. Where previously there had been curiosity, suddenly there was panic. This was compounded by the police, who, still following strict orders, would not allow anyone to pass through the gates without showing their identification first.

When the last of the *Stikine*'s crew appeared to have disembarked, Captain Naismith reboarded the ship by himself and carried out a personal check of the crew's quarters. He had just got back on to the quayside when, with cataclysmic force, the ship blew up, killing him instantly and many of those around him. The time was 4.06. It was possible to establish the time precisely because the dock clock stopped at that moment and remained at 4.06 for several months to come. The explosion was colossal. The tremor was recorded on a seismograph 1,000 miles away in Simla. The 4,500-ton steel ship simply disintegrated. Pieces of flying metal hurtled through the air and were deposited up to a mile away. The *Jalapadma*, a 4,000-ton ship berthed next to the *Stikine*, was lifted right out of the water and deposited on the quay wall. One of the *Stikine*'s huge anchors was caught in the rigging of a ship in the neighbouring dock. Eleven ships were now on fire and four were sunk or sinking. There were fires everywhere, in the godowns and the dock buildings, and in the shanty town of Bombay itself. Many of the godowns were themselves full of explosives. Worse was to come. At 4.40 the explosives in what was left of the aft end of the *Stikine* blew up. The second explosion was twice as powerful as the first. Debris flew 3,000 feet into the air.

The fight to save what was left of the docks continued all through that night and most of the next day. Military and civilian forces were drafted in, working alongside untold numbers of volunteers. There was no single overall authority and yet somehow the worst of the raging fires were contained and many of the injured were brought out of the inferno. It was a night that showed the English and the Indians working together at their very best and that saw many individual acts of heroism. After the first explosion twenty or so people found themselves trapped on a jetty with no means of reaching the quayside, surrounded by water full of burning cotton and metal debris. There was one small boat nearby which was, with some difficulty, reached. Half of the stranded got into the boat and it set off for the quayside. Once there, the half who had been rescued forgot about those left behind and headed for the gates. One of those remaining dived into the dock, swam to the boat, rowed it back to those who were still left stranded and brought them all off. It was only a matter of minutes before the second explosion. Another hero of a different kind was Ali Mecklai, a local businessman, who spent the night touring the city's chemist shops in a hired taxi collecting drugs and medicines to take to the overstretched hospitals. Two other brave men managed to get an ammunition train moving and out of the danger zone just minutes before it too blew up. There were countless other examples of selfless dedication to duty during the long night, but particular mention has to be made of the Bombay Fire Service. Out of 156 firemen involved, sixty-five were killed and eighty wounded. In total 233 people were killed and 476 injured. The dock itself was devastated, as were most of the ships in it.

Once the immediate threat of fire had been extinguished, the authorities' thoughts inevitably turned to the question of what had happened to the *Stikine*'s gold. The answer was soon pretty obvious. It had been blown sky high and scattered over an area about a mile wide. When Burjorji Motiwala, a 70-year-old pensioner living in a fourth-floor flat, heard a thump, for instance, he naturally went out to see what had happened. He was somewhat surprised to discover that a gold bar had been deposited on his balcony. He handed the bar in to the police and later received a substantial reward of 999 rupees. He gave his entire reward to the disaster relief fund.

In total less than half the bars were recovered, of which most were found lying on land. The dock was drained and labourers were employed to wade through the mud waist deep in the hope of finding further bars, but only about half a dozen were dredged up in this manner. Expert opinion was that the bars had probably turned end on and sunk through the mud to the clay bottom about ten feet down. The dock is regularly dredged, and now and again the odd bar comes to the surface.

LEFT: *Damaged ships and collapsed buildings littering the docks in the aftermath of the fire.*

THE I.52
OPERATION MOMI

ABOVE: *Lt Commander Jesse Taylor was the first airman from Task Group 22-2 to spot the surfaced Japanese submarine. He described it over his radio as 'very large and very pointed at bow and stern'. He dropped two Mk 54 depth bombs and one Mk 24 mine or acoustic torpedo.*

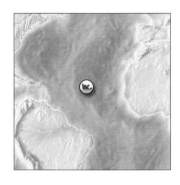

I N THE LATE AUTUMN of 1994 two privately sponsored salvage missions, one British and one American, were about to get underway. Both had been many years in the planning, and during that time all concerned had been very careful to keep their intentions from becoming known to the world at large, particularly potential rivals. The problem was that both groups had the same objective, namely finding the location of a giant cargo-carrying Japanese submarine the *I.52*. The fact that the two competing groups were to set sail within weeks of each other for the same destination was not altogether a coincidence. The *I.52*, with over two tons of gold ingots on board, was known to be lying in an area of ocean at least 5,000 metres deep. The technology for locating ships in very deep water had only recently been developed. Once it had become technically possible both to search those depths and to retrieve objects from them, it was inevitable that the *I.52* would be targeted sooner or later. An equally important factor was that the Cold War was now over and a new, market-oriented Russia was keen to exploit its sophisticated technical hardware in return for badly needed Western currency. Both the American and the British teams were to make use of Russian search ships and Russian equipment.

The *I.52* had been constructed in the Kure Navy Yard, near Hiroshima, and completed on 18 December 1943. Designed specifically as a long-range cargo carrier, it was 356.5 feet long and had a displacement of 2,095 tons and a top speed of 17.75 knots when on the surface and 6.5 knots when submerged. It carried 19 torpedoes, was capable of diving to a depth of 330 feet, and its extra large fuel tanks gave it a massive range, at 12 knots, of 27,000 nautical miles. In March 1944, following its sea trials, the *I.52* (codenamed Momi) slipped out of Kure harbour to begin a most remarkable maiden voyage. Its destination was the port of Lorient, in German-occupied France. The submarine was under the command of Captain Kameo Uno, and had a hand-picked crew of ninety-three. In addition to the crew there was a small group of elite passengers on board, skilled technical personnel

OPPOSITE: *A German seaman scans the air from the conning tower of his submarine. They were at their most vulnerable when exposed above water, but the* I.52 *and the* U-530 *both needed to surface in order to make their rendezvous – it was to prove the undoing of the* I.52.

involved in the critical exchange of scientific military information with Germany. Shortly before departure the *I.52* received a last-minute surprise delivery of 146 gold bars in 49 boxes. The gold was sent to the dockyard under heavy guard from the Osaka branch of the Bank of Japan.

Ahead lay what was undoubtedly one of the most daunting and dangerous tasks undertaken by any ship of any nation during the war. It involved sailing half-way round the world, not only alone but, because the ship was mainly journeying through enemy-controlled waters, also largely in a submerged mode. The conditions on board were spartan in the extreme. Space was constricted, the food monotonous (mainly steamed rice and tinned beans), and all surfaces were wringing wet with condensation, so that before long clothes were covered in mildew and skin rashes were the norm. It was not a voyage for the faint-hearted.

The submarine's only port of call was Singapore, which had been under Japanese occupation for two years, and it arrived there in late March 1944. Here it took on board 230 tons of the metals wolfram, molybdenum and tin, 54 tons of rubber, and five tons of quinine. It is arguable that this part of the cargo was even more important to Germany than the gold and technical experts that were also on board. One of Germany's greatest problems during the Second World War was a shortage of strategic supplies, in particular rubber and metals used in the arms industry, such as wolfram and tin. Germany's main ally, Japan, had access to these supplies in abundance, particularly after Japan's successful invasion of Malaya in 1942. Transportation of these items to German-occupied Europe, however, proved extremely problematic. Russia blocked the land route, while the navies of the United States and Great Britain were in control of the North and South Atlantic. From 1941 Germany made a number of attempts to ship strategic supplies both on the Northabout route (via the Arctic Ocean and the Barents Sea) and the Southabout route (via the South China Sea and the Indian and Atlantic Oceans). As the war progressed, Germany's losses by surface ship became

BELOW: *The* I.52 *submarine preparing for its maiden voyage somewhere in Eastern waters with the crew enjoying some fresh air and sunshine. The six-month voyage half way around the world was to be conducted almost entirely in darkness. Surfacing for the vital recharging of batteries could only occur under cover of nightfall.*

LEFT: *The USS aircraft carrier* Bogue *at anchor in Bermuda in 1945. The* Bogue *was the senior ship in Task Group 22-2. When searching for the wreck fifty years later, the German U-boat log proved more accurate than the log of the carrier. This photograph provides a good view of the TBM planes on the foredeck.*

unacceptably high, while its need for the vital materials grew ever more urgent. Towards the end of 1943 the desperate strategy of using cargo-carrying submarines was developed.

The *I.52* left Singapore for Lorient on 23 April 1944. As the Japanese submarine headed across the Indian Ocean and then turned northwards up the South Atlantic, the German submarine *U–530* left the German port of Kiel and headed south. The two submarines were scheduled to meet in mid Atlantic at position 15° North 40° West at 9.15 p.m. (dusk) on 22 June. The purpose of the rendezvous was to transfer, from the German submarine to the Japanese, a liaison officer and two technicians with the latest radar search equipment in order to facilitate the safe conduct of the Japanese submarine through the perilous Bay of Biscay area. Inferior radar equipment was the bugbear of the Japanese submarines, allowing them to be caught off guard by the Allies time and time again. Ironically, it was just when the *I.52* surfaced to take on board the superior German equipment that was to help guarantee its safety, that it was finally spotted by an American pilot.

The Japanese submarine reached the rendezvous position just one day late. The meeting was successfully achieved at the first attempt and the transfer of crew and radar equipment was made. It was an impressive feat of navigation for the two submarines to meet up in the middle of the Atlantic in this way approximately 800 miles southwest of the Azores, the nearest point of land. But it was an ill-fated union. Just minutes after the transfer, Lieutenant-Commander Taylor in a TBM aircraft launched from USS Aircraft Carrier *Bogue*, part of Task Group 22.2, spotted a surfaced submarine that fitted the description of a Japanese cargo carrier. 'Very large and very pointed at bow and stern' was what he immediately radioed back to the *Bogue*. His radio was not functioning properly and his message never reached the control ship. Luckily for the Allies, another pilot called Hirsbrunner, also flying a TBM, did pick up the signal and was able to relay it back to the carrier.

Lieutenant-Commander Taylor's sighting was not purely fortuitous. Unknown to either the Japanese or the Germans, Allied interception and decoding of enemy radio signals had provided them with detailed knowledge of the movements of both submarines throughout their entire voyages. USS *Bogue* had been detached from the main South Atlantic Fleet, together with five destroyers, to attack and sink both submarines.

Taylor had first picked up evidence of a submarine in the vicinity on his radar at around 11.40 p.m. (he was using American time, which was about two hours behind German time), and at a distance of about ten miles. When he was one mile away he dropped two smoke lights and a purple-coloured sonar buoy. At this point the plane was at an altitude of 1,500 feet and travelling at approximately 120 knots. As soon as the sonar buoy hit the water Taylor was able to hear the sound of the submarine's propellor. At half a mile's distance from the target Taylor dropped a flare and immediately the submarine was clearly visible below him, fully surfaced. He flew over the submarine, made a tight turn and came in on its port bow at a height of 300 feet and a speed of 175 knots. He dropped two Mark 54 depth bombs set to explode hydrostatically at 25 feet. By now the submarine was diving for cover, with only its conning tower and stern still visible. Both bombs exploded, one very close to the submarine and the other about 75 feet away. Taylor dropped another sonar buoy, orange this time, and then turned for a second attack, now intending to deploy the MK 24 mine that he also carried on board. The MK24 was not actually a mine at all but a recently developed and highly sensitive acoustic torpedo that homed in on the propellor noise of its target. The first time Taylor tried to launch the MK24 he failed because he had forgotten to switch his selector from bombs to torpedoes. He made another tight turn, came in a third time and on this occasion he succeeded in dropping the torpedo about 200 feet astern of the turbulence created by the diving submarine. He could still hear the propellor noises of the submarine on his orange sonar buoy. He listened intently for a further three or four minutes, after which he heard a loud explosion. The propellor sounds ceased. He then heard what he later described as a crackling, crunching noise – 'like the noise made when a tin can is crushed'. The noises picked up by the sonar buoys and relayed to the plane cockpit were all recorded on a special sonar buoy wire recorder and still exist in the confidential files of the National Archives in Washington. The time of the MK24 explosion recorded by Taylor was 11.50 p.m.

At 1.00 a.m. Lieutenant Gordon arrived on the scene, also in a TBM plane, and Taylor returned to base. Gordon had on board Price Fish, a civilian underwater sounds expert, who had been central to the development of the sonar buoy system. This was the first time that sonar buoys had been used in action, and Price Fish was eager to observe for himself exactly how well they functioned. More sonar buoys were dropped in the area by Gordon's plane, and further faint propellor noises were detected. At 1.45 a.m. the noises appeared to be getting stronger and Gordon decided to drop his MK24 mine. At 2.13 a.m. an enormous explosion was heard, after which no further propellor noises were detected.

The following morning the destroyers *Janssen* and *Haverfield* were detached from the task group to investigate an oil slick that had been spotted by another TBM plane circling above the scene of the previous night's action. A boat was lowered from the *Janssen* and samples of the oil were taken. It was thought to be either lubricating oil or sludge. A large quantity of crude rubber was observed floating in the area, some of which was collected. Also picked up was a rubber sandal with a Japanese inscription, some wood thought to be Philippine mahogany, some light black silk fishing line, and 'one piece of flesh tissue, about

LEFT: *The crew of the* USS Bogue *trying to raise a crashed plane on the flight deck. Allied intelligence knew exactly where the German and Japanese submarines were proposing to rendezvous because they were intercepting German and Japanese radio signals and had already cracked the codes being used.*

12 ozs, identified by the pharmacist's mate as human tissue probably from the abdomen of an oriental'. A large number of sharks were also observed in the area, which it was thought might explain the small quantity of human flesh recovered.

American naval intelligence carried out a very lengthy and detailed analysis of the entire incident. They concluded that a Japanese submarine had been sunk. Whether the German submarine had also been sunk was more problematic. Gordon's sonar recordings suggested that a second submarine had been attacked and destroyed. The possibility of it having been the same submarine that was attacked by both Taylor and Gordon was considered unlikely, because all propellor noise had ceased after Taylor's attack, and when Gordon picked up renewed propellor noise it was from a different position. It was considered that the submarine could not have got from one position to the other without restarting its engines and therefore transit propellor noise would have been heard. The only factor giving the Americans any doubt was that they had not managed to collect any debris which would suggest German origin. However, on balance they considered it probable that the German submarine had also been destroyed. In conclusion it was reported that the use of MK24 mines in conjunction with sonar buoys was a significant advance in anti-submarine technology, which undoubtedly it was.

As it happened, the submarine *U–530* was neither sunk nor even damaged in this attack, but survived and eventually returned safely to Kiel. In its log-book, which still exists in the German naval war archive in Freiburg, it is recorded that one hour after a successful rendezvous with the Japanese submarine, the Germans heard explosions approximately twenty miles to the north in an area which, they calculated, the Japanese submarine would quite probably have reached. American intelligence was, of course, not privy to German U-boat logs when they carried out their analysis. The only conclusion that can be drawn from both American and German records is that both Taylor's and Gordon's attacks were directed against the Japanese submarine *I.52*. The mystery is how and in what shape the *I.52*

AC-6

RIGHT: *One of the many posters designed to encourage the American war effort at home.*

survived the first MK24 explosion, what it was doing between the time of the first attack and the time of the second attack some ninety minutes later, and how it moved from one position to another without any apparent propellor noise being picked up on the sonar buoys.

Both rival salvage groups analysed all the available data, German, American and Japanese, and interestingly came to broadly the same conclusions about the likely sinking position of the *I.52*. The American data, by far the most prolific and detailed, was the main determinant. The British group, headed by lawyer Clive Hayley and merchant banker Simon Fraser, was to be the first in the water. The Russian research ship *Keldysh* sailed from Southampton early in January 1995. Of the two expeditions, the British was significantly more ambitious. The intention was to locate the *I.52* and to salvage the gold in the one visit. The latter was to be carried out by deploying the two Russian *Mir* submersibles that were on board. The submersibles were equipped with articulated arms on the outside of the tiny hulls which could deploy specially constructed cutting tools and pick up objects such as gold bars. The British group also had a second target in mind after the completion of the *I.52* operation. The American expedition was limited to the one target and initially only to locating that target. Salvage was to be put off to a later date.

The British expedition experienced a number of teething problems, but by the time the ship reached the search area everyone was working well together. The sonar fish was towed by the *Keldysh* over the surface of the ocean bed by means of a very long cable, and the resulting sonar traces were printed out in graphic form as well as being recorded on computer discs. In the positions where anomalies showed up on the sonar recordings the *Mir* would carry out a dive from the mother ship so that the anomaly could be investigated. This was a more thorough means of investigation than was possible by remotely operated cameras, as it enabled a pair of human eyes to look directly at whatever had caused the aberration in the sonar trace, but because of the length of time involved while the *Mir* descended it was also a slow and painstaking process. One by one the anomalies were checked out and, to the increasing disappointment of the salvage team, one by one they proved negative. Soon the entire designated search area had been covered, with no positive results. The decision was taken to abort this part of the project and move on to the second target.

On 12 April 1995 the American group, led by Paul Tidwell, departed from Bridgetown, Barbados, in the Russian research vessel *Yuzhmorgeologiya*. Again the main search tool was side-scan sonar, this time backed up with cameras fixed to a towed sledge. In determining the search area, careful allowance had been made for wind direction during the night when the *I.52* sank, the prevailing currents and the likely angle of descent as the damaged submarine plunged downwards. The search continued for two weeks, covering essentially the same area as the British had covered a few months earlier. The results were the same. No evidence of a large steel shipwreck of any kind was detected.

Those on board the *Yuzhmorgeologiya* began to question whether the *I.52* had after all been sunk by the two attacks carried out by the American TBM aircraft. Perhaps there was another explanation for the events of the night of 23 April 1944. Interestingly, and worryingly, there had always been another theory about what had happened to the *I.52*. Official Japanese war records had their submarine listed as having been sunk in the Bay of Biscay around 1 August 1944. This was not just wild speculation on the part of the Japanese, but was based on clear evidence recorded in the German Naval High Command war diaries, which again are still preserved at Freiburg. On 30 July 1944 German Naval Headquarters had received a signal from the Japanese U-boat *Fohre* (another code name for the *I.52*) indicating that it was thirty-six hours from the rendezvous point for entering the port of Lorient in the Bay of Biscay. This signal was received over one month after the Americans thought they had sunk the Japanese submarine and indicated a new position several thousand miles from the supposed scene of destruction. The following day two more signals were received, stating the same information and setting a new time for rendezvous. However, although the Germans sent escort ships out to the agreed meeting place, no Japanese submarine appeared. The escort ships were sent out again on 1 and 2 August, but still no submarine appeared. By 4 August, in the absence of further signals, the Germans reluctantly concluded that the submarine must have been sunk some time after sending out the second set of signals on 31 July. The signals had no signature, but the Germans were convinced of their authenticity because they made use of Flieder cypher instructions, 'and must therefore originate from *Fohre*'.

The salvors on board the Russian research ship began to consider the unthinkable, namely that the *I.52* had, after all, survived the attack launched from USS *Bogue* and limped on into the Bay of Biscay before being finally annihilated. It seemed unlikely. After all there was the wealth of debris picked up by the destroyer *Janssen*, including human flesh. And yet it was not unknown for Japanese submarines to release detritus in a deliberate attempt to deceive the Allies. An alternative possible explanation was that the Biscay signal was an Allied ruse intended to deceive the Germans and lure their escort ships into the open. But, if this was the case, why was no Allied attack carried out against those ships when they came out on two consecutive nights? And why was it that the Allies themselves seemed later to have forgotten about their own fake signal? Because in 1954 American and British intelligence gave serious consideration to trying to salvage the lost gold on the basis that the wreck was lying in relatively shallow waters in the Bay of Biscay.

The American salvage group, in a last-minute decision before leaving port, had decided to employ the services of a small high-tech company called Meridian Sciences Inc., that

ABOVE: *A Russian* Mir *submersible used both by the British team and later by Paul Tidwell during his second expedition to the wreck site. The photograph shows the* Mir *being launched.*

ABOVE: *Paul Tidwell with some of the items he has salvaged from the* I.52 *debris field. Tidwell has taken great care to treat the sunken submarine with the kind of respect appropriate to a grave site including returning personal items to members of the bereaved families.*

specialized in computer analysis of navigation systems, to carry out a renavigation on all the data relating to the *I.52* sinking. In simplistic terms the logs of all the US ships involved were analysed for errors in their original navigation, and these error patterns were then applied to their data on the day of the sinking. This analysis came up with the startling conclusion that the Japanese submarine, always presuming that it had indeed sunk, would be found lying a good ten miles from the official US navy position. Interestingly, the new position was significantly closer to the one that had been indicated by the original German log-book. These conclusions were hastily e-mailed to the search ship, and the *Yuzhmorgeologiya*, with rapidly dwindling fuel supplies, started combing the new area.

With just one day left before the search was due to be terminated, the sonar on board the *Yuzhmorgeologiya* came up with a superb image of what was quite clearly a large steel wreck. Impressive photography from the camera sledge showed beyond doubt that it was a submarine. The *I.52* was the only submarine known to have sunk in the area. It was a remarkable find and the British team were quick to congratulate their rivals on their success.

As it turned out salvor Paul Tidwell's problems were only just starting. It took him nearly four years to organise a return visit to the wreck site. This was not because he had lost interest in the project but because salvage is so often a more complex business than it first seems. However, in November 1998, this time using the Russian research ship *Keldysh* and the *Mir* submersibles, previously used by the British team, he finally set out again. The *Keldysh*'s satellite navigational system deposited the *Mir*s to within a few hundred yards of the sunken submarine on the first dive. There was a short wreath laying ceremony to commemorate the dead Japanese sailors and the three German technicians who had also been on board at the point of sinking. The sight of the wreck close up had a haunting effect on all who saw it but this must have been particularly true for William Gordon who was one of the original pilots involved in the submarine's sinking, and who was included in the *Keldysh* party.

The wreck lies upright on a hard sandy bottom listing slightly to the port side close to a small outcrop of rock. There is some silting up but most of the wreck is clearly exposed. A part of the bow section is missing and there is some damage in the forward section but generally the submarine is in remarkably good shape. There was no longer any room for doubt that Tidwell's first expedition had located the right wreck because the numbers *I.52* were still clearly identifiable on either side of the central conning tower. At this depth there is no coral growth so details such as the deck guns and even the deck binoculars stood out clearly. The *Mir*s recovered various items from the debris field using their manipulators, including personal artefacts as well as items of cargo such as tin ingots which it is known the submarine was carrying at the time of its loss. Tidwell has since travelled to Japan to return the personal items to members of the Bereaved Relatives Association. No gold was discovered in the debris field but this was hardly surprising as the gold was stowed well within that area of the hull which remains in tact. Penetrating the hull was not attempted on this expedition. This would have been politically far more sensitive because of the war graves issue and technically far more difficult. To complicate matters further Japan has now made a formal claim of ownership.

The gold bars are definitely there. It would be possible to put an X on the chart to mark the spot. But picking them up will not be easy. The *I.52* story has some way to go yet

THE JOHN BARRY

ARABIAN SILVER

THE *JOHN BARRY* WAS ARGUABLY the most mundane-looking treasure ship of all. It looked in fact exactly like what it was, a cheap, functional and efficient freighter, capable of 12 knots and of carrying approximately 9,000 tons of cargo. It was one of over 2,700 almost identical ships built in the United States between 1941 and 1945. They were called Liberty ships, for the very good reason that they helped keep the vital Allied supply routes open for most of the war. Built to a simple sixty-year-old British design, they were mass-produced, many of their parts having been prefabricated, and their giant steel plates were welded rather than riveted together, all of which allowed for rapid construction. One of these workhorses of the war, the *Robert E. Peary*, was built in a record-breaking four and a half days, an amazing industrial feat. For all its lack of the finer architectural details lavished on other ships, the *John Barry*'s claim to be a treasure ship is indisputable. Nor was it just any old treasure ship but, according to some fervent believers, the richest, certainly the most controversial, of its era.

The *John Barry*, launched in 1941, was one of the earliest models, built by the Oregon Shipbuilding Corporation of Portland, Oregon, and owned by the United States Maritime Commission. It was 416 feet long, with two decks, five holds and a gross tonnage of 7,176 tons. Its early crossings of the Atlantic were relatively uneventful. Then, in early July 1944, it was detailed to sail for the Saudi Arabian port of Ras Tanurah and another 'port unspecified in the Persian Gulf'. The apparent vagueness of its ultimate destination was later to help convince researchers that it was on a special mission.

The *John Barry* left Hampton Roads, Norfolk, in convoy on 24 July 1944, having previously berthed in New York. On board, in addition to its forty-four crew members, were 27 US navy gunners, who were to defend the ship in the event of attack. The ship carried in its holds a typical mixed general war cargo, much of it Lend-Lease material. This included trucks, cranes, steel pipe and beer. In addition, carefully stowed in its No. 2 hold, were 750

boxes containing exactly three million Saudi Riyals, silver coins of 91 per cent purity. They had 'struck in Mecca' stamped on them in Arabic, a convenient gloss on the truth which was to cause some embarrassment to the Saudi Arabian government 50 years later when they were finally hauled out of the ocean in a blaze of publicity. They had, of course, been minted in the United States, but this could hardly have been stamped on a coin that was to be circulated in Arabia. The Saudi authorities neatly explained away the apparent subterfuge by claiming that they had been conceived in Mecca and merely manufactured in the United States. Whatever their provenance, the Saudi Riyals were real enough and could be clearly traced in historical documents. They were catalogued as Lend-Lease requisition no. SZ-505 A2 (AB). The amount allocated to the United States Treasury was $753,607.99, which represented 1,031,250 fine ounces of silver. The US Mint records showed 'Lost at Sea 1,031,250 fine ounces of silver'. It could not be neater. But the main object of fascination for future treasure-hunters was not the presence of Saudi Riyals. They were just the icing on the cake. What whetted the appetite of restaurateur Jay Fiondella and United States naval officer Brian Shoemaker was the further evidence that Shoemaker claimed to have unearthed in US archives to the effect that the *John Barry* was carrying a huge quantity of silver bullion, some 1,500 tons of it, in addition to the Saudi coins. This discovery turned the humble Liberty ship overnight into the richest treasure ship of the twentieth century and led to newspaper headlines like that of the *Telegraph* of 30 September 1991, 'Treasure hunters aim to raise £142m silver from wreck', or *The Times* of 6 January 1993, 'Salvage divers find £200m treasure', or the *News of the World* of 27 November 1994, '£200m splash and grab'.

The *John Barry*'s convoy arrived at Port Said in Egypt, at the northern entrance to the Suez Canal, on 19 August, and at Suez, at the southern end of the canal, on the 20 August. It sailed from there on the 21st and arrived in Aden on the 26th. After Aden the convoy dispersed and the *John Barry* was routed independently. It left again on the same day and sailed alone across the Arabian Sea, zigzagging in accordance with instructions issued by Naval Control Aden, *en route* for Ras Tanurah in the Persian Gulf. On the evening of the 28th the sea was rough. All observers were agreed about that, but not about how clear the weather was. Captain Joseph Ellerwald, who was in charge of the *John Barry*, thought that it had been a hazy evening, whereas most of the other observers, including Oberleutnant Horst Klatt on the submarine *U-859*, remembered it as having been one of bright moonlight.

The *U-859* was one of the IXD2 class of cargo-carrying U-boats with a range of 30,000 miles. It was equipped with twenty-four torpedo tubes, had a crew of sixty-nine and was under the command of Kapitan Jebsen. It had left the German port of Kiel on 4 April 1944, nearly five months earlier, for the long and arduous voyage to Penang, in Malaya. The scheduled route involved a first call at Kristiansand on the southern tip of Norway and then a wide sweep southwards around the west of the British Isles, down through the Atlantic, around the Cape of Africa and back up the Indian Ocean. The crew were handpicked and highly disciplined, but even so the strain of the long voyage was beginning to tell. For five months these men had been in almost continual darkness, only surfacing for an hour each night to recharge the submarine's batteries, living under claustrophobic and cramped conditions, their only contact with the outside world the occasional radio report that described the worsening military situation back home. It was hardly surprising, then, that tempers were getting shorter and differences of opinion louder. They suffered alternately from excessive cold and excessive heat. Choking carbon dioxide fumes were continuously causing sore eyes. The food was monotonous. And always at the back of their thoughts was the knowledge that their chances of survival were at the best only slim. Of the 45 U-boats that sailed for the Far East, only four made it back to Germany, thirty-four sunk *en route*. However, the traffic was considered to be so vital to the Axis powers that they pursued the strategy despite the appalling losses. The *U-859* was carrying 30 tons of mercury, together with much-needed radar parts and all-important technical information.

The Allies were not unaware of the *U-859's* movements and had already instructed the South African air force to attack it as and when an opportunity arose. On 5 July, at around dawn, a Catalina flying boat spotted the submarine, while the latter was enjoying one of its rare moments on the surface. The Catalina promptly dropped depth charges that damaged one of the submarine's fuel tanks, killed a seaman and seriously injured one of the officers. The *U-859* returned fire from its deck guns, damaging the Catalina, and then hastily submerged in case Allied reinforcements were in the vicinity. It was a close escape and a reminder of the dangers of surfacing even in semi light, however great the temptation.

At dusk on 28 August the *U-859* surfaced as usual to obtain a positional fix and recharge its batteries. It established its position as being approximately 15.10° North, 55.18° East. Kapitan Jebsen was then surprised and delighted to observe an unescorted enemy merchant ship, in almost total black-out, zigzagging erratically. The U-boat manoeuvred into position and waited at periscope level for the merchant ship to approach. Jebsen estimated its tonnage at 8,000 tons, which was a pretty good guess. The unescorted merchant ship zigzagging towards him was the *John Barry*.

When the *John Barry* was at a distance of approximately 850 yards, Kapitan Jebsen gave the order to fire off three torpedoes. According to Oberleutnant Klatt, only one of the torpedoes hit its target. The *John Barry* survivors gave differing accounts in their evidence as to how many torpedoes struck in that first attack. Most agreed that the first torpedo hit around 10.00 p.m. in the forward part of No. 3 hold on the starboard side. Some claimed that a second torpedo struck shortly afterwards, also on the starboard side. Most agreed that another torpedo struck on the port side about 45 minutes after the first attack, causing the ship to break in two and sink. This version of events is also corroborated by German survivor accounts. Klatt recalls how those on the U-boat observed the Americans hastily abandoning their ship. They then noticed that the *John Barry* did not appear to be sinking. The U-boat manoeuvred around it and fired a torpedo into the port side. This torpedo struck its target about midships. All observers are agreed that the *John Barry* then appeared to break in two and sank almost immediately.

Interestingly, Captain Ellerwald stated that the second attack torpedo struck the starboard side, with no torpedoes striking on the port side. He seemed to be alone in this opinion. There are other contradictions in the evidence. According to Captain Ellerwald's account of events, immediately the first torpedo struck he left his cabin and went on to the bridge, where he gave the order to abandon ship. In other accounts the impact of the first hit strained the ship's structure, so that Ellerwald had difficulty getting out of his cabin and it was some minutes before he arrived on the bridge. Similarly, Ellerwald stated that as soon as the first torpedo hit the *John Barry* it began to sink by the bows. According to Oberleutnant Klatt, the *John Barry* showed no signs of sinking to begin with, which is why after about half an hour they decided to fire the second torpedo. Significantly the summary of survivors' reports, drawn up in Washington by Lieutenant Barbara Conrad on 5 October 1944, includes the following remark: 'Interviewing officer at Basra, Iraq, stated that whilst the Master described the crew as behaving in an orderly manner, this statement is doubtful since the ship was quickly abandoned without orders and while there was reason to think it was not in a sinking position. Ship was then left an easy target for the second torpedo.' The purpose of going into this matter in some detail is not to point the finger at Captain Ellerwald and his crew over 50 years after the event. Some degree of confusion and panic when under submarine attack is all too understandable and human. It is rather to emphasize how easy it is for confusion to arise in connection with a catastrophic event like a shipwreck, and how this can lead to all kinds of further misunderstandings later on for those who come to investigate it.

Two of the *John Barry*'s lifeboats were destroyed before they could be launched, but two others were successfully got away. Those in Captain Ellerwald's boat were picked up by another American Liberty ship, the *Benjamin Bourne*, while those with Mr Richards, the purser, and Mr Bolton, the Chief Engineer, were picked up by a Dutch ship, the *Sunetta* and taken to Aden. Two men had been injured and two had lost their lives. The *U-859* continued on its route to Penang. The German submarine should have been escorted into harbour for the last leg of its journey, but the Japanese escort ships were unable to make the rendezvous because of foggy weather. The *U-859* was consequently instructed to try to make it into port by itself. Like so many others, it failed to do so. It was sunk by a torpedo from the British submarine *Trenchant*, only two hours' sailing from its destination and with large loss of life. Eleven survivors were fished out of the sea. The British submarine had been

LEFT: *A quantity of Saudi silver Riyals before being cleaned. Over one and one half million coins were salvaged in total. However, the fabled silver bullion cargo amounting to over 1,500 tons in bars was not discovered.*

well aware of the existence and even the movements of the *U-859*, as signals from the German U-boat were constantly being intercepted and the information relayed to the *Trenchant*'s commander.

The first substantive clue that led to the belief that the *John Barry* was carrying a vast quantity of silver bullion as well as Saudi Riyals was the official statement made after the sinking by the ship's purser, G.L. Richards, to Lieutenant-Commander C.A. Woods at Aden. This mentioned that the *John Barry*'s cargo included $26 million in silver, listed as government Lend-Lease. This information was repeated in a US Intelligence report of 3 September and a US observer's report, also written at Aden, on 7 September. The same information was repeated again in the written statement drawn up in Washington on 5 October. It was repeated yet again in the written statement made by Captain Joseph Ellerwald to the US Coastguard on 23 March 1945. $26 million in silver bullion was the equivalent of approximately 1,500 tons of silver. If true, this had to be the biggest shipment of silver in one vessel ever known. The problem was: where was the silver destined for? At first India was thought to be the most likely candidate. It was known that large quantities of silver were shipped to India from the US at this period under the Lend-Lease scheme. A telling discovery was a letter written by the Director of the US Mint in June 1944, the month before the *John Barry* sailed, which referred to supplying India with 90 million ounces of silver. One problem with the India theory was that neither India nor Britain claimed any knowledge of a loss of silver bullion on their accounts on the *John Barry*. Another was that the *John Barry* was not even scheduled to call at an Indian port. However, a large part of the cargo was Lend-Lease destined for Russia. The unnamed port on the Persian Gulf was Abadan, which was a main supply route for Russia. After that it was only a small step to the conclusion that the shipment of silver bullion was for the Russian account, and now the belief in the bullion theory snowballed. Even the problem of stowage appeared to be solved. A *John Barry* survivor came forward who vividly remembered truck load after truck load of silver being brought to the ship's side under heavily armed guard and loaded into No. 3 hold.

ABOVE: *A Saudi Riyal in close up. The coins were manufactured in the United States and were in the process of being shipped to Saudi Arabia when the* John Barry *was sunk.*

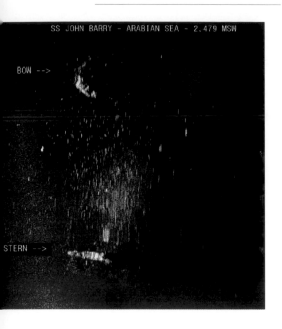

ABOVE: *A side-scan sonar survey shows the wreck on the seabed at a depth of 2,580 metres.*

When the American Maritime Administration put the salvage rights for the American-owned cargo on the *John Barry* up for tender in the late 1980s, specific mention was made of the silver bullion as well as the Saudi Riyals. Shoemaker, Fiondella and partners were among those bidding, and won the contract for salvage. This, however, was only the first stage in a delicate series of political negotiations that had to be concluded before the search for the *John Barry* could begin. The ship had been sunk in a position approximately 150 miles off the coast of Oman. According to the United Nations Convention of the Sea this was in international waters, but it was also within Oman's economic zone and Oman laid claim to the shipwreck. As it happened, Oman had already entered into a contract with Keith Jessop, of HMS *Edinburgh* fame, in conjunction with Sheikh Ahmed Farid al Aulaqi, to salvage the *John Barry*. There were now two independent groups from different countries with separate claims to the *John Barry* cargo. It was the sort of problem that besets the salvage industry and which so often ends in acrimony and the courts. Fortunately, in this instance, an amicable agreement was reached.

From this point onwards the *John Barry* project was very different from the great majority of treasure-hunting projects, in so far as it was properly financed and professionally managed. Sheikh Farid insisted on deploying only the very best equipment and the most professional personnel. An initial side-scan sonar survey, carried out in the early 1950s, identified a wreck on the seabed in approximately 8,500 feet of water that was in the right position for being the *John Barry*. Positive identification was subsequently carried out by David Mearns of Eastport International, using the *Magellan* RoV. It was clear that the shipwreck lay on the seabed in two pieces. The ship had fractured in the area of No. 3 hold. A large amount of debris had spilled from the hold on to the seabed, but there was no evidence of any silver bars.

RIGHT: *One of the* John Barry's *lifeboats still secured to the wreck. Only two of the four lifeboats were launched.*

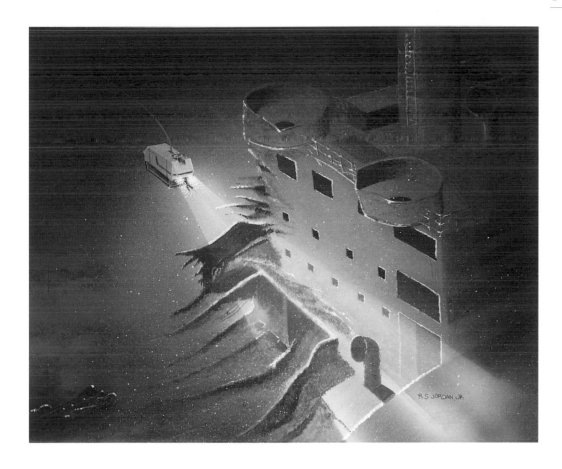

LEFT: *An artist's impression of an RoV investigating the* John Barry.

It was evident that explosives would be necessary to open up the ship for further investigation. At this point the French underwater specialists IFREMER were brought in. Detonating explosives at a depth of 8,500 feet was an extremely delicate operation, and there were only a handful of navies and private companies around the world with the necessary expertise. IFREMER not only had this expertise but they also had a three-man submersible called *Cyana* which could be used for close-up inspection of the wreck before and after a series of controlled explosions. However, the explosives achieved very little. Entry to No. 2 hold, where it was known that the Saudi Riyals were stowed, was still blocked by a large amount of wreckage and overburden. IFREMER were therefore commissioned to build a giant intelligent grab, to be deployed from the surface, to remove the weight of obstructions and bring up the treasure cargo. Grabs, of course, had been in use for many years, particularly by Risdon Beazley, in the salving of valuable cargoes. But the deepest Risdon Beazley or anyone else had ever gone was 1,000 feet. To deploy a grab at 8,500 feet would require the transmission of enormous power and a highly sophisticated controllable tool. The only previous use of anything remotely like it had been when the *Glomar Explorer* was commissioned by the CIA to salvage a Russian nuclear submarine that had sunk in a similar depth in the 1970s. That had cost half a billion dollars and ended in disaster. IFREMER set about designing what was necessary on a slightly more modest scale. It was at this stage that the financial resources of Sheikh Farid and his consortium were most necessary, because so far not an ounce of silver had been recovered.

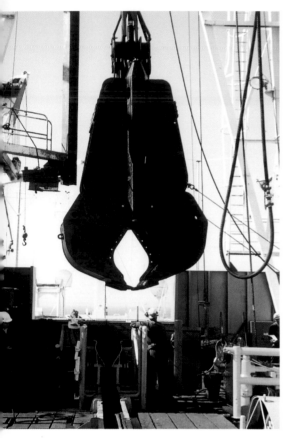

ABOVE: *The giant intelligent grab, designed and built by IFREMER, was equipped with thrusters and cameras to enable it to be deployed accurately on the seabed to within a few inches. The drill pipe from which it was suspended meant that the grab could exert approximately one hundred tons of pulling power.*

By 1994 the new technology was in place. The grab was to be deployed from a drill ship, the unglamorously named *Flex LD*, through its moon pool by means of the drill string. This enabled a hundred tons of pulling power to be communicated to the ocean bed. The grab itself was manoeuvred by computer-controlled thrusters to within a few inches of accuracy and was equipped with underwater cameras so that the operator on the surface ship could see what was happening. Clarity of vision was enhanced by pumping down clean water.

The new technology was operated by a specialist company, Blue Water Recoveries, formed specifically for the purpose of the *John Barry* salvage. It was in 1994 that, after four years of effort in the field, preceded by many more years of patient research in the archives, one and a half million Saudi Riyals spilled on to the deck of the *Flex LD*. In one grab alone some half million coins were brought up. Technically it was a highly successful operation, largely planned and managed by Robert Hudson of the Blue Water group. Financially, however, it was something of a qualified success. Excavations inside what remained of No. 3 hold revealed no sign of any silver bars.

The lack of silver bars prompts one to look again, a little more sceptically this time, at the evidence that convinced Shoemaker and Fiondella that the silver hoard was there in the first place. There are five official statements, all of which refer to $26 million of silver having been on board. These are the statement of the purser to Lieutenant-Commander Woods, in Aden, the US Intelligence Report of 3 September, the statement of the survivors to the US officer in Aden of 7 September, the US summary of survivors' statements drawn up in Washington, dated 5 October, and finally Captain Ellerwald's statement to the US Coastguard on 23 March 1945. The survivors arrived in Aden on 2 September, and it seems quite probable that the purser's statement was made the same day. If that was the case, it also seems quite probable that all the other statements were based on the purser's initial remark. It is particularly significant that in his original lengthy statement on the sinking made in Khorramshahr, in Persia (now Iran), Captain Ellerwald made no mention of the $26 million. It is also somewhat suspect that all the statements refer to exactly the same number of dollars' worth of silver. There is no reference to numbers of ounces or boxes, or any of the other ways in which a silver cargo could have been denominated. Rather more seriously undermining to the treasure hoard theory is that, according to my sources, during a confidential interview conducted in the 1980s, the purser equivocated as to whether his original remark had referred to bars of silver or whether he had all along been thinking of the Saudi Riyals. This would suggest that a chance verbal error by a man, understandably somewhat shell-shocked, having just been torpedoed out of his ship, may well have led to one of the greatest wild goose chases of all time. It is quite possible that the purser had simply got his quantities mixed up, in much the same way that Captain Ellerwald was not too sure which side of the ship the second torpedo hit or whether indeed it was the second torpedo or the third. It has to be remembered that these men were in the middle of a war, and whether there was 15 tons of silver on board or 1,500 tons was of very little practical consequence. It was 8,500 feet down, and in 1944 nobody dreamed of picking it up. A small error at the time may well have resulted in a much larger miscalculation fifty years later.

The faith of those who continue to believe that the 1,500 tons of silver really was stowed on board the *John Barry* has not been shaken. Indeed, when the sceptic points out that not only was not a single bar found, but also no country, be it Russia, the United States, Britain

LEFT: *Loading silver coins on board the* Flex LD, *a drill ship used to prospect for oil under the sea bed but converted specifically for use on the* John Barry *project.*

or India, has ever come forward and claimed ownership, the 'treasure hoard' proponents simply reply that there has been a conspiracy of silence by the authorities. It is this latter theory that John Besant expounds at some length in his fascinating book, *Stalin's Silver*, published in 1995, after the conclusion of the salvage project. Besant contends that Roosevelt had the silver bullion shipped, off the record, as a sweetener for Stalin, a view that some academic historians, such as Dr Charmley of the University of East Anglia, have hastened to support. The conspiracy theory is always a difficult one to argue against, because the lack of evidence is regarded as part of the proof. Again, however, when examined closely the hard evidence that Besant does supply to support his argument begins to look fairly tenuous. For instance, one of the main items that he produces in his book is a letter from Art Markel, who was a senior executive of the Reynolds Submarine Service Corporation, owners of the *Aluminaut* submarine. Dated 29 November 1967, the letter states: 'In researching the Maritime Administration Records, we find that the manifest of this vessel contained building materials, but an annotation stated that a large quantity of silver bullion was also carried.' Today Washington archivists deny all knowledge of any *John Barry* manifest as mentioned by Markel. Besant concludes that this must mean the manifest has been suppressed by the authorities at some date since 1967. I would rather contend that it suggests that Markel used the words manifest and bullion very loosely. Many laymen regard any listing of cargo as a manifest, which of course it is not, and many likewise use the word bullion without making a distinction between silver bars and silver coins. As it happens, I have correspondence from Markel myself from throughout this period of late

ABOVE: *A US Second World War truck still lashed on to the deck of the* John Barry *and in a surprisingly well preserved condition.*

1967 and early 1968. At the time Markel was interested in trying to salvage various deep wrecks, including the *John Barry*, with the *Aluminaut* submarine. In a letter of 19 January 1968 he wrote: 'In regard to the *John Barry*, I have not been able to ascertain any additional treasure in excess of the 1,031,250 ounces of silver mentioned. This information comes from the US Maritime Administration, the Department of State, and the Department of the Treasury. At this time, unless further values can be substantiated, the degree of salvage difficulty concerning the *John Barry* would probably make it an unlikely prospect for the near future.' This is hardly the statement of a man convinced that he has glimpsed a silver cornucopia, and it illustrates once again the danger of taking a remark out of context.

There is a curious footnote to the *John Barry* story. Sailing across the Mediterranean as part of convoy UGS.48, about one week ahead of the *John Barry*, was another Liberty ship called the *Samsylarna*. This ship was carrying 7,600 bars of silver of approximately one hundredweight each, amounting in total to 250 tons. This was not quite the enormous hoard fabled to be on the *John Barry*, but still a significant quantity. The silver was destined for Bombay. On 4 August 1944 the *Samsylarna* was bombed and abandoned. The silver was salvaged a few days later and taken to Port Said – at just about the time that the *John Barry* was passing through.

THE AWA MARU
THE ACCURSED SHIP

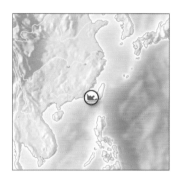

Being a submariner was arguably the toughest and most dangerous job in the war. One in five of American submarine crews did not return, a much higher casualty rate than in other branches of the forces. This statistic reflected the fact that when a submarine was hit it was not uncommon for the entire crew to be killed. It induced an intense bonding between men as well as a fierce desire to attack first and sink the enemy, before lethal reprisals in the shape of depth charges began exploding around the submarine's fragile hull. An understanding of the mind-set that this created is important to an understanding of the *Awa Maru* disaster.

Admiral Charles Andrews Lockwood, who was in charge of the American Pacific submarine fleet, based at Saipan, in the Mariana Islands, ran his men as if they were competing in a baseball league team. 'Sink 'em all' was his slogan – and the eventual title

ABOVE: *Admiral Charles Andrews Lockwood Jr who was in command of the American Pacific fleet based at Saipan.*

LEFT: *The* USS Queenfish *performing sea trials in the Pacific. The* Queenfish *had an impressive track record of hits but was going through a lean period before the sinking of the* Awa Maru.

of his autobiography – and it summed up the blunt, go-getting qualities of the man. He was
a very successful and effective commander. Crews were highly competitive, and numbers of
kills were everything.

On the evening of Sunday, 1 April 1945, USS *Queenfish* (SS393) was patrolling the
waters of the Taiwan Straits, an area notorious for its mists. The *Queenfish* was the latest
design of American submarine, a sleek and lethal killer, 311 feet long with a beam of only
twenty-seven feet, capable of travelling at 20 knots on the surface and 9 knots when
submerged. It was equipped with twenty torpedoes, much improved in accuracy since the
early days of the war when American torpedoes had been notorious for their waywardness.
Launched just over a year previously, the *Queenfish* was on its fourth patrol. Its Captain,
Commander Charles Loughlin, and a large number of its officers and crew had been with
the *Queenfish* since the beginning. Loughlin's first two patrols had been signally successful,
sinking nearly 100,000 tons of enemy shipping, but its third patrol had been disappointing,
with only one kill, and its fourth was proving still worse. After twenty-four days at sea they
still had nothing to show for it.

By 1 April the crew of the *Queenfish* in their cramped and dank quarters were getting
bored and restless. They were desperate for a score. They had no wish to incur the taunts of
rival submarine teams by returning with a blank sheet. Then, at 10.00 p.m., the radar
operator noticed a blip on the screen. There was a target at a distance of 17,000 yards
travelling very fast in a northeasterly direction. From the image it made, lying low in the
water, it appeared to Loughlin to resemble a destroyer. Its speed also suggested an enemy
warship. It was not zigzagging and it was not travelling in convoy, either of which might
have suggested a merchant ship. Earlier that day another submarine in the same hunting pack

as the *Queenfish*, called USS *Sea Fox*, had had a contact with a Japanese convoy, and Loughlin guessed that a Japanese destroyer might be rushing to some scene of action involving this convoy. In the space of just a few seconds the mood on board the *Queenfish* was entirely changed. Everyone was suddenly tense and alert. The submarine closed on its target to a distance of 3,600 yards. Those men who were topside, including Loughlin, could make out nothing in the darkness and the fog. The order was given to fire four stern torpedoes.

Japan had never been a signatory to the 1929 Geneva Convention, and they refused the Red Cross permission to monitor their prison camps or establish minimum standards of welfare. By early 1944 the United States was becoming increasingly concerned about the deteriorating condition of their prisoners of war in Japanese internment. More and more stories were reaching the American public about how their young loved ones were suffering from near starvation, a total lack of medical supplies, and appalling sanitation. Typhoid and dysentry were rife. Relatives were understandably demanding that something should be done, and there was growing support for reprisals against the Japanese interned inside American camps. The American administration was astute enough to realize that reprisals would just make matters worse. To a certain extent the Americans were victims of their own increasing military success. As they sank more and more Japanese shipping, the very life-blood of the Japanese economy, Japanese soldiers found themselves reduced to skeleton rations, and so, hardly surprisingly, they became less and less concerned about the welfare of their prisoners. Towards the end of 1944, American diplomats came up with a skilfully crafted solution. The United States would permit certain clearly designated ships free passage from Japan to Japanese overseas territories and back again, provided that those ships carried and delivered Red Cross relief supplies to prisoners of war. By the end of 1944 Japan's strategic position was so dire that it was prepared to swallow the bait, with the proviso that the United States did not attempt to stop or search any of the ships involved. The first two mercy missions carried out by the *Hakusan Maru* and the *Hoshi Maru* were successfully accomplished. The third, and by far the most ambitious, was undertaken by the *Awa Maru*. It ended in the worst American submarine error of the war, resulted in years of behind-the-scenes diplomatic cover-ups and eventually led to five separate nations competing in the biggest treasure hunt of modern times.

LEFT: *A rare photograph of the* Awa Maru *travelling at speed. The* Awa Maru *was being used as a hospital ship on its final voyage, sanctioned both by the United States and Britain. Under Red Cross protocol a hospital ship was immune from attack.*

The *Awa Maru* was an 11,378-ton ship built in 1942 by Mitsubishi, originally intended as a luxury passenger liner, but quickly converted for use as a freighter cum transport ship with much more rudimentary accommodation. Its owners were the famous Japanese shipping line Nippon Yusen Kaisha, better known as NYK, and its captain was Hamada Matsutaro, who soon established a reputation for reliability and skill. He manoeuvred the *Awa* safely through a number of close encounters with the enemy, supplying Japan's southern dependencies with vital supplies. It was not long before the *Awa* had acquired a reputation for being a lucky ship. This reputation was not to last. After the sinking it came to be known as 'the Accursed Ship'.

In the Japanese port of Kobe the *Awa* loaded 800 tons of Red Cross emergency relief supplies that had been delivered to Japan via Soviet Russia. This left plenty of space in its capacious holds for further cargo, the nature of which the Japanese had no intention of revealing to the United States or its allies. As a further precaution the *Awa* was equipped with primed explosives, so that in the event of the ship being boarded it could immediately destroy itself. The secret cargo included aeroplane parts and munitions, the presence of which was strictly illegal according to established international law, but which were urgently needed to help bolster the failing Japanese war effort. Also loaded was a quantity of gold and paper currency, placed inside a specially constructed safe in the *Awa*'s holds for shipment to Bangkok. This was not the first time the Japanese had used a hospital ship for the shipment of gold. Just a few weeks earlier the *Hoshi Maru* had transported fifteen tons of gold from Kobe to Shanghai.

The *Awa Maru* left the port of Moji in Japan on 17 February 1945. It first headed southwest to Taiwan, then on to Hong Kong, Saigon and Singapore, its final destination being Jakarta. It had four large white crosses painted on its sides, two on either side, designating it as a hospital ship on a mission of mercy. The relief supplies were distributed as had been agreed with the USA authorities. The gold was taken off at Singapore, as were the munitions. American intelligence quickly confirmed that the *Awa Maru* had carried military supplies, and when this information came before Admiral Lockwood he promptly requested permission from his superior, Admiral Chester Nimitz, to sink the *Awa* on its return voyage. Nimitz refused permission. It seems highly probable that senior American officials had known all along that the *Awa* was intended to carry military supplies as well as Red Cross relief. The Japanese would not have told them as much directly, but the requirement that the *Awa* should be allowed to travel without being stopped, boarded and searched was tantamount to stating that there would be items shipped that did not fall into the category of humanitarian aid. The Americans had presumably come to the conclusion that at this stage of the war it was more important to get aid through to their POWs than it was to prevent military supplies getting through. It was, no doubt, a tough and difficult decision, but Nimitz was adamant. The *Awa* was to be allowed safe passage. Signals to this effect were broadcast to all operating submarines three times in early March and again in late March. On each occasion submarine commanders were updated on the *Awa*'s latest designated route and schedule.

On the return voyage the *Awa Maru* was crowded with over 2,000 passengers, including many women and children and high-ranking officials, all anxious to leave Japan's increasingly vulnerable southern outposts in Indonesia and Malaya. It called in again at Singapore, and then the course was set across the South China Sea for the Taiwan Straits and the homeland of Japan. The *Awa* made good speed, approximately 18 knots, and kept all its lights blazing so that no enemy could be unaware of its special protected status. In the darkness and fog of the night of 1 April 1945, however, Commander Loughlin on the bridge of USS *Queenfish* saw no evidence of lights nor of white crosses – but it was clear from what happened on the radar screen that the four torpedoes fired had hit their target. The image broke in two and then promptly disappeared—a perfect kill. A surge of joy went through the entire crew. Loughlin waited some minutes, his sonar operators listening carefully to determine whether there was a possibility of further enemy ships in the vicinity. In the absence of any propellor noise being picked up he cautiously reapproached the area of sinking. A number of people were observed swimming in the oily water. The *Queenfish* crew threw lifebelts towards them. According to later crew reports the shipwrecked Japanese refused all assistance, preferring certain death in the water. Only one man clung on to a belt and was hauled aboard the *Queenfish*. He was a ship's steward, named Shimoda Kantaro, and would prove to be the only survivor. Straight away he was interrogated as to the identity of his ship. When he spelt out the name *Awa*, Loughlin immediately realized he had made a most disastrous error.

Admiral Lockwood had considerable sympathy for the predicament of his submarine commander, but he had no choice but to recall him immediately and relieve him of his post pending a court martial. Loughlin was found guilty of negligence in carrying out orders. It was the least severe of the available reprimands, but none the less Loughlin was devastated. He maintained throughout and continues to maintain to this day that, although his action turned out to be an error, he did nothing wrong and, faced with the same situation, he would do the same again. The United States government, after some hesitation, contacted Japan, accepted responsibility and promised compensation, including a replacement ship. The last thing the Americans wanted was to jeopardize Japanese goodwill in the development of the humanitarian aid programme to POWs. The compensation was never paid. Once again the *Awa Maru* story became engulfed in larger political issues that complicated any simple rights or wrongs. A few months after the sinking the war with Japan was over and the United States was faced with the task of trying to reconstruct the Japanese economy. Millions of dollars of aid were poured in to this programme. In this context it would have been politically embarrassing for the Americans to have to pay compensation for an act of war when it was now accepted between the two nations that Japan had been the original aggressor in that war. Payment of such compensation could jeopardize American public support for the aid programme. Japanese Prime Minister Yoshida could see the logic of this argument, and in April 1949 he signed the Awa Maru Claims Resolution Settlement by which, in recognition of the generous aid the United States had provided to help with Japan's reconstruction, Japan absolved the United States of any need to pay compensation.

There were doubtless those in both governments who would have been more than happy for the matter to be forgotten from that point on, and the *Awa Maru* left quietly buried on the bottom of the sea. There was little chance of this happening, however, once rumours began circulating about the fabulous treasures the *Awa* had carried on its final voyage. Its status was also complicated by the fact that the relatives of the victims did not see the Claims Resolution Settlement in the same way that their government had. Many of them were dissatisfied with the financial recompense they had received and felt that if the *Awa* wreck

ABOVE: *Commander Frank N. Shamer who took over the command of* USS Queenfish *from Commander Charles Loughlin, celebrates the safe homecoming of the ship and crew in San Francisco, October 1945.*

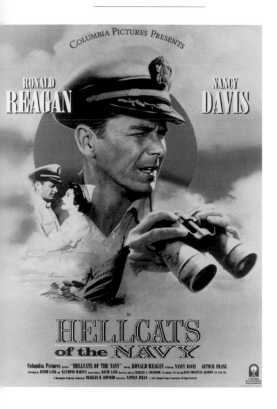

ABOVE: *Poster made for one of the many patriotic American films made during the war to boost morale, starring the future president, Ronald Reagan.*

contained valuables, then those valuables rightly belonged to them. They also wanted the remains of their loved ones returned for a proper burial. The Awa Maru Bereaved Families Association was formed to pursue their interests.

As early as 1947 the Japanese government had put forward plans for salvaging the rubber known to have formed part of the cargo on the Awa Maru. At this early stage, interestingly, the Japanese acknowledged that the tin, also known to have been on board, had been looted from Singapore, and therefore they would have difficulties claiming ownership of this part of the cargo, even if they salvaged it. The occupying Americans, however, did not want the *Awa* controversy stirred up again and put an end to the Japanese salvage plans. After this initial setback a former Japanese naval captain named Tamiya went to Taiwan and persuaded the Chinese Nationalist government to get involved. The Taiwanese, in the shape of a Mr Sakuma, approached the British Treasury in 1953, asking Britain to accept ownership of the cargo and enter into a salvage contract. The Treasury approached Malaya on the subject, and Malaya responded to the effect that they could not claim definite ownership until the cargo had been salvaged and markings on the tin ingots and other commodities supposedly on board had been examined. A cautious British Treasury procrastinated, neither denying nor accepting ownership. At this point the cargo under discussion included 3,357 tons of tin, 2,800 tons of crude rubber, shellac, mica, beeswax, lacquer, aluminium, mercury, beryllium, oil, asbestos, sugar, rice, salt, coconut oil and tobacco. It was clearly a very valuable cargo, but there was no mention at this stage of any exotic treasure.

Tamiya carried out searches throughout 1953 and 1954, but without success. In 1956 he died and the initiative was taken up by a former Japanese Admiral named Fukuda. In 1953 my father's contacts had brought him information on the cargo of the *Awa Maru*, and in 1958, as a result of this, Risdon Beazley Marine Ltd, the British company that he worked closely with, who were at the time the leading world experts in salvage, approached the Foreign Office regarding the diplomatic implications of undertaking a search for the *Awa Maru*. The Foreign Office were not encouraging. They were not prepared to approach the Chinese Communist government or the Chinese Nationalist government on the matter, as Risdon Beazley had requested, because it was felt any such approach might suggest that the governments concerned had some kind of legitimate interest in the *Awa Maru* cargo, an impression the Foreign Office was anxious not to give. For their part, Risdon Beazley were not prepared to venture around the other side of the world without Foreign Office protection, and so shelved the project in favour of other shipwrecks closer to hand.

Throughout the late 1950s and 60s a whole series of mainly Japanese salvage projects were initiated to try to find the *Awa Maru*. Most of them were poorly financed and none had any success. In 1968 Risdon Beazley again approached the British Foreign Office about the *Awa Maru*. This time the Foreign Office was more relaxed about an approach to the Chinese but advised 'waiting until the situation had quietened down'. So, once again, my father and Risdon Beazley put the project on the back burner. More years went by, but still the *Awa Maru* was not forgotten. Then, on 17 November 1976, the whole world suddenly woke up to the *Awa Maru* story as a result of an article printed in the *San Diego Evening Tribune*. The article referred to an application by an American named Bill Brunton to the Republic of China to salvage the treasure of the *Awa Maru*, now valued at $5 billion. The treasure consisted, it was claimed, of forty tons of gold ingots, twelve tons of platinum, 150,000 carats of uncut diamonds, bales of paper currency of various denominations and forty cases of looted art treasures. It would be easy to dismiss these claims as typical treasure-hunter hyperbole. However, a close examination of the circumstances surrounding the *Awa*'s departure from Singapore on its return voyage suggests that there might be some basis for them. Hidaka Shinsaku, who headed naval intelligence in Malaya and Singapore, specifically referred to three large safes, loaded with British and American currency, diamonds and gold, being put on board the *Awa* before it left Singapore for the last time. Furthermore, at the Yokohama war crimes trials, Hidaka's statement about the loading of valuables was confirmed by General Inada Seijun who had been in charge of the ship's loading.

In the wake of this American proposal to the Chinese, Risdon Beazley made a third attempt to interest the British Foreign Office in a British-backed salvage project. A delegation of Chinese salvage experts were due to visit Britain in the company of the Chinese Foreign Minister in November 1977. Risdon Beazley Marine Ltd obtained Foreign Office permission to entertain them. The visit went well, the Chinese showing great interest in the practical problems of salvage, while the management of Risdon Beazley expressed its keen interest in salvaging the *Awa Maru* and asked for its proposal to be put before the appropriate authorities in Beijing. In retrospect both the Americans and the British had been a little naive in their approaches to the Chinese, underestimating their ability to go it alone.

The following report written in 1986 by Yao Gen-Fu, Deputy Chief Engineer of the China Salvage Company, is of some interest.

> Commencing in 1977, the China Salvage Company undertook a salvage operation on *Awa Maru* and found the ship was broken in two. We demolished the upper deck, main deck, and shell [deck] in way of the holds, to the extent that it was above the seabed. Also some superstructure, deck houses were removed step by step. The fore part of *Awa Maru* was lifted out after underwater cutting.
>
>   Divers searched compartments including the accommodations and cleared the holds as far as the bilge brackets and pried up some of the bottom ceilings (floors) before demolishing. Our divers operated underwater approximately 6,100 man hours of bottom time. We had a general plan drawing of *Awa Maru* and other information, but divers did not find any safe (box) or piece of gold or diamonds. Our government has volunteered to turn over to Japan the remains and personal effects which were recovered by our Company.'

It later transpired that in 1976 Richard Nixon had presented the Chinese with a satellite chart showing the exact location of the *Awa Maru* as part of his building of bridges with Communist China – reinforcing the impression that the ship's fate has always been determined by larger diplomatic considerations. The salvage work which was continued by the Chinese into the 1980s recovered nearly all the tin that was known to have been on board. As to the fabled treasure, there are a number of theories. One is that it was never there in the first place. Another is that the Chinese recovered it but are not admitting to it. A third is that it was recovered by another group before the Chinese got there in 1977. It is to this theory that Yao Gen-Fu lends some credence further on in his report, where he states: 'I estimate that it is possible that some unknown teams dived on *Awa Maru* in the period 1945–1977 before our company undertook the salvage.' And the fourth theory is that it is still there, waiting to be discovered.

BELOW: *A sombre memorial in the Zojoji Temple in Tokyo for the two thousand or more Japanese citizens who lost their lives when the* Awa Maru *was sunk.*

THE GAZETTEER

The 17 ships in this book are by no means
the only treasure ships of the 20th century. More than 170
shipwrecks are plotted on this map, covering the whole array of
treasure ships: those that have been salvaged to yield magnificent
treasures, those that have flattered to deceive, and those
that remain unfound. For each plot, corresponding
information about the ship, including the date on which
it sank, its location, cargo, and route, and the salvage history
where known, can be found in the Gazetteer.

THE GAZETTEER

1 ABOSSO
24 April 1917
LOCATION: 180 miles WbyN from Fastnet, Eire
CARGO: Gold
SALVAGE: None
ROUTE: Bathurst, W. Africa–Liverpool, UK
TYPE: 7782T; Elder Dempster; British
COMMENT: Sunk by *U-43*

2 ADMIRAL NAKHIMOV
28 May 1905
LOCATION: 6 miles E of Kami Tsushima, Japan
CARGO: Included gold, platinum; recent newspaper estimates value the cargo at $3,774 million
SALVAGE: Many attempts
ROUTE: Russia–Far East
TYPE: 8524T; Russian cruiser
COMMENT: *See Chapter*

3 AEOLIAN SKY
4 November 1979
LOCATION: Off Anvil Point, 12 miles EbyS from Bill of Portland
CARGO: £1.2 million Seychelles rupees
SALVAGE: Rupees apparently not discovered by divers
ROUTE: London–Dar-es-Salaam, Tanzania
TYPE: 6540T; Greek
COMMENT: Cargo contains dangerous chemicals and other hazards

4 AGBERI
28 December 1917
LOCATION: 18 miles NW half W of Bardsey Island, UK
CARGO: Silver specie and ivory
SALVAGE: None known of
ROUTE: Dakar, W. Africa–Liverpool, UK
TYPE: 4821T; Elder Dempster; British
COMMENT: Sunk by *U-87*

5 ALIAKMON RUNNER
February 1983
LOCATION: 10.01°N 63.18°E
CARGO: $13 million worth of antique temple artefacts
SALVAGE: None
ROUTE: Singapore–Piraeus, Greece
TYPE: Greek
COMMENT: Ship caught fire, crew rescued by Japanese vessel

6 ALNWICK CASTLE
19 March 1927
LOCATION: 310 miles WbyS from Bishop Rock, Scilly Isles, UK
CARGO: Silver
SALVAGE: None
ROUTE: Plymouth, UK–S. Africa
TYPE: 5900T; Union Castle; British
COMMENT: Sunk by German submarine *U-81*. Chief Officer's lifeboat with 31 people drifted for 9 days before being picked up

7 AMANDA
4 March 1927
LOCATION: 18.08°S 49.22°E
CARGO: Silver
SALVAGE: Not known
ROUTE: Not known
TYPE: 1170T; J. P. Pedersen & Son; Norwegian
COMMENT: Lost during a cyclone

8 ANCONA
8 November 1915
LOCATION: Off Cape Carbonara, near Sardinia
CARGO: 12 barrels of gold coin
SALVAGE: Unsuccessful salvage attempt in 1990. A later attempt also failed
ROUTE: Naples, Italy–New York, US
TYPE: 8210T; Italia steamship Co.; Italian
COMMENT: Sunk by German *U-38* disguised as an Austrian U-boat when Italy had not yet entered the war

9 ANDAMAN
24 May 1953
LOCATION: 51.08.21°N 01.33.57°E
CARGO: 1 box of gold plus 8 ingots of silver, each weighing 30 lbs
SALVAGE: Gold and one ingot of silver
ROUTE: Gothenberg, Sweden–Calcutta, India
TYPE: 4765T; Swedish
COMMENT: Collided with SS *Fortune* during fog

10 ANDANIA
27 January 1918
LOCATION: 2 miles NNE of Rathlin Island, UK
CARGO: Silverware and diamonds
SALVAGE: None
ROUTE: Liverpool, UK–New York, US
TYPE: 13405T; Cunard; British
COMMENT: Sunk by German submarine *U-46*

11 ANDREA DORIA
26 July 1956
LOCATION: 40.37°N 69.37°W
CARGO: Supposedly containing gold
SALVAGE: Salved by Peter Grimble in 1984 in conjunction with Oceaneering International without significant recoveries
ROUTE: Genoa, Italy–New York, US
TYPE: 29083T; Italia Line; Italian
COMMENT: Sunk as a result of collision with SS *Stockholm*

12 ANTIOPE
27 October 1941
LOCATION: 53.13°N 01.08°E
CARGO: Silver, silverware, china and antiques
SALVAGE: No official reports of salvage
ROUTE: London, UK–New York US
TYPE: 4545T; New Egypt and Levant Shipping Co.; British
COMMENT: Sunk by bombing. Ship dispersed after the war

13 APAPA
28 November 1917
LOCATION: 53.26.45°N 04.18.50°W
CARGO: Silver specie and ivory
SALVAGE: Commercial salvage during 1970s. Recent recoveries by Chorley Subaqua Club include an intact electric light bulb
ROUTE: W. Africa–Liverpool, UK
TYPE: 7832T; Elder Dempster; British
COMMENT: Sunk by German submarine *U-96*

14 APAPA
15 November 1940
LOCATION: 54.34°N 16.47°W
CARGO: Gold (£19,188)
SALVAGE: None
ROUTE: Freetown, W. Africa–Liverpool, UK
TYPE: 9333T; Elder Dempster; British
COMMENT: Bombed by Focke-Wulf FW200

15 APPAM
15 January 1916
LOCATION: Not Available
CARGO: Gold
SALVAGE: Never discovered
ROUTE: W. Africa–UK
TYPE: 7781T; Elder Dempster; British
COMMENT: Ship did not sink – treasure supposedly hidden on Haiti. *See Chapter*

16 ARABIA
6 November 1916
LOCATION: 35.56°N 20.15°E
CARGO: Silver and jewels
SALVAGE: None
ROUTE: Sydney, Australia–London, UK
TYPE: 7933T; Peninsular and Oriental; British
COMMENT: Torpedoed by German submarine *UB-43* and sank in 10 minutes

17 ARABIC
19 August 1915
LOCATION: 50.50°N 8.32°W
CARGO: Much rumour that a large quantity of gold was on board
SALVAGE: Salvaged twice in late 1990s but no gold discovered
ROUTE: Liverpool, UK–New York, US
TYPE: 15801T; White Star; British
COMMENT: Sunk by German *U-24*; the incident caused a furore between the US and Germany, anticipating the *Lusitania*

18 AREQUIPA
2 June 1903
LOCATION: 4.75 cables 84° NW from the main pier, Valparaiso port, Chile
CARGO: Gold
SALVAGE: None known of
TYPE: 2953T; Pacific Steam Navigation Company; British
COMMENT: Lost during violent storm while loading cargo

19 ASHIGARA
8 June 1945
LOCATION: 01.59°S 104.57°E
CARGO: Gold
SALVAGE: Worked by joint Japanese/ Indonesian salvage venture in 1988
ROUTE: Indonesia–Japan
TYPE: 12700T; Japanese heavy cruiser
COMMENT: Sunk by British submarine

20 ASIATIC PRINCE
24 March 1928
LOCATION: 24°N 155°W
CARGO: Approx. 2 tons gold
SALVAGE: None
ROUTE: New York, US–Yokohama, Japan
TYPE: 5800T; Prince Line; British
COMMENT: Ship passed through an area of cyclone north of Hawaii and was never heard of again. There were no survivors

21 ATLANTIAN
25 June 1918
LOCATION: 110 miles NbyWhalfW from Eagle Island, Eire
CARGO: Gold and silver
SALVAGE: None
ROUTE: Galveston, US–Liverpool, UK
TYPE: 9399T; Leyland & Co; British
COMMENT: Sunk by German submarine *U-86*

22 AWA MARU
1 April 1945
LOCATION: 24.40°N 119.45°E
CARGO: Gold and treasure
SALVAGE: Only tin and rubber recovered by Chinese salvage company
ROUTE: Singapore–Japan
TYPE: 11378T; Nippon Yusen Co; Japanese
COMMENT: *See Chapter*

23 BADAGRI
13 July 1918
LOCATION: 425 miles WNW of Cape St Vincent
CARGO: £25,000 in gold, silver and coin
SALVAGE: None
ROUTE: Liverpool, UK–Sierra Leone
TYPE: 2956T; Elder Dempster; British
COMMENT: Sunk by German U-boat *U-91*

24 BALLARAT
25 April 1917
LOCATION: 49.33°N 05.36°W
CARGO: Gold rumoured
SALVAGE: Salvaged by Risdon Beazley in 1950s, but no gold recovered
ROUTE: Melbourne, Australia–London, UK
TYPE: 11,120T; P&O; British
COMMENT: Gold was definitely put on board in South Africa on final voyage but was probably transferred in W. Africa

25 BARENTSZ
1945
LOCATION: Tjilatjiap Harbour, Indonesia
CARGO: 20 tons of gold
SALVAGE: If quantities of gold true almost certainly salvaged
ROUTE: Indonesia–Japan
TYPE: Japanese
COMMENT: Burnt out and sunk

26 BATAVIER V
17 May 1916
LOCATION: Half mile E (magnetic) of North buoy, Inner Gabbard, North Sea
CARGO: 14 cases of gold each containing £5,000
SALVAGE: Salvage carried out by HMS ships, 26 May–1 June 1916
ROUTE: London, UK–Rotterdam, Holland
TYPE: 1569T; Wm H. Muller & Co; Dutch
COMMENT: Ship was mined

27 BEAVERBRAE
25 March 1941
LOCATION: 60.12°N 09.00°W
CARGO: Gold, 25 boxes of platinum grain, 1 parcel of rough diamonds
SALVAGE: None
ROUTE: Liverpool, UK–St Johns, Canada
TYPE: 9956T; Canadian Pacific; Canadian
COMMENT: Bombed and caught fire

28 BEGA
29 March 1908
LOCATION: Tanga Point, 160 miles from Sydney, Australia
CARGO: 561 ozs gold. Also presentation silver plate belonging to Rev. Briscombe
SALVAGE: Some salvage at time of loss
ROUTE: Tathra, Australia–Sydney, Australia
TYPE: 567T; Illawarra Shipping Co; British
COMMENT: Vessel foundered

29 BENMOHR
5 March 1942
LOCATION: 06.05°N 14.15°W
CARGO: 1.5 million ozs silver bullion
SALVAGE: None
ROUTE: Bombay, India–Freetown, W. Africa–Oban, Scotland
TYPE: 5920T; Ben Line; British
COMMENT: Sunk by German submarine U-505

30 BENVRACKIE
13 May 1941
LOCATION: 00.49°N 20.15°W
CARGO: Bullion
SALVAGE: None
ROUTE: Tyne, UK–Cape Town, S. Africa
TYPE: 6434T; Ben Line; British
COMMENT: Torpedoed by German submarine U-105. Of the 85 persons on board 59 survived, 58 of whom were in one lifeboat for 13 days

31 BOX
1914–18
LOCATION: Sierra Leone
CARGO: Box of gold
SALVAGE: Not recovered
COMMENT: Lost during transhipment in port

32 BREMEN
1916
LOCATION: 300 miles south of Iceland
CARGO: Valuables and precious stones
SALVAGE: None
ROUTE: Kiel, Germany–Norfolk, US
TYPE: 7911; Cargo-carrying submarine; German
COMMENT: Never heard of again after departure. British Cruiser *Mantua* reported colliding with submarine-like object south of Iceland

33 CALEDONIA
4 December 1916
LOCATION: 125 miles EbyS Malta
CARGO: Silver coin
SALVAGE: None
ROUTE: Aden, Egypt–UK
TYPE: 9223T; Anchor Line; British
COMMENT: Sunk by German submarine U-65

34 CALIFORNIA
11 July 1943
LOCATION: 41.15°N 15.24°W
CARGO: 7 boxes of diamonds, valued at £72,250
SALVAGE: None
ROUTE: Glyde, UK–Freetown, W. Africa
TYPE: 16792T; Anchor line; British
COMMENT: Bombed and sunk by German aircraft while in convoy and being used as a troopship

35 CEREBOLI
11 April 1929
LOCATION: Massan Brot, Sudan
CARGO: 17 cases of specie
SALVAGE: £3,000 saved
ROUTE: Massowah, Eritrea–Jeddah, Saudi Arabia

36 CITY OF BATH
1 December 1942
LOCATION: 09.50°N 59.25°W
CARGO: Platinum
SALVAGE: None known of
ROUTE: Mombasa, Kenya–Trinidad, West Indies
TYPE: 5079T; Ellerman Lines; British
COMMENT: Torpedoed by German submarine U-508, 6 crew killed

37 CITY OF BIRMINGHAM
16 August 1940
LOCATION: 53.35°N 00.07°E
CARGO: Platinum matte
SALVAGE: Salvaged by Risdon Beazley Marine
TYPE: 5309T; British
COMMENT: Sunk by mine

38 CITY OF CAIRO
6 November 1942
LOCATION: 23.30°S 05.30°W
CARGO: 3.25 million ozs silver
SALVAGE: None
ROUTE: Table Bay, S. Africa–Pernambuco, Brazil
TYPE: 8034T; Ellerman Lines; British
COMMENT: Sunk by German submarine U-68

39 CITY OF MELBOURNE
13 May 1942
LOCATION: 15.00°N 54.40°W
CARGO: Gold
SALVAGE: None
ROUTE: S. Africa–US
TYPE: 6630T; Ellerman lines; British
COMMENT: Torpedoed by German submarine U-156

40 CITY OF NEW YORK
30 March 1942
LOCATION: 35.16°N 74.25°W
CARGO: Diamonds
SALVAGE: None known of
ROUTE: Lourenco Marques, Mozambique–Norfolk, US
TYPE: 8272T; American South African Lines; American
COMMENT: Sunk by German submarine U-160

41 CITY OF RIO DE JANIERO
22 February 1901
LOCATION: Mile Rock, San Francisco, US
CARGO: Gold
SALVAGE: None known of
ROUTE: Yokohama, Japan–San Francisco, US
TYPE: 3548T; Pacific Mail SS Co.; American
COMMENT: Lost in thick fog; 104 lives lost out of 201 on board

42 CITY OF WELLINGTON
21 August 1942
LOCATION: 07.29°N 14.40°W
CARGO: Platinum
SALVAGE: None
ROUTE: Mossel Bay, S. Africa–Freetown, W. Africa
TYPE: 5733T; Ellerman lines; British
COMMENT: Sunk by German submarine U-506

43 CLARION
8 December 1909
LOCATION: Lake Erie, Canada
CARGO: Gold and silver
SALVAGE: None known of

44 COLOMBIA
9 August 1907
LOCATION: 06.28°S 80.50°W
CARGO: Specie
SALVAGE: Part salved
ROUTE: Payta, Peru–Eten, Peru
TYPE: 3335T; Pacific Steam Navigation Co., British
COMMENT: Struck on a rock and wrecked

45 COLORADAN
9 October 1942
LOCATION: 33.47 S 14.34 E
CARGO: Gold
SALVAGE: None
ROUTE: S. Africa–US
TYPE: 6557T; American Hawaiian Steamship Co; American
COMMENT: Sunk by German submarine U-159

46 COLUMBIA
13 September 1931
LOCATION: Point Tosca, Margarita Isle Lower California, US
CARGO: $700,000 bar silver
SALVAGE: $600,000 recovered
ROUTE: New York–San Francisco, US
TYPE: Grace Line, American
COMMENT: Wrecked

47 CORREGIDOR
1942
LOCATION: Corregidor Island, Manila Bay, Philippines
CARGO: 15,792,000 silver pesos
SALVAGE: Largely salvaged during war but it has been estimated that in excess of 1 million pesos remain unsalved
COMMENT: Dumped by the US minelayer *Harrison* to avoid seizure by Japanese

48 DARU
15 September 1941
LOCATION: 51.56°N 05.58°W
CARGO: 50 boxes of coin
SALVAGE: None known of
ROUTE: Duala, W. Africa–Liverpool, UK
TYPE: 3854T; Elder Dempster; British
COMMENT: Sunk by German aircraft of Gruppe 406, Luftflotte 3, while travelling in convoy HG72. Bombed and caught fire. No loss of life

49 DELHI
13 December 1911
LOCATION: 2 miles off Cape Spartel, Morocco
CARGO: £295,925 gold and silver bullion
SALVAGE: Salvaged at time of loss
ROUTE: London, UK–India, Bombay
TYPE: 8090T; Peninsular & Orient; British
COMMENT: Wrecked during storm. Duke and Duchess of Fife were passengers

50 DUNBAR CASTLE
9 January 1940
LOCATION: 2 miles NE of North Goodwins Light, English Channel
CARGO: Jewellery
SALVAGE: Not known
ROUTE: London, UK–Beira, Mozambique
TYPE: 10002T; Union Castle; British
COMMENT: Sunk by magnetic mine

51 EDINBURGH
2 May 1942
LOCATION: 72°N 35°E
CARGO: £45 million gold
SALVAGE: Salvaged in 1980s by Keith Jessop's consortium
ROUTE: Russia–UK
TYPE: 10000T; Cruiser class warship; British
COMMENT: *See Chapter*

52 EGYPT
20 May 1922
LOCATION: Near Ushant, 20 miles off Armen, France
CARGO: Gold and silver valued in excess of £1 million
SALVAGE: 98% recovered by the Italian company Sorima
ROUTE: London, UK–Bombay, India
TYPE: 7941T; Peninsular & Orient; British
COMMENT: Hit rocks during thick fog

53 ELINGAMITE
9 November 1902
LOCATION: West Island, Three Kings, New Zealand
CARGO: £17,300 in silver and gold
SALVAGE: Salvaged several times but most of the treasure still remains
ROUTE: Sydney, Australia–Auckland, New Zealand
TYPE: 2585T; Huddart Parker & Co, New Zealand
COMMENT: Ship hit rocks

54 ELISABETHVILLE
6 September 1917
LOCATION: 10 miles south of Belle Isle, France
CARGO: Uncut diamonds valued at $2.6 million in safe and 10 tons of ivory
SALVAGE: Ivory recovered but not diamonds
ROUTE: W. Africa–Falmouth, UK
TYPE: 7017T; Cie Belge Maritime du Congo; Belgian
COMMENT: Sunk by German submarine

55 EMPIRE KOHINOR
2 July 1917
LOCATION: 06.20°N 16.30°W
CARGO: 2 parcels of diamonds
SALVAGE: None
ROUTE: Table Bay, S. Africa–UK
TYPE: 5225T; Anchor Line; British
COMMENT: Sunk by German submarine U 618

56 EMPIRE MANOR
27 January 1944
LOCATION: 44.05°N 52.10°W
CARGO: 10 kegs of gold – 7 bars to the keg totalling 28,569 oz
SALVAGE: Partially salvaged in the 1970s by Risdon Beazley Marine
ROUTE: New York, US–Halifax, Canada
TYPE: 7071T; Ministry of transport; British
COMMENT: Collided with SS *Edward Kavanagh*, travelling in same convoy

57 EMPRESS OF BRITAIN
26 October 1940
LOCATION: 55.16°N 09.50°W
CARGO: Gold
SALVAGE: Attempted at least once
ROUTE: Capetown, S. Africa–Liverpool UK
TYPE: 42348T; Canadian Pacific; Canadian
COMMENT: *See Chapter*

58 EMPRESS OF CANADA
13 March 1943
LOCATION: 01.13°S 09.57°W
CARGO: Gold
SALVAGE: None
ROUTE: Cape Town, S. Africa–US
TYPE: 20325T; Canadian Pacific; Canadian
COMMENT: 1400 Greek and Polish refugees and Italian prisoners of war on board. Sunk by Italian submarine *Leonardo da Vinci*

59 EMPRESS OF CHINA
1911
LOCATION: Yokohama, Japan
CARGO: Silver bullion
SALVAGE: Salvaged at time of loss
ROUTE: US–Japan
TYPE: Canadian Pacific; Canadian
COMMENT: Wrecked during fog

60 EMPRESS OF IRELAND
29 May 1914
LOCATION: 5 miles E of Father Point,
mouth of St Lawrence River, Canada
CARGO: Silver
SALVAGE: Largely salvaged at time of loss
ROUTE: Quebec, Canada–Liverpool, UK
TYPE: 14191T; Canadian Pacific; Canadian
COMMENT: Sunk as a result of collision
with Norwegian collier *Storstad*
during fog

61 EUPHRATES WRECK
2 October 1916
LOCATION: S of Hadethah, Persian Gulf
CARGO: Gold
SALVAGE: Attempted by Germans in 1917
TYPE: Shaktur

62 FELTRE
17 February 1937
LOCATION: Near Prescott, River Columbia,
Oregon, US
CARGO: $185,000 bar silver
SALVAGE: Largely salved at time of loss
TYPE: Italian

63 FLORENTINE
1951
LOCATION: 22.30°N 140.28°E
CARGO: Gold
SALVAGE: None
TYPE: American

64 FLYING ENTERPRISE
10 January 1952
LOCATION: 50 miles off Falmouth
CARGO: $156,000 in bank notes, plus
£5,000 in English Treasury notes in
8 postal bags
SALVAGE: Sorima carried out salvage but
$100,000 unsalved
ROUTE: Hamburg, Germany–US
TYPE: 6711T; Isbrandtsen Company;
American
COMMENT: Damaged in storm and then
sank while on tow

65 FORT STIKINE
14 April 1944
LOCATION: Bombay Harbour, India
CARGO: £1 million in gold
SALVAGE: Approx. 50% recovered
ROUTE: Birkenhead, UK–Bombay, India
TYPE: 7142T; Ministry of War Transport;
British
COMMENT: *See Chapter*

66 GAIRSOPPA
16 February 1941
LOCATION: 300 miles SW of Galway Bay
CARGO: 3 million ozs of silver and gold
SALVAGE: None
ROUTE: India–UK
TYPE: 5237T; British India Steam
Navigation Co.; British
COMMENT: Sunk by German submarine
U-101, only one survivor. Searched for
several times but not discovered

67 GALICIA
10 June 1917
LOCATION: 49.00°N 10.00°W
CARGO: 9 cases of silver, plus ivory
SALVAGE: None
ROUTE: Malaysia–London, UK
TYPE: 1400T; J. Hall Jnr & Co; British
COMMENT: Sunk by German submarine
U-70

68 GALWAY CASTLE
12 September 1918
LOCATION: 160 miles SWhalfS from
Fastnet, Eire, but floated for a further
3 days
CARGO: £21,600 silver
SALVAGE: None
ROUTE: Plymouth, UK–Durban, S. Africa
TYPE: 7988T; Union Castle Line; British
COMMENT: Sunk by German submarine
U-82. 150 drowned as the result of an
over-hasty abandonment of the ship

69 GEORGES PHILIPPAR
16 May 1932
LOCATION: 145 miles NNE of Cape
Gardafui, Gulf of Aden
CARGO: £30,000 silver
SALVAGE: None
ROUTE: Yokohoma, Japan–Marseilles,
France
TYPE: 17359T; Messageries Maritime;
French
COMMENT: Ship caught fire; 54 passengers
lost

70 GOLD COAST
19 April 1917
LOCATION: 52.00N 07.50W
CARGO: Gold bullion
SALVAGE: None
ROUTE: W. Africa–Liverpool, UK
TYPE: 4255T; Elder Dempster; British
COMMENT: Sunk by German submarine

71 GORIZIA
30 April 1917
LOCATION: 50.36°N 02.53°W
CARGO: 800 cases of brass and $5,000 gold
coin in safe
SALVAGE: Bulk of the brass, but not the
gold, salvaged by Risdon Beazley Ltd
ROUTE: New York, US–Le Havre, France
TYPE: 1957T; Uruguayan
COMMENT: Sunk by German submarine
UC-61, the submarine went alongside the
Gorizia and attached bombs to it

72 GOVERNOR
1 April 1921
LOCATION: Near Port Townsend, Strait of
Juan de Fuca
CARGO: Large quantity of money in safe
SALVAGE: Some salvage by Robert Mester
in 1987
ROUTE: Victoria, Canada–Seattle, USA
TYPE: 5474T; Pacific Mail; American
COMMENT: In collision with *West
Hartland*

73 HAGURA
16 May 1945
LOCATION: 30 miles SW of Penang,
Malaysia
CARGO: Gold
SALVAGE: Not known
ROUTE: Malaysia–Japan
TYPE: 10,000T; Heavy Cruiser; Japanese
COMMENT: Sunk by torpedos from British
destroyers, *Suamarez, Venus, Verulam,
Vigilant,* and *Virago*

74 HAMPSHIRE
5 June 1916
LOCATION: 1.5 miles offshore between
Brough of Birsay and Marwick Head,
Orkneys, UK
CARGO: £2 million gold rumoured
SALVAGE: One attempt in the 1930s
ROUTE: Scapa Flow, Orkneys–Murmansk,
Russia
TYPE: 10850T; Armed Merchant Cruiser;
British
COMMENT: *See Chapter*

75 HAROLD
27 September 1903
LOCATION: Off Sewaren, New Jersey, US
CARGO: Silver ingots
SALVAGE: Partly salvaged
TYPE: American

76 HAZEL BRANCH
12 November 1907
LOCATION: Adelaide Patch, Straits of
Magellan, Chile
CARGO: Silver
SALVAGE: Some salvage
ROUTE: Antofagusta, Chile–Liverpool, UK
TYPE: 2623T; F. & W. Ritson; British
COMMENT: Wrecked

77 HEALDTON
21 March 1917
LOCATION: Off Holland
CARGO: $3 million gold rumoured
SALVAGE: None known of
ROUTE: Holland–UK
TYPE: American tanker
COMMENT: Sunk by German submarine.
Doubtful that gold is there

78 HENRY STANLEY
6 December 1942
LOCATION: 40.35°N 39.40°W
CARGO: 3 boxes of diamonds
SALVAGE: None
ROUTE: Liverpool, UK–Freetown, W. Africa
TYPE: 5026T; Elder Dempster; British
COMMENT: Torpedoed and sunk by
German submarine *U-103*. Only the ship's
captain survived. He was captured and
taken on board the U-boat

79 HIGHLAND WARRIOR
3 October 1915
LOCATION: Near Cape Prior, Spain
CARGO: Gold
SALVAGE: Not known
ROUTE: London, UK–Buenos Aires,
Argentina
TYPE: 7485T; Nelson line; British
COMMENT: Wrecked

80 HIKAWA MARU NO. 2
19 August 1945
LOCATION: 35.45°N 135.30°E
CARGO: Gold, treasures, war booty
SALVAGE: Supposedly located by Japanese
salvage company in 1980s
ROUTE: Returning to Japan at end of war
TYPE: 6076T; Previously Dutch hospital ship
Op Ten Noort
COMMENT: Scuttled on instructions of
Japanese after signing of armistice

81 HOSPITAL SHIP
1945
LOCATION: 16.22°N 119.49°E
CARGO: Bullion
SALVAGE: None known of
ROUTE: Philippines–Japan
TYPE: Japanese hospital ship

82 I.34
12 November 1943
LOCATION: 05.17°N 100.05°E
CARGO: Half a ton of gold
SALVAGE: Salvaged but no reports of gold
having been found
ROUTE: Japan–Singapore–Germany
TYPE: 2198T; B class Japanese submarine
COMMENT: Sunk by UK submarine *Taurus*

83 I.52
24 June 1944
LOCATION: 15.16°N 39.55°W
CARGO: Gold
SALVAGE: Found but not yet salvaged
ROUTE: Japan–Lorient, France
TYPE: 2095T; Japanese submarine
COMMENT: *See Chapter*

84 ISLANDER
15 August 1901
LOCATION: Stevens Passage, near Juneau,
Alaska
CARGO: $3 million gold
SALVAGE: Largely salvaged in 1930s
ROUTE: Alaska, US–Vancouver, Canada
TYPE: 1495T; Canadian Pacific Navigation
Co.; Canadian
COMMENT: *See Chapter*

85 ITSUKISHIMA
17 October 1944
LOCATION: 05.27°S 112.43°E
CARGO: 2 tons of gold
SALVAGE: Many attempts at salvage
ROUTE: Indonesia–Japan
TYPE: 1970T; Japanese minelayer
COMMENT: Sunk by Dutch submarine
Zwaardvisch

86 JEBBA
18 March 1907
LOCATION: Near Bolt Tail, Devon, UK
CARGO: Specie, ivory, palm oil, fruit and
mails – total value £200,000
SALVAGE: Largely salved at time of loss
ROUTE: W. Africa–Plymouth and Liverpool,
UK
TYPE: 3813T; Elder Dempster; British
COMMENT: Wrecked

87 JOHN BARRY
28 August 1944
LOCATION: 15.10°N 55.18°E
CARGO: 3 million Saudi Arabian silver
reals plus possibility of further 1,500 tons of
bar silver
SALVAGE: Recently located in 8000 ft of
water; salvage operations carried out
ROUTE: Norfolk, US–Riyadh, Saudi Arabia
TYPE: 7176T; Liberty Ship; American
COMMENT: *See Chapter*

88 KALEWA
1 August 1942
LOCATION: 30.16°S 13.38°E
CARGO: Specie
SALVAGE: None
ROUTE: UK–Aden
TYPE: 4389T; British & Burmese Navigation
Co.; British
COMMENT: Sank after collision with
Boringia

89 LA SEYNE
14 November 1909
LOCATION: 01.01°N 104.12°E
CARGO: Diamonds
SALVAGE: Not known
ROUTE: France–Singapore
TYPE: 2379T; Messageries Maritimes; French
COMMENT: Sank in two minutes after
collision with British India liner *Onda*

90 LACONIA
12 September 1942
LOCATION: 05.05°S 11.38°W
CARGO: Platinum
SALVAGE: None
ROUTE: Suez–Liverpool, UK via Cape
Town, S. Africa
TYPE: 19695T; Cunard–White Star Line; British
COMMENT: Sunk by German submarine
U-156. 1,500 Italian prisoners of war on
board at time

91 LACONIA
25 February 1917
LOCATION: 160 miles NWbyW from
Fastnet
CARGO: 1,060,665 ozs silver including 132
boxes of specie
SALVAGE: Found and partially opened up
but no recoveries made
TYPE: 18099T; Cunard; British
ROUTE: New York, US–Liverpool, UK
COMMENT: Sunk by German submarine
U-50

92 LAFIAN
24 September 1941
LOCATION: 31.12°N 23.32°W
CARGO: Bullion
SALVAGE: None
ROUTE: Port Harcourt, W. Africa–
Liverpool, UK
TYPE: 4876T; Elmina Ltd; British
COMMENT: Sunk by German submarine
U-107

93 LAURENTIC
23 January 1917
LOCATION: 10 miles N of Lough Swilly,
Eire
CARGO: £5 million gold
SALVAGE: All salvaged apart from 20 gold
bars and approx. £60,000 of ships money.
Many recent attempts to salvage remainder
ROUTE: Liverpool, UK–Halifax, Canada
TYPE: 14892T; White Star; British
COMMENT: See Chapter

94 LUSITANIA
7 May 1915
LOCATION: 12 miles S of Old Head of
Kinsale, Eire
CARGO: Unconfirmed rumours of bullion
and valuables
SALVAGE: Salvaged more than once
ROUTE: New York US–Liverpool, UK
TYPE: 30396T; Cunard; British
COMMENT: See Chapter

95 MADEIRA
17 November 1914
LOCATION: 47.59°N 06.28°W
CARGO: Gold
SALVAGE: None
ROUTE: W. Africa–Liverpool, UK
TYPE: 1773T; Elder Dempster; British
COMMENT: Foundered while on tow

96 MALOJA
27 February 1916
LOCATION: 2 miles SW of Dover Pier, UK
CARGO: Diamonds, gold, silver bar and
silver coin
SALVAGE: Dispersed by Trinity House in
1919
ROUTE: London, UK–Bombay, India
TYPE: 12431T; Peninsular & Orient; British
COMMENT: Struck mine

97 MANTOLA
9 February 1917
LOCATION: 49.45°N 13.20°W
CARGO: 600,000 ozs silver
SALVAGE: None
ROUTE: UK–India
TYPE: 8260T; British India Steam
Navigation Co.; British
COMMENT: Sunk by German submarine
U-81

98 MARERE
18 January 1916
LOCATION: 236 miles E of Malta
CARGO: Bullion rumoured
SALVAGE: None
ROUTE: Moudhros, Greece–UK
TYPE: 6443T; Commonwealth & Dominion,
British
COMMENT: Sunk by gunfire from German
submarine *U-35*

99 MEDINA
28 April 1917
LOCATION: Near Start Point, UK
CARGO: 1 box of silver bullion as well as the
Viceroy of India's jewels valued at £10
million
SALVAGE: Several attempts in 1970s
and 1980s
ROUTE: India–London, UK
TYPE: 12358T; Peninsular & Orient; British
COMMENT: Torpedoed by German
submarine *UB-31*

100 MELISKERK
8 January 1943
LOCATION: Near Durban, S. Africa
CARGO: Bullion
SALVAGE: Salvaged at time of loss
TYPE: Dutch

101 MERIDA
12 May 1911
LOCATION: 55 miles from Cape Charles, US
CARGO: 480,000 ozs silver
SALVAGE: Salvaged in 1930s by Venturi and
more than once in 1980s – results unclear
ROUTE: Vera Cruz, Mexico–New York, US
TYPE: 6207T; New York and Cuba Mail SS
Co.; American
COMMENT: Collision with *Admiral
Farragut*

102 MILTON
15 June 1911
LOCATION: Near Cape Espichel, Portugal
CARGO: Specie
SALVAGE: Not known
ROUTE: London, UK–Santos, Brazil
TYPE: 2679T; Lamport & Holt; British
COMMENT: Wrecked

103 MINAS
15 February 1917
LOCATION: 160 miles W of Cape Matapan,
Greece
CARGO: 3 million marks in gold
SALVAGE: None
ROUTE: Naples, Italy–Salonica, Greece
TYPE: 2854T; Soc. Anon. A. Parodi; Italian
COMMENT: Sunk by German submarine
U-39

104 MINIOTA
31 August 1917
LOCATION: 13 miles SW of Portland Bill, UK
CARGO: 120,000 ozs silver
SALVAGE: Recently located but silver not
recovered
ROUTE: Montreal, Canada–Southampton,
UK
TYPE: 6422T; Canadian Pacific Railway;
Canadian
COMMENT: Sunk by German submarine
U-19

105 MINNA
1959
LOCATION: Bullock Harbour, China
CARGO: Treasure
SALVAGE: Not known
ROUTE: Foochoo, China–Shanghai, China
TYPE: Sailing vessel

106 MINNEHAHA
7 September 1999
LOCATION: 12 miles SE of Fastnet, Eire
CARGO: Gold rumoured
SALVAGE: None
ROUTE: London, UK–New York, US
TYPE: 13714T; Atlantic Transport Line
COMMENT: Torpedoed and sunk by
German submarine *U-48*

107 MIRA
15 May 1916
LOCATION: 50 miles SE of Siracuse, Italy
CARGO: Gold rumoured
SALVAGE: None
TYPE: 3050T; French Soc. Gen. de
Transports Maritimes, French
COMMENT: Sunk by German submarine
U-34

108 MONGOLIA
23 June 1917
LOCATION: 50 miles SbyW of Bombay,
India
CARGO: Large quantity of currency
SALVAGE: None known of
ROUTE: London, UK–India and Australia
TYPE: 9505T; Peninsular & Orient; British
COMMENT: Sunk by mine

109 MOOLTAN
26 July 1917
LOCATION: 37.56°N 08.34°E
CARGO: Gold
SALVAGE: None
ROUTE: Bombay, India–UK
TYPE: 9723T; Peninsular & Orient; British
COMMENT: Sunk by German submarine
UC-27

110 NAMUR
29 October 1917
LOCATION: 36.05°N 04.15°W
CARGO: Gold
SALVAGE: Recently salvaged
ROUTE: Penang, Malaysia–London, UK
TYPE: 6701T; Peninsular & Orient; British
COMMENT: Sunk by German submarine
U-35

111 NEW GUINEA WRECK
1943
LOCATION: Off Sepik, Papua New Guinea
CARGO: $1.68 billion gold rumoured
SALVAGE: Attempted by Singapore-based
group
TYPE: Japanese
COMMENT: Supposedly sunk by British
submarine

112 NEW TORONTO
5 November 1942
LOCATION: 05.57°N 02.30°E
CARGO: Gold
SALVAGE: None
ROUTE: Lagos, W. Africa–Liverpool, UK
TYPE: 6568T; Elder Dempster; British
COMMENT: Sunk by German submarine
U-126

113 NIAGARA
18 June 1940
LOCATION: 35.53°S 174.54°E
CARGO: £2,500,000 gold
SALVAGE: £2,379,000 recovered in 1942
and £120,000 in 1953, the latter by
Risdon Beazley
ROUTE: Auckland, New Zealand–
Vancouver, Canada
TYPE: 13415T; Canadian Australian Line;
British
COMMENT: Sunk by mine

114 NIDARLAND
11 November 1942
LOCATION: 11.41°N 60.42°W
CARGO: 175 bars of silver
SALVAGE: None known of
ROUTE: Santa Fe, Argentina–Trinidad, West
Indies
TYPE: 6076T; Rederi a/s Nidaros;
Norwegian
COMMENT: Sunk by German submarine
U-67

115 NEUVO MORTERA
27 July 1905
LOCATION: Off Vuevitas, Cuba
CARGO: 230,000 specie
SALVAGE: Largely salvaged at time of loss
ROUTE: Havana, Cuba–Santiago, Cuba
TYPE: Cuban

116 OCEANA
16 March 1942
LOCATION: 50.43°N 0.27°E
CARGO: Silver, gold and ivory. £747,610
specie
SALVAGE: Largely salvaged at time of loss
ROUTE: London, UK–Bombay, India
TYPE: 6610T; Peninsular & Orient; British
COMMENT: In collision with German
barque *Pisagua*

117 OCEANIC
10 September 1914
LOCATION: Hoevdi Grund, SE of Isle of
Foula, Shetlands
CARGO: Silver bullion rumoured
SALVAGE: Several times
TYPE: 17274T; Oceanic Steamship
Navigation Co.; British
COMMENT: Ran ashore on the rocks

118 ORAVIA
12 November 1912
LOCATION: Billy Rock, Port Stanley,
Falklands
CARGO: Specie
SALVAGE: Saved
ROUTE: Liverpool, UK–Callao, Peru
TYPE: 5374T; Pacific Steam Navigation Co.;
British
COMMENT: Wrecked

119 ORCADES
10 October 1942
LOCATION: 35.51°S 14.40°E
CARGO: Platinum
SALVAGE: None
ROUTE: Cape Town, S. Africa–UK
TYPE: 23456T; Orient Steam Navigation
Co, British
COMMENT: Torpedoed by German
submarine *U-172*

120 ORIGEN
30 June 1918
LOCATION: 47.28°N 08.20°W
CARGO: Specie
SALVAGE: Saved at time of loss
ROUTE: London, UK–Oporto, Brazil
TYPE: 3545T; Booth Steamship Co.; British
COMMENT: Torpedoed by German
submarine *U-86*

121 PASIR
1945
LOCATION: Tjilatjiap Harbour, Indonesia
CARGO: 5 tons of gold rumoured
SALVAGE: If true almost certainly salvaged
ROUTE: Indonesia–Japan
TYPE: 1187T; Japanese
COMMENT: Burnt out and sunk

122 PEARY
19 February 1942
LOCATION: Darwin, Australia
CARGO: £1 million gold bullion rumoured
SALVAGE: Not known
TYPE: US destroyer
COMMENT: Bombed and sunk by Japanese

123 PERSIA
30 December 1915
LOCATION: 71 miles SEbyS of Cape
Martello, Crete
CARGO: 400,000 ozs silver bullion and
specie, and diamonds
SALVAGE: None
ROUTE: London UK–India, via Marseilles
TYPE: 7974T; Pensinsular & Orient; British
COMMENT: Sunk by German submarine
U-38. 334 persons out of 501 on board
were lost

124 PHEMIUS
19 December 1943
LOCATION: 05.01°N 00.17°W
CARGO: Specie
SALVAGE: Not known
ROUTE: UK–W. Africa
TYPE: 7406T; Ocean Steamship Company;
British
COMMENT: Sunk by German submarine
U-515

125 PILOT BOAT 19
11 May 1940
LOCATION: Near Rozenburg Island, Holland
CARGO: 200 boxes of gold each weighing 125 lbs
SALVAGE: Mainly salved
ROUTE: Holland–UK
TYPE: 300T; Pilot steamer; Dutch
COMMENT: *See Chapter*

126 PIPESTONE COUNTY
19 March 1942
LOCATION: 37.43°N 66.16°W
CARGO: £17,600 gold
TYPE: 5102T; Sea Shipping Co Inc; US
SALVAGE: None
COMMENT: Sunk by German submarine *U-576*

127 POLYDORUS
27 November 1942
LOCATION: 09.01°N 25.38°W
CARGO: Specie
SALVAGE: None
ROUTE: Liverpool, UK–Freetown, W. Africa
TYPE: 5922T; Nederlandsche Stoom. Maats; Dutch
COMMENT: Sunk by German submarine *U-176*

128 PORT MONTREAL
1942
LOCATION: 12.17°N 80.20°W
CARGO: Diamonds
SALVAGE: None
TYPE: 5882T; Port Line; British
COMMENT: Sunk by German submarine *U-68*

129 PRESIDENT LINCOLN
31 May 1918
LOCATION: 350 miles W of Brest, France
CARGO: Gold
SALVAGE: None
ROUTE: France–US
TYPE: 18168T; American (originally a German liner taken as a prize by the US)
COMMENT: Sunk by German submarine *U-90*

130 PRINCESS SOPHIA
26 October 1918
LOCATION: Lynn Canal, Alaska, US
CARGO: £200,000 gold
SALVAGE: Some salvage at time of loss
ROUTE: Skagway, Alaska–Vancouver, Canada
TYPE: 2320T; Canadian Pacific Railway Company; Canadian
COMMENT: Struck reef during a snow storm

131 PRINCIPE DE ASTURIAS
5 March 1916
LOCATION: 3 miles E of Ponta Boi, near Santos, Brazil
CARGO: £1 million gold and £500,000 in jewels rumoured
SALVAGE: Various attempts at salvage
ROUTE: Barcelona, Spain–Buenos Aires, Argentina
TYPE: 8371T; Pinillos Line; Spanish
COMMENT: Struck rocks during fog

132 PRINZ ADALBERT
October 1915
LOCATION: Coast of Libau, Lithuania
CARGO: Gold rumoured
SALVAGE: Not known
TYPE: 9050T; German cruiser
COMMENT: Sunk by British submarine *E8*

133 RAHMANI
14 July 1943
LOCATION: 14.52°N 52.06°E
CARGO: Gold sovereigns
SALVAGE: Not known
ROUTE: Bombay, India–Jeddah, Saudi Arabia
TYPE: 5463T; Mogul Line; Indian
COMMENT: Sunk by Japanese submarine *I.29*

134 RAMONA
20 November 1911
LOCATION: Cape Decision, Canada
CARGO: Gold
SALVAGE: Some salvage at time of loss
ROUTE: Skagway, Alaska–Seattle, US

135 RANGITANE
26 November 1940
LOCATION: 36.58°S 175.22°W
CARGO: Silver
SALVAGE: None
ROUTE: New Zealand–Panama
TYPE: 16712T; New Zealand Shipping Co.; British
COMMENT: Sunk by German surface raider

136 RENATE LEONHARDT
August 1917
LOCATION: 5 miles off the Texel, Holland
CARGO: 454 cases gold, silver and jewels
SALVAGE: Numerous attempts that have produced no results
ROUTE: Rotterdam, Holland–Germany
TYPE: German
COMMENT: Sunk by British warships

137 REPUBLIC
23 January 1909
LOCATION: 40.23°N 69.36°W
CARGO: $3 million in gold coins
SALVAGE: Many attempts without results
ROUTE: New York, US–Genoa, Italy–Alexandria, Egypt
TYPE: 15378T; Oceanic Steam Navigation Co; British
COMMENT: *See Chapter*

138 ROMMEL'S GOLD
18 September 1943
LOCATION: Corsica, Italy
CARGO: £30 million of looted treasure
SALVAGE: French government financed a search in 1949; several subsequent attempt, but without any results
ROUTE: Bastia, Corsica–Italy
TYPE: Small launch
COMMENT: *See Chapter*

139 RUPERRA
20 June 1917
LOCATION: 36.44°N 13.60°E
CARGO: Gold
SALVAGE: One box of gold removed before sinking
ROUTE: Sudan–London, UK
TYPE: 4232T
COMMENT: Sunk by German submarine *UC-27*

140 SAKKARAH
13 May 1902
LOCATION: Guamblin, off Socorro Island, Chile
CARGO: $1.5 million gold and specie
SALVAGE: Partly salvaged at time of loss
ROUTE: Valparaiso, Chile–Hamburg, Germany
TYPE: German
COMMENT: Wrecked

141 SALAZIE
21 November 1912
LOCATION: Nosykomba Reefs, Madagascar
CARGO: Specie
SALVAGE: Not known
ROUTE: Marseille, France–Mauritius
TYPE: Messageries Maritimes; French

142 SALYBIA
24 March 1916
LOCATION: 4 miles SWbyW Dungeness, UK
CARGO: Gold
SALVAGE: Probably salvaged
ROUTE: Dominica, West Indies–London, UK
TYPE: 3352T; Royal Mail Steamship; British
COMMENT: Sunk by German submarine *UB-29*

143 SAMOA
14 June 1916
LOCATION: 37.30°N 72.10°W
CARGO: Silver
SALVAGE: None known of
ROUTE: S. Africa–New York, US
TYPE: 1137T; Jacobsen & Thon; Norwegian
COMMENT: Sunk by German submarine

144 SANSEI MARU
28 June 1944
LOCATION: 33.53°N 129.01°E
CARGO: Large quantity of coin supposedly on board
SALVAGE: Salvage results disappointing
ROUTE: Indonesia–Japan
TYPE: 2386T; Yamashita Kisen KK; Japanese
COMMENT: Sunk by US submarine *Sealion*

145 SANTA RITA
9 July 1942
LOCATION: 26.11°N 55.40°W
CARGO: £20,000 gold
SALVAGE: None
ROUTE: Suez–Philedelphia, US
TYPE: 8379T; Grace Line; American
COMMENT: Sunk by German submarine *U-172*

146 SHINKO MARU
24 December 1918
LOCATION: Nabeshima, Japan
CARGO: Gold
SALVAGE: None known of
ROUTE: Chemulpo, Japan–Osaka, Japan
TYPE: Japanese

147 SHIRANGUI MARU
14 March 1945
LOCATION: 22.18°N 114.10°E
CARGO: Gold and silver
SALVAGE: Several salvage attempts
ROUTE: Malaysia–Japan
TYPE: 1300T; Japanese
COMMENT: Bombed

148 SHIRALA
2 July 1918
LOCATION: 4 miles NEbyEhalfE from Owers L.V., UK
CARGO: 4 packages of diamonds and elephants tusks
SALVAGE: Tusks recovered 1978 but no record of diamonds being recovered
ROUTE: London, UK–Bombay, India
TYPE: 5306; British India Steam Navigation Co.; British
COMMENT: Sunk by German submarine *UB-27*

149 SILVER MAPLE
26 February 1944
LOCATION: 04.44°N 03.20°W
CARGO: Specie
SALVAGE: None
ROUTE: Bathurst, W. Africa–Takoradi, W. Africa
TYPE: 5313T; Silver Line; British
COMMENT: Sunk by German submarine *U-66*

150 SIRIS
12 July 1942
LOCATION: 31.20°N 24.48°W
CARGO: Gold coin and bar
SALVAGE: None
TYPE: 5242T; Royal Mail; British
COMMENT: Sunk by German submarine *U-201*

151 SOCOTRA
30 November 1915
LOCATION: Near Le Touquet, France
CARGO: £18,100 in bullion
SALVAGE: Probably salvaged at time of loss
ROUTE: Brisbane, Australia–London, UK
TYPE: 6009T; Peninsular & Orient; British
COMMENT: Wrecked

152 SOEKABOEMI
28 December 1942
LOCATION: 47.25°N 25.20°W
CARGO: Connected with loss of precious stones
ROUTE: Glasgow, UK–Bahia, Brazil
SHIP TYPE: 7051T; Rotterdamsche Lloyd; Dutch
SALVAGE: None
COMMENT: Sunk by German submarine *U-356*

153 SOMALI
26 March 1941
LOCATION: Off Blyth, UK
CARGO: 80 boxes of liquid gold and 1616crts precious stones
SALVAGE: None known of
ROUTE: London, UK–Methil, UK
TYPE: 6809T; Peninsular & Orient; British
COMMENT: Bombed by German aircraft

154 SPARTAN PRINCE
11 September 1908
LOCATION: 00.13°N 35.37°W
CARGO: Specie
SALVAGE: Not known
ROUTE: New York, US–Plate River, Argentina

155 STENTOR
27 October 1942
LOCATION: 29.13°N 20.53°W
CARGO: 5000 ozs gold
SALVAGE: None
ROUTE: Lagos, W. Africa–Liverpool, UK
TYPE: 6148T; China Mutual Steam Navigation Co.; British
COMMENT: Sunk by German submarine *U-509*

156 SURINAME
13 September 1942
LOCATION: 12.07°N 63.32°W
CARGO: Gold
SALVAGE: None
ROUTE: Mombasa, Kenya–New York, US
TYPE: 7915T; Netherlands West Indies Govt; Dutch
COMMENT: Sunk by German submarine *U-558*

157 TANNENFELS
25 August 1944
LOCATION: 44.57.02°N 00.32.07°W
CARGO: Gold, silver and loot
SALVAGE: Some salvage at time of loss by Les Abeilles
TYPE: 7840T; Deutsche dampfs.; German
COMMENT: Scuttled by Germans

CARGO ROUTE LISTINGS

158 TARQUAH
7 July 1917
LOCATION: 10 miles S of Bull Rock, Eire
CARGO: Gold
SALVAGE: Salvaged in 1980s but no gold recovered
ROUTE: Sierra Leone, W. Africa–Liverpool, UK
TYPE: 3359T; Elder Dempster; British
COMMENT: Sunk by German submarine *U-57*

159 TILAWA
23 November 1912
LOCATION: 07.36°N 61.08°E
CARGO: Gold
SALVAGE: None known of
ROUTE: Bombay, India–Mombasa, Kenya–UK
TYPE: 10006T; British India Steam Navigation Company; British
COMMENT: Sunk by Japanese submarine *I.29*

160 TITANIC
15 April 1912
LOCATION: 41.43.35°N 49.56.55°W stern; 41.43.55°N 49.56.50°W bow
CARGO: Miscellaneous
SALVAGE: Some artefacts recently recovered
ROUTE: Southampton, UK–New York, US
TYPE: 46392T; White Star; British
COMMENT: *See Chapter*

161 TOONAN
10 July 1933
LOCATION: 36.52.30°N 122.47.30°E
CARGO: $1,500,000 sycee silver
SALVAGE: Salvage carried out by Tokyo Salvage Company
ROUTE: Newchwang, China–Shanghai, China
TYPE: 1482T; China Merchants Steam Navigation Co.; Chinese
COMMENT: Collision with *Chosun Maru*

162 TOYOURA MARU
6 May 1944
LOCATION: 32.18°N 127.11°E
CARGO: Gold
SALVAGE: None known of
ROUTE: Shanghai, China–Japan
TYPE: 2510T; Nippon Yusen KK; Japanese
COMMENT: Sunk by US submarine *Spearfish*

163 TUBANTIA
16 March 1916
LOCATION: 4 miles ENE of North Hinder Light ship, Holland
CARGO: Diamonds; also rumours of gold
SALVAGE: Attempted during 1920s without results
ROUTE: Amsterdam, Holland–Buenos Aires, Argentina
TYPE: 14053T; Koninklijke Hollandsche Lloyd Line; Dutch
COMMENT: *See Chapter*

164 U-1062
30 September 1944
LOCATION: Mid-Atlantic
CARGO: Gold rumoured
SALVAGE: None
ROUTE: Japan–Germany
TYPE: German cargo-carrying submarine

165 U-534
5 May 1945
LOCATION: Island of Anholt, Denmark
CARGO: Secret cargo that was rumoured to include gold or documents
SALVAGE: Salvage carried out in 1993 but no gold or documents recovered, only vintage wine and contraceptives
TYPE: German U-boat
COMMENT: Sunk by RAF Liberator

166 U-853
6 May 1945
LOCATION: Off Block Island, US
CARGO: Rumours of gold doubtful, mercury more likely
SALVAGE: Many attempts at salvage
TYPE: German submarine
COMMENT: Sunk by the US navy frigate *Moberly* and US navy destroyer *Atherton*

167 UMGENI
9 November 1917
LOCATION: N of Shetlands, UK
CARGO: 12 boxes of silver coin
SALVAGE: None
ROUTE: Clyde, UK–Lagos, W. Africa
TYPE: 2662T; Bullard King & Co; British
COMMENT: Missing ship. Last seen by SS *Salaga*

168 VYNER BROOKE
13 February 1942
LOCATION: 15 miles N of Muntok, Banka Island, Indonesia
CARGO: Jewellery
SALVAGE: None known of
ROUTE: Singapore–Australia
TYPE: 1670T; Sarawak Steamship Co; Sarawak
COMMENT: Bombed by Japanese aircraft

169 WARATAH
1909
LOCATION: Between Durban and Cape Town, S. Africa
CARGO: Rumoured to be bullion
SALVAGE: None
ROUTE: Sydney, Australia–London, UK
TYPE: 9339T; Blue Anchor Line; British
COMMENT: Missing ship

170 WELSH PRINCE
7 December 1941
LOCATION: 53.23.40°N 00.58.55°E
CARGO: Silverware and antiques
SALVAGE: Dispersed
ROUTE: Southend, UK–Methil, UK
TYPE: 5148T; Prince Line; British
COMMENT: Sunk by mine

171 WEST IMBODEN
21 April 1942
LOCATION: 41.14°N 65.55°W
CARGO: £29,000 gold
SALVAGE: None
TYPE: 5751T; United States Maritime Commission; American
COMMENT: Sunk by German submarine *U-752*

172 WEST LASHAWAY
30 August 1942
LOCATION: 350 miles E of Trinidad
CARGO: Gold
SALVAGE: None
ROUTE: W. Africa–US
TYPE: 5637T; American West Africa Line; American
COMMENT: Sunk by German submarine *U-66*

173 WILLIAM WILBERFORCE
9 January 1943
LOCATION: 29.20°N 26.53°W
CARGO: Gold
SALVAGE: None
ROUTE: Lagos, W. Africa–Liverpool, UK
TYPE: 4013T; Elder Dempster; British
COMMENT: Sunk by German submarine *U-571*

174 YASAKA MARU
21 December 1915
LOCATION: 60 miles off Port Said, Egypt
CARGO: £200,000 gold sovereigns
SALVAGE: Some salvage at time of loss
ROUTE: London, UK–Japan
TYPE: 10932T; Nippon Yusen; Japanese
COMMENT: Sunk by German submarine

The following appendices detail the main movements of gold carried out under British control. The act of moving gold during war time was kept highly secret for obvious reasons. This confidentiality makes it difficult for the researcher today to establish exactly what amounts of gold went on which ships. In many instances the records are oblique, obscure, contradictory or missing. But the difficulty is not simply the result of understandable government caution, poor record keeping and the atrophying effects of time. The logistics of the operation itself causes difficulty. On several occasions, but especially in June 1940, there was enormous pressure to ship gold out as fast as possible because of the threat of imminent invasion. There was also the need to support Britain's credit with its main supplier of arms and raw materials, the United States. Only gold was considered adequate for the purpose. The British Navy was also engaged in action all over the world. It is therefore not surprising that dates of sailings were frequently changed at the last minute, that quantities of gold shipped were subject to unexpected fluctuations, and a ship's availability was altered as other demands became of paramount importance. In view of this it is necessary to treat sailing dates in the following tables with some degree of caution.

Considering the problems that the British Admiralty and Treasury faced, they did a remarkably good job. This was largely a result of some astute decision making. Ships were classified by certain criteria – especially defensive armament, wireless communication and speed – for carrying gold and limits were imposed accordingly. In autumn 1939 warships were limited to carry £2 million for transatlantic shipments, fast unescorted liners £1 million; slower cargo ships were not used at all. By the end of June 1940 the situation had become so desperate that up to £50 million was permitted on warships, £14 million on liners over 15,000 tons and £5 million on cargo boats under 10,000 tons. There was careful regulation of the routes, according to the continually changing strategic situation.

The following tables do not take into account private shipments of gold, or silver and precious stone shipments, whether private or state. Nor is it within the scope of these appendices to concern itself with shipments of gold by other countries such as France, Germany, Japan or the US. The gazetteer of lost ships does, however, provide examples of all of these categories

50 tons of gold consisted of approximately 3,550 bars packed in 890 boxes, each box weighed 125 lbs when full and the dimensions of each box were 13" x 9 x 7". The total cubic capacity of all 890 boxes took up approximately 440 cubic feet of space.

GOLD SHIPMENTS–WORLD WAR ONE

NAME OF SHIP	DATE	QUANTITY	
SOUTH AFRICA–UK			
(Usually Cape Town to Plymouth)			
HMS Albion	09/01/1915	£4,000,000	*Some transhipment of these*
HMS Cornwall	09/01/1915	£4,000,000	*three cargoes at St Helena*
HMS Cordelia	14/02/1915	£4,000,000	*and Gibraltar*
SS Saxon	06/11/1915	£500,000	
SS Llandovery Castle	27/11/1915	£358,750	
SS Balmoral Castle	04/12/1915	£500,000	
SS Durham Castle	11/12/1915	£500,000	
SS Norman	18/12/1915	£500,000	
SS Galway Castle	25/12/1915	£500,000	
SS Kenilworth Castle	04/01/1916	£310,907	
SS Walmer Castle	14/01/1916	£623,662	
SS Llanstephan Castle	15/01/1916	£630,000	
SS Saxon	29/01/1916	£630,000	
SS Galway Castle	21/06/1916	£250,000	
SS Laconia	24/06/1916	£4,000,000	
SS Llanstephen Castle	01/07/1916	£250,000	
SS Glenart Castle	06/07/1916	£250,000	
SS Saxon	08/07/1916	£200,000	
SS Balmoral Castle	19/07/1916	£375,000	
SS Gaika	24/07/1916	£494,829	
SS Norman	29/07/1916	£499,525	
SS Berwick Castle	05/08/1916	£498,002	

NAME OF SHIP	DATE	QUANTITY	
SS Kenilworth Castle	12/08/1916	£499,292	
SS Walmer Castle	22/08/1916	£496,087	
SS Durham Castle	08/09/1916	£493,974	
SS Galway Castle	12/09/1916	£496,644	
SS Dunvegan Castle	16/09/1916	£494,407	
SS Llanstephan Castle	20/09/1916	£497,334	
SS Saxon	27/09/1916	£499,658	
SS Balmoral Castle	07/10/1916	£497,678	
SS Norman	14/10/1916	£497,104	
SS Comrie Castle	14/10/1916	£499,802	
SS Kenilworth Castle	28/10/1916	£500,000	
SS Walmer Castle	06/11/1916	£499,521	
SS Carlisle Castle	10/11/1916	£496,371	
SS Durham Castle	21/11/1916	£497,116	
SS Dunvegan	29/11/1916	£500,000	
SS Saxon	07/12/1916	£499,513	
SS Llanstephan	21/12/1916	£500,000	
SS Balmoral	23/12/1916	£500,000	
SS Norman	04/01/1917	£500,000	
HMS Kent	10/01/1917	£3,985,000	
SS Durham Castle	10/01/1917	£500,000	
SS Balmoral Castle	15/01/1917	£500,000	
SS Llanstephan Castle	15/01/1917	£500,000	
SS Norman	29/01/1917	£500,000	
SS Dunvegan Castle	19/02/1917	£500,000	
SS Anchises	24/02/1917	374 boxes	
SS Ulimaroa	24/02/1917	350 boxes	
HMS Marmora	22/03/1917	£4,337,276	*£3,386,192 transhipped at Sierra Leone for Halifax, Canada; £300,000 in gold loaded Sierra Leone for UK*
HMS Kent	07/07/1917	£1,866,052	
HMS Himalaya	01/03/1918	£990,000	*via Rio de Janeiro*
SS Saxon	04/03/1918	£500,000	
SS Walmer Castle	28/04/1918	£997,836	*both ships left Cape Town with £500,000; picked up balance at Sierra Leone*
SS Norman	28/04/1918	£986,381	

SOUTH AFRICA–CANADA
(Cape Town to Halifax, unless otherwise stated)

NAME OF SHIP	DATE	QUANTITY	
HMS Orbita	28/08/1915	£4,000,000	
HMS Orbita	27/11/1915	£4,000,000	
SS Laconia	24/06/1916	£4,000,000	
HMS Kent	01/08/1916	£4,000,000	*transhipped to Highflyer at St Vincent and then to Isis at Bermuda*
SS Armadale Castle	20/09/1916	£4,000,000	
HMS Kent	28/09/1916	£4,000,000	*transhipped on to French cruiser Desaix at Dakar and then to the Laurentide at Bermuda*
HMS Isis	00/11/1916	636 boxes	
HMS Duke of Ediburgh	16/12/1916	£5,000,000	
HMS Cornwall	16/01/1917	1131 boxes	*gold of this convoy of six ships was transhipped at Sierra Leone onto the Donegal and French ship Dupleix and transhipped at Bermuda onto the Isis and the Berwick*
SS Medic	as above	90 boxes	
SS Berrima	as above	364 boxes	
SS Orsova	as above	329 boxes	
SS Mendi	as above	240 boxes	
SS Kenilworth Castle	as above	£500,000	
SS Militiades	24/02/1917	429 boxes	*gold of this convoy of five ships transhipped at Sierra Leone onto Britannia and Kleber and then onto Donegal and Isis*
HMS Orcoma	as above	1283 boxes	
SS Walmer Castle	as above	£500,000	
SS Ulimaroa	as above	350 boxes	
SS Anchises	as above	374 boxes	
HMS Kent	15/03/1917	£8,000,000	*gold on this convoy transhipped at Sierra Leone onto Highflier and Carnarvon*
SS Osterley	as above		
SS Galway Castle	as above		
SS Wiltshire	as above		
SS Norman Castle	as above		
SS Balmoral Castle	as above		
HMS Orama	22/06/1917	£4,000,000	
HMS Calgarian	20/07/1917	£3,000,000	

SOUTH AFRICA–USA
(Cape Town to New York)

NAME OF SHIP	DATE	QUANTITY	
SS Gordon Castle	04/12/1915	£1,000,000	
SS Corfe Castle	17 /12/1915	£1,000,000	
SS Susquehanna	23/06/1916	£500,000	
HMS Laurentic	30/07/1916	£4,000,000	
SS York Castle	09/08/1916	£500,000	
SS Chepstow Castle	26/08/1916	£500,000	
SS Aros Castle	09/09/1916	£500,000	
SS Cluny Castle	13/11/1916	£500,000	
SS Caronia	18/03/1918	£1,000,000	*picked up a further £3 million at Sierra Leone*

SOUTH AFRICA–WEST AFRICA
(Cape Town to Sierra Leone unless otherwise stated; see also certain shipments listed above on the South Africa–Canada and South Africa–US routes, which went via Sierra Leone)

NAME OF SHIP	DATE	QUANTITY
SS Medea	20/02/1917	350 boxes
SS Seangbee	23/03/1917	268 boxes
SS Ballarat	23/03/1917	346 boxes
SS Durham Castle	24/03/1917	£1,501,362
HMS Africa	00/07/1917	£4,000,000
HMS Africa	19/09/1917	£3,984,406
HMS Britannia	27/09/1917	£3,976,854
HMS Himalaya	18/10/1917	£3,969,230
HMS Britannia	28/10/1917	£1,993,172
HMS Kent	15/11/1917	£1,963,916
HMS Britannia	25/11/1917	£1,988,894
HMS Kent	04/01/1918	£3,993,689
HMS Britannia	05/02/1918	£3,986,155
HMS Kent	04/03/1918	£6,987,423
SS Briton	04/03/1918	as above
SS Kingfauns Castle	04/03/1918	as above
HMS Britannia	02/04/1918	£3,626,886
HMS Africa	06/04/1918	£4,000,000
HMS Britannia	23/05/1918	£3,912,072
HMS Britannia	01/07/1918	£2,002,314

SOUTH AFRICA–AUSTRALIA
(Cape Town to either Melbourne or Sydney)

NAME OF SHIP	DATE	QUANTITY
SS Corinthic	09/02/1918	£386,031
SS Orontes	19/04/1918	£257,193
SS Tofua	22/05/1918	£425,319
SS Essex	07/07/1918	£409,000
SS Matatua	24/07/1918	£1,000,000
SS Rimutaka	14/08/1918	£1,000,000
SS Boonah	21/08/1918	£1,000,000
SS Malta	00/09/1918	£1,000,000
SS Cluny Castle	00/10/1918	£1,000,000
SS Barambah	05/07/1917	Unknown

SOUTH AFRICA–INDIA
(Durban to Bombay)

NAME OF SHIP	DATE	QUANTITY
SS Dilwara	13/03/1916	£400,000
SS Palamcotta	07/04/1916	£400,000
SS Dilwara	12/06/1916	£400,000
SS Palamcotta	12/06/1916	£400,000
SS Aratoon Apcar	29/07/1916	£500,000
SS Dilwara	22/08/1916	£500,000
SS Karoa	10/09/1916	£500,000
SS Dilwara	01/11/1916	£500,000
SS Karoa	18/11/1916	£500,000
SS Dunera	29/11/1916	£500,000
SS Dilwara	08/01/1917	£500,000
SS Karoa	15/01/1917	£500,000
SS Dunera	08/02/1917	£500,000
SS Aragon	25/04/1917	£500,000
SS Caronia	14/07/1917	£1,000,000

NAME OF SHIP	DATE	QUANTITY	

WEST AFRICA–UK

(All shipments from West Africa carried gold originally from South Africa and transshipped at Sierra Leone, except where marked as *, indicating West Africa as the origin of the gold)

NAME OF SHIP	DATE	QUANTITY	
SS Abosso	29/06/1916	£99,732*	
SS Abinsi	10/07/1916	£99,800*	
SS Tarquah	15/07/1916	£99,830*	
SS Karina	27/07/1916	£98,942*	
SS Burutu	29/07/1916	£99,664*	
SS Elmina	14/08/1916	£99,686*	
SS Apapa	23/08/1916	£99,665*	
SS Mendi	29/08/1916	£99,889*	
SS Abosso	07/09/1916	£79,782*	
SS Abinsi	21/09/1916	£49,766*	
SS Tarquah	27/09/1916	£49,837*	
SS Borda	26/08/1916	154 boxes*	
SS Karina	05/10/1916	£22,076*	
HMS Weymouth	15/05/1917	£1,520,000	
SS Euripedes			
HMS Mantua	29/05/1917	308 boxes	plus £298,000*
SS Aeneas	as above	154 boxes	
SS Commonwealth	as above	154 boxes	
SS Devon	as above	154 boxes	
SS Ceramic	as above	154 boxes	
SS Nestor	as above	154 boxes	
HMS Marmora	14/06/1917	£1,300,000	plus £299,736*
HMS Mantua	04/07/1917	£1,866,052	plus £299,788*
SS Marathon	as above		
SS Ascanius	as above		
SS Exmouth	03/08/1917	£149,954*	
SS Hororata	14/08/1917	154 boxes*	
HMS Morea	14/08/1917	£1,982,934	plus £149,000*
HMS Motagua	22/08/1917	£998,000	plus £149,000*
SS Mantula	12/09/1917	£59,431	
HMS Motagua	28/09/1917	£1,994,236	
HMS Marmora	06/10/1917	£998,140	
HMS Kildonan Castle	13/10/1917	£1,054,613	
HMS Morea	24/10/1917	£1,959,000*	
HMS Armadale Castle	01/11/1917	£1,961,000	
HMS Moldavia	06/11/1917	£1,948,031	
HMS Kildonan Castle	15/11/1917	£1,993,000	plus £150,000*
HMS Mantua	23/11/1917	£2,021,199	
HMS King Alfred	01/12/1917	£1,964,000	plus £150,000*
HMS Moldavia	18/12/1917	£1,989,000	
HMS Armadale Castle	16/01/1918	£1,016,239	
HMS Moldavia	27/01/1918	£1,013,697	
HMS Glasgow	27/01/1918	£1,039,860	
HMS Marmora	04/02/1918	£923,893	
HMS Morea	18/02/1918	£996,765	
HMS Mantua	25/02/1918	£985,573	
HMS Armadale Castle	06/03/1918	£996,186	
HMS Marmora	14/03/1918	£995,169	
HMS Gloucestershire	22/03/1918	£999,669	
HMS Mantua	01/04/1918	£997,295	
SS Saxon	01/04/1918	£499,191	
HMS Charamulula	02/04/1918	£171,011	
HMS Artois	15/04/1918	£996,960	plus £150,000*
HMS City of London	08/05/1918	£492,369	via Rio de Janiero
SS Dunvegan Castle	15/05/1918	£633,535	
HMS Kent	22/05/1918	£992,738	
SS Kenilworth Castle	22/05/1918	£990,897	
HMS Artois	31/05/1918	£991,000	
HMS Orcoma	08/06/1918	£746,853	plus £299,000*
HMS Amethyst	12/06/1918	£998,864	
HMS Himalaya	17/06/1918	£999,853	
HMS Macedonia	24/06/1918	£989,355	
HMS Marmora	27/06/1918	£999,000	via Rio de Janiero
HMS Ebro	03/07/1918	£923,980	plus £150,000*
HMS Hildebrand	04/08/1918	£998,084	
HMS Morea	13/08/1918	£1,004,230	plus £150,000*
HMS Mantua	23/08/1918	£149,959	
HMS Almanzora	22/09/1918	£149,000	

GHANA–SIERRA LEONE

NAME OF SHIP	DATE	QUANTITY
SS Karina	07/05/1917	£149,090
SS Akabo	19/05/1917	£149,417
SS Apapa	04/06/1917	£149,744
SS Elmina	09/06/1917	£149,292
SS Tarquah	20/06/1917	£149,954
SS Abinsi	30/06/1917	£149,054
SS Karina	14/07/1917	£149,954
SS Akabo	04/08/1917	£148,920
SS Apapa	12/08/1917	£149,905
SS Abinsi	05/09/1917	£59,431
SS Apapa	05/11/1917	£149,732
SS Abinsi	26/11/1917	£149,717
SS Burutu	08/04/1918	£149,891
SS Elmina	27/05/1918	£149,421
SS Mandingo	31/05/1918	£149,878
SS Burutu	23/06/1918	£149,746
SS Akabo	31/07/1918	£149,840
SS Elmina	18/08/1918	£149,959
SS Burutu	04/09/1918	£149,620

UK/FRANCE–US/CANADA

(UK to Halifax, unless otherwise stated)

NAME OF SHIP	DATE	QUANTITY	
HMS Lowestoff	05/08/1915	£4,016,000	
HMS Carnarvon	17/08/1915	£4,016,000	
HMS Argyll	28/08/1915	£1,614,000	
		£2,390,000	
HMS Roxburgh	14/09/1915	£4,000,000	
HMS Lowestoff	13/09/1915	£4,000,000	
HMS Devonshire	20/09/1915	£4,000,000	
HMS Donegal	08/10/1915	£5,000,000	
HMS Carmania	10/10/1915	£5,000,000	
SS Baltic	17/11/1915	£250,000	
SS New York	17/11/1915	£250,000	
SS Adriatic	23/11/1915	£250,000	
SS St Louis	26/11/1915	£250,000	
SS Cymric	01/12/1915	£400,000	to New York
SS Tuscania	01/12/1915	£500,000	to New York
SS Philadelphia	02/12/1915	£446,550	
SS California	10/12/1915	£446,550	
SS St Paul	10/12/1915	£446,550	
SS Lapland	16/12/1915	£446,550	
SS New York	18/12/1915	£446,550	
SS Baltic	22/12/1915	£190,250	
HMS Drake	29/04/1916	£4,001,100	
HMS Drake	01/06/1916	£4,001,586	
SS St Paul	16/06/1916	£2,002,999	
HMS Cumberland	20/06/1916	£4,006,657	
HMS Berwick	28/06/1916	£4,003,887	
SS Metagama	20/07/1916	£500,442	
SS Athenia	25/07/1916	£501,125	
HMS Drake	26/07/1916	£4,004,820	
SS Grampian	27/07/1916	£502,884	
SS Saturnia	31/07/1916	£497,108	
SS Tuscania	04/08/1916	£878,394	
		£705,988	
HMS Celtic	04/08/1916	£1,035,917	
SS Cassandra	04/08/1916	£500,981	
SS Missanabic	10/08/1916	£502,824	
HMS Laurentic	10/08/1916	£4,000,000	
SS Laconia	16/08/1916	£507,582	
HMS Roxburgh	18/08/1916	£4,000,938	
SS Scandinavian	22/08/1916	£497,078	
HMS Antrim	22/08/1916	£4,003,283	
SS Metagama	24/08/1916	£501,474	
SS Northland	25/08/1916	£502,499	to New York
SS Athenia	28/08/1916	£500,450	
HMS Carnarvon	28/08/1916	£4,003,712	to New York
SS Grampian	31/08/1916	£500,809	
HMS Leviathan	01/09/1916	£4,002,247	
SS Saturnia	04/09/1916	£501,601	to New York
SS Corsican	07/09/1916	£501,780	
SS Southland	07/09/1916	£502,234	

NAME OF SHIP	DATE	QUANTITY	
SS Dupetit Thouars	09/09/1916	£4,000,000	*from Brest*
SS Cassandra	11/09/1916	£504,892	
SS Missanabie	14/09/1916	£506,238	
HMS Drake	23/09/1916	£1,784,904	
		£2,217,663	
SS Scandanavian	26/09/1916	£187,373	
		£192,085	
		£21,128	
SS Dupetit Thouars	16/10/1916	£4,000,000	*from Brest*
HMS Roxburgh	30/10/1916	£4,000,000	
HMS Drake	04/11/1916	£2,403,820	
		£1,600,000	
HMS Calgarian	07/11/1916	£4,000,000	
HMS Devonshire	13/11/1916	£4,000,000	
Unknown	04/12/1916	Unknown	*from Cherbourg*
Unknown	12/12/1916	Unknown	*from Cherbourg*
HMS Duke of Edinburgh	15/12/1916	£5,000,000	
Unknown	20/12/1916	Unknown	*from Cherbourg*
SS Corsican	20/12/1916	£1,000,000	
Unknown	23/12/1916	£5,000,000	
SS Celtic	27/12/1916	£1,000,000	*to New York*
SS Missanabie	29/12/1916	£1,000,000	
SS Laconia	30/12/1916	£1,000,000	*to New York*
HMS Calgarian	01/01/1917	£5,000,000	
HMS Laurentic	23/01/1917	£5,000,000	*lost en route*
Unknown	09/01/1917	£5,000,000	*from Calais*
Unknown	17/01/1917	Unknown	*from Calais*
HMS Cochrane	17/01/1917	£5,000,000	
HMS Calgarian	19/02/1917	658 boxes	
HMS Calgarian	01/03/1917	838 boxes	
HMS Drake	15/03/1917	782 boxes	
HMS Berwick	24/03/1917	£5,000,000	
HMS Calgarian	12/04/1917	£5,000,000	
HMS Devonshire	25/05/1917	£3,000,000	
HMS Calgarian	03/06/1917	579 boxes	
HMS Cumberland	15/06/1917	£3,000,000	
HMS Calgarian	19/07/1917	£3,000,000	
HMS Roxburgh	29/07/1917	£3,000,000	
HMS Calgarian	00/08/1917	444 boxes	
HMS Andes	18/02/1918	£250,000	
HMS Olympic	11/03/1918	£454,000	
		143 boxes	
HMS Isis	14/03/1918	£241,300	
		76 boxes	
HMS Donegal	16/03/1918	£525,000	
		170 boxes	
HMS Leviathan	22/03/1918	£491,000	
		162 boxes	
HMS Columbella	30/03/1918	£266,177	
		75 boxes	
HMS Cumberland	03/04/1918	£468,237	
		136 boxes	
HMS Mauretania	04/04/1918	£491,436	
		143 boxes	
HMS Teutonic	04/04/1918	£239,152	
		74 boxes	
HMS Aquitania	21/04/1918	£1,039,860	
		321 boxes	
HMS Olympic	22/04/1918	£1,013,697	
		320 boxes	
HMS Isis	26/04/1918	£220,563	
		65 boxes	
HMS Donegal	08/05/1918	£997,295	
		317 boxes	
HMS Mauretania	10/05/1918	£990,232	
		307 boxes	
HMS Isis	12/05/1918	65 boxes	

FRANCE–UK
(Cherbourg to Portsmouth, unless otherwise stated)

NAME OF SHIP	DATE	QUANTITY	
Torpedo Boat	24/02/1916	£4,000,000	
Torpedo Boat	16/03/1916	£4,000,000	
Torpedo Boat	16/03/1916	£4,000,000	
SS Dunois	08/06/1916	£4,000,000	
SS Cerbere	08/06/1916	£4,000,000	
SS Pertuisane	08/06/1916	£4,000,000	
SS Durandal	08/08/1916	£4,000,000	
SS Cerbere	08/08/1916	£4,000,000	
Unknown	13/08/1916	£4,000,000	
SS Princess Victoria	05/09/1916	£4,000,000	*final part of special shipment from France of £40 million in addition to regular shipments of French and Italian gold*
Unknown	26/10/1916	471 boxes	*Boulogne–Dover*
HMS Crusader	11/11/1916	240 boxes	*Boulogne–Dover*
HMS Phoenix	11/11/1916	251 boxes	*Boulogne–Dover*
SS Rouen	13/12/1916	Italian gold	*port of origin unknown*
Torpedo Boat	18/02/1917	15 tons Italian gold	

UK–SOUTH AFRICA

NAME OF SHIP	DATE	QUANTITY	
SS Kildonan Castle	08/1914	£50,000	
SS Llandovery Castle	12/09/1914	£100,000	*£500,000 shipped in total over 5 weeks*

UK–NORWAY
Shipments of £125,000 per time – details not provided

UK–HOLLAND

NAME OF SHIP	DATE	QUANTITY
Unknown	14/06/1917	£1,000,000
Unknown	23/06/1917	£1,000,000
Unknown	21/07/1917	£1,000,000
Unknown	28/07/1917	£1,000,000
Unknown	03/08/1917	£250,000
Unknown	09/08/1917	£800,000
Unknown	27/08/1917	£600,000
Unknown	12/09/1917	£800,000
Unknown	10/10/1917	£800,000
Unknown	10/11/1917	£1,000,000
Unknown	17/11/1917	£800,000
Unknown	13/12/1917	£600,000
Unknown	21/12/1917	£700,000
Unknown	09/01/1918	£800,000
Unknown	30/01/1918	£400,000
Unknown	02/02/1918	£400,000

MALTA–UK

NAME OF SHIP	DATE	QUANTITY	
HMS Jupiter	20/11/1916	£50,000	
Unknown	03/1917	£40,000	
HMS Implacable	05/08/1917	£65,000	*via Gibraltar*

GIBRALTAR–UK

NAME OF SHIP	DATE	QUANTITY
HMS Duncan	06/03/1917	£25,000
HMS Savage	10/12/1917	£25,000

MALTA–GIBRALTAR

NAME OF SHIP	DATE	QUANTITY
HMS Celandine	06/05/1917	£20,000
HMS Narcissus	09/05/1917	£20,000

MALTA–EGYPT

NAME OF SHIP	DATE	QUANTITY
HMS Honeysuckle	15/03/1918	£25,000
HMS Ribble	05/07/1918	£25,000
HMS Honeysuckle	09/07/1918	£25,000
HMS Honeysuckle	01/09/1918	£25,000

INDIA–UK
(All shipments from Bombay unless otherwise stated)

NAME OF SHIP	DATE	QUANTITY	
HMS Moldavia	24/10/1915	£200,000	
SS Caledonia	31/10/1915	£200,000	
SS Khyber	07/11/1915	£200,000	
SS Persia	14/11/1915	£200,000	
SS Medina	21/11/1915	£200,000	
SS Kaisar-i-hind	28/11/1915	£200,000	
HMS Salsette	05/12/1915	£200,000	*transhipped onto Mongolia at Aden*

NAME OF SHIP	DATE	QUANTITY	
SS Khiva	12/12/1915	£200,000	
SS Kashgar	26/12/1915	£200,000	*transhipped onto* Malwa *at Aden*
SS Salsette	02/01/1916	£200,000	*transhipped onto* Mooltan *at Aden*

RUSSIA–JAPAN

NAME OF SHIP	DATE	QUANTITY
SS Satsuma	22/12/1916	Russian gold
SS Nisshin	22/12/1916	Russian gold

JAPAN–INDIA

NAME OF SHIP	DATE	QUANTITY
Unknown	28/02/1917	£260,000
Unknown	20/03/1917	£150,000

JAPAN–CANADA
(To Vancouver, unless otherwise stated)

NAME OF SHIP	DATE	QUANTITY	
SS Tokiwa	17/02/1916	Unknown	*gold in these two shipments*
SS Chitose	17/02/1916	Unknown	*transferred to* Rainbow
SS Tokiwa	17/05/1916	Unknown	
SS Idzumo	Unknown	Unknown	*to Victoria*
SS Iwate	Unknown	Unknown	*to Victoria*
SS Nisshin	Unknown	Unknown	*to Victoria*

AUSTRALIA–CANADA
(Sydney to Vancouver, unless otherwise stated)

NAME OF SHIP	DATE	QUANTITY
SS Niagara	03/08/1916	£500,000
SS Makura	31/08/1916	£500,000
SS Niagara	28/09/1916	£500,000
SS Waikawa	10/10/1916	£500,000
SS Wairuna	21/10/1916	£500,000
SS Makura	31/10/1916	£500,000
SS Niagara	23/11/1916	£500,000
SS Waetotara	24/11/1916	£500,000
SS Makura	21/12/1916	£500,000
SS Niagara	18/01/1917	£500,000
SS Makura	15/02/1917	£500,000
SS Niagara	15/03/1917	£500,000
SS Manuka	04/04/1917	£250,000
SS Niagara	15/05/1917	£500,000

NEW ZEALAND–US
(Wellington to San Francisco, unless otherwise stated)

NAME OF SHIP	DATE	QUANTITY	
SS Moana	03/08/1916	£500,000	
SS Maitai	14/09/1916	£500,000	
SS Moana	12/10/1916	£500,000	
SS Maitai	08/11/1916	£500,000	
SS Moana	07/12/1916	£500,000	
SS Moana	01/02/1917	£500,000	
SS Waikawa	02/02/1917	£500,000	
SS Paloona	01/03/1917	£500,000	
SS Moana	29/03/1917	£500,000	
SS Paloona	26/04/1917	£500,000	*retained in New Zealand because of raider threat*

AUSTRALIA–INDIA
(Sydney to Calcutta, unless otherwise stated)

NAME OF SHIP	DATE	QUANTITY	
SS Chindwara	26/07/1917	£250,000	
SS Waihara	31/07/1917	£250,000	
SS Waitorus	01/08/1917	£250,000	
Unknown	20/11/1917	£250,000	
SS Carina	18/05/1918	£1,500,000	*from Melbourne*
SS Khiva	04/06/1917	£250,000	*Fremantle–Bombay*
SS Mooltan	15/06/1917	£250,000	*Fremantle–Bombay*
SS Aratoon Apcar	00/07/1917	£257,000	*Fremantle–Bombay*
SS Somali	03/07/1917	£515,000	*Fremantle–Bombay*
SS Manora	12/07/1917	£515,000	*Fremantle–Bombay*
SS Mongolia	30/07/1917	£500,000	*Fremantle–Bombay*

INDIA–AUSTRALIA

NAME OF SHIP	DATE	QUANTITY	
SS Carina	06/08/1918	£500,000	*Calcutta–Melbourne*

AUSTRALIA–EGYPT

NAME OF SHIP	DATE	QUANTITY
SS Wiltshire	31/01/1918	£400,000
SS Ormonde	28/02/1918	£200,000
Unknown	00/06/1918	£400,000
SS Assist	00/08/1918	£400,000
SS Dorset	21/07/1918	£400,000
SS Port Darwin	26/08/1918	£400,000
SS Malta	00/11/1918	£500,000

AUSTRALIA–SOUTH AFRICA

NAME OF SHIP	DATE	QUANTITY
SS Commonwealth	14/03/1918	£250,000
SS Orontes	16/03/1918	£250,000
SS Boonah	25/04/1918	£500,000

AUSTRALIA–CHILE

NAME OF SHIP	DATE	QUANTITY
SS Osterley	08/05/1918	£263,000(sovs)

INDIA–HONGKONG–CANADA
(Bombay to Vancouver. The vessels that they were transhipped onto are listed)

NAME OF SHIP	DATE	QUANTITY	
SS Dilwara	06/09/1917	£500,000	Empress of Asia
SS Dunera	20/10/1917	£500,000	Empress of Japan
SS Dilwara	21/11/1917	£500,000	Empress of Russia
SS Dunera	06/01/1918	£500,000	Empress of Asia
SS Dilwara	11/02/1918	£500,000	Empress of Russia
SS Dunera	15/04/1918	£500,000	Empress of Japan
SS Hedjaz	21/06/1918	Unknown	

BRAZIL–UK

NAME OF SHIP	DATE	QUANTITY
HMS Himalaya	00/04/1918	£1,000,000

BRAZIL–US
(Rio de Janiero to New York)

NAME OF SHIP	DATE	QUANTITY
SS Vauban	24/09/1917	£10,800
SS Vasari	25/10/1917	£13,582
SS Vestris	10/12/1917	£10,949

BORNEO/SINGAPORE–UK

NAME OF SHIP	DATE	QUANTITY
SS Protesilaus	00/03/1916	2616 ozs
SS Cyclops	00/02/1917	3778 ozs
SS Peleus	00/03/1917	1529 ozs
SS Hyson	00/05/1917	1502 ozs
SS Agamemnon	00/06/1917	1448 ozs
SS Glaucus	00/06/1917	1899 ozs
SS Mooltan	00/09/1917	2362 ozs
SS Manora	00/09/1917	1719 ozs

GOLD SHIPMENTS WORLD WAR TWO

GOLD ON WATER AT THE OUTBREAK OF THE WAR 03/09/1939

NAME OF SHIP	DATE	QUANTITY	
UK–US			
SS Queen Mary		£9,908,000	
SS Samaria		£2,688,000	
SS Arandora Star		£3,025,000	
SS Van Dyck		£3,024,000	
UK–Canada			
SS Montrose		£3,204,000	
SS Antonia		£3,205,000	
SS Empress of Britain		£3,009,000	
SS Empress of Australia		£5,229,000	*French gold*

NAME OF SHIP	DATE	QUANTITY	

Argentina–UK

SS Almanzora		£300,000	*in sovereigns*

South Africa–UK

SS Warwick Castle		£2,112,000	
SS Athlone Castle		£869,000	

GOLD SHIPPED DURING HOSTILITIES

UK–CANADA
(Portland to Halifax, unless otherwise stated)

NAME OF SHIP	DATE	QUANTITY	
HMS Revenge	07/10/1939	£2,000,000	
HMS Resolution	07/10/1939	£2,000,000	
HMS Emerald	07/10/1939	£2,000,000	*from Plymouth*
HMS Enterprise	07/10/1939	£2,000,000	*from Plymouth*
HMS Caradoc	07/10/1939	£2,000,000	*from Plymouth*
HMS Asacania	27/10/1939	£2,000,000	
HMS Alaunia	05/11/1939	£2,000,000	
HMS Assinboine	07/11/1939	£1,000,000	*from Plymouth*
HMS Effingham	07/11/1939	£2,000,000	*from Plymouth*
HMS Emerald	12/11/1939	£3,000,000	*from Plymouth*
HMS Resolution	17/11/1939	£5,000,000	*from Plymouth*
HMS Ausonia	25/11/1939	£2,000,000	*from Plymouth*
HMS Letitia	15/12/1939	£2,000,000	*from Southampton*
HMS Resolution	22/12/1939	£5,000,000	*from Greenock*
HMS Enterprise	31/12/1939	£3,000,000	*from Portsmouth*

UK–US
(Liverpool to New York, unless otherwise stated)

NAME OF SHIP	DATE	QUANTITY	
SS Brittanic	01/1940	£500,000	
SS Lancastria	01/1940	£1,300,000	
SS Scythia	01/1940	£750,000	
SS Port Freemantle	01/1940	£1,400,000	
SS Samaria	01/1940	£1,500,000	
SS Northern Prince	01/1940	£300,000	*from London*
SS Georgic	01/1940	£200,000	
HMS Emerald	05/01/1940	£3,000,000	
HMS Royal Sovereign	07/01/1940	£5,000,000	
HMS Alaunia	11/01/1940	£2,000,000	*from Southampton*
HMS Revenge	24/01/1940	£10,000,000	*from Plymouth*
HMS Laconia	26/01/1940	£2,000,000	*from Portland*
SS Cameronia	02/1940	£48,000	*from Glasgow*
SS Brittanic	02/1940	£645,000	
SS Lancastria	02/1940	£1,057,000	
SS Malayan Prince	02/1940	£63,000	*from London*
SS Georgic	02/1940	£690,000	
SS Samaria	27/02/1940	£1,283,000	
SS Western Prince	02/1940	£192,000	*from London*
SS De Grasse	13/02/1940	£1,750,000	
SS Tokai Maru	03/1940	£266,000	*port of origin unknown*
SS Scythia	03/1940	£1,061,000	
SS Western Prince	05/03/1940	£1,000,000	*from London*
SS Lancastria	08/03/1940	£750,000	
SS Georgic	18/03/1940	£1,000,000	
SS Eastern Prince	20/03/1940	£500,000	*from London*
SS Brittanic	22/03/1940	£1,000,000	
SS Cameronia	26/03/1940	£1,000,000	*from Glasgow*
SS De Grasse	30/03/1940	£1,000,000	
SS Pacific Grove	04/1940	£542,000	*from London*
HMS Enterprise	12/04/1940	£5,000,000	*from Portsmouth*
SS Lancastria	17/04/1940	£550,467	
SS Cameronia	24/04/1940	£550,615	*from Glasgow*
SS Georgic	04/1940	£1,058,077	
SS Eastern Prince	04/1940	£552,588	*from London*
SS Northern Prince	11/04/1940	£500,000	*from London*
SS Samaria	11/04/1940	£1,000,000	
SS Western Prince	19/04/1940	£750,000	*from London; came under air attack but not sunk*
SS Antonia	29/05/1940	£1,750,000	
SS Clydesbank	05/1940	£387,760	*port of origin unknown*
SS Western Prince	05/1940	£1,122,260	*from Southampton*

NAME OF SHIP	DATE	QUANTITY	
SS Brittanic	02/05/1940	£2,151,890	
HMS Ausonia	04/05/1940	£3,000,000	*from Southampton*
SS Cameronia	08/05/1940	£1,500,000	
French Ship	15/05/1940	£1,000,000	*port of origin unknown*
SS Eastern Prince	17/05/1940	£750,000	*from Southampton*
SS Samaria	20/05/1940	£2,000,000	
SS Northern Prince	30/05/1940	£750,000	*from Southampton*
SS Port Freemantle	06/1940	£42,600	*port of origin unknown*
SS Eurybates	06/1940	£547,150	*port of origin unknown*
SS Aracatata	06/1940	£210,440	*port of origin unknown*
Unknown	06/1940	£30,750	*port of origin unknown*
SS Volendam	06/1940	£54,380	*port of origin unknown*
SS Kaituna	12/06/1940	£2,000,000	*from Swansea*
SS Kent	12/06/1940	£3,000,000	*from Southampton*
SS Western Prince	12/06/1940	£4,500,000	*from Southampton*
SS Crispin	12/06/1940	£2,000,000	
SS Cameronia	13/06/1940	£6,500,000	*from Glasgow*
SS Port St John	21/06/1940	£2,000,000	*from Avonmouth*
SS Samaria	26/06/1940	£10,000,000	
SS Northern Prince	28/06/1940	£4,500,000	*from Southampton*
SS Crispin	07/1940	£217,894	*port of origin unknown*
SS Samaria	07/1940	£4,096,358	
SS Northern Prince	07/1940	£1,499,014	*port of origin unknown*
SS Western Prince	07/1940	£1,462,030	*port of origin unknown*
SS Canada	07/1940	£394,803	*port of origin unknown*
SS Aracatata	07/1940	£169,227	*port of origin unknown*
SS British Prince	01/07/1940	£3,000,000	*from Southampton*
SS Eastern Prince	04/07/1940	£6,000,000	*from Southampton*
SS Eurylochus	06/07/1940	£3,000,000	
SS Port Freemantle	06/07/1940	£3,000,000	
SS Toronto City	09/07/1940	£3,000,000	*from Bristol*
SS Opawa	10/07/1940	£6,000,000	*from Southampton*
SS Empire Penguin	11/07/1940	£2,000,000	*from Glasgow*
SS Pacific President	13/07/1940	£2,000,000	*from Southampton*
SS Cameronia	19/07/1940	£6,000,000	*from Glasgow*
SS Pacific Shipper	20/07/1940	£2,000,000	*from Southampton*
SS Britanic	20/07/1940	£6,000,000	
SS Welsh Prince	20/07/1940	£2,000,000	*from Glasgow*
SS Nerissa	20/07/1940	£2,000,000	
SS Port Brisbane	26/07/1940	£2,000,000	
SS Scythia	31/07/1940	£6,000,000	
SS Dundrum Castle	31/07/1940	£3,000,000	*from Southampton*
HMS Emerald	03/08/1940	£10,000,000	*from Greenock*
HMS Revenge	10/08/1940	£14,500,000	*from Greenock*
SS Eastern Prince	15/08/1940	£120,000	*from Southampton*
SS Cameronia	27/08/1940	£750,000	*from Glasgow*
SS Britannic	27/08/1940	£500,000	
HMS Ripley	08/04/1942	10 tons	*from Clyde*
HMS Piorun	08/04/1942	Russian gold	*from Clyde*
HMS Churchill	08/04/1942	Russian gold	*from Clyde*
HMS Chesterfield	08/04/1942	Russian gold	*from Clyde*
HMS Liverpool	Unknown	21 tons	*port of origin unknown*

UK–CANADA
(Liverpool to Ottawa, unless otherwise stated)

NAME OF SHIP	DATE	QUANTITY	
SS Duchess of Richmond	16/02/1940	£1,000,000	*to Halifax*
SS Scythia	20/02/1940	£1,784,000	*to Halifax*
HMS Ascania	22/02/1940	£3,000,000	*port of origin unknown; to Halifax*
HMS Malaya	22/02/1940	£10,000,000	*Greenock–Halifax*
SS Samaria	02/03/1940	£1,250,000	*to Halifax*
SS Duchess of Bedford	02/03/1940	£1,000,000	*to Halifax*
SS Antonia	09/03/1940	£500,000	
HMS Orion	14/03/1940	£5,000,000	
SS Duchess of York	16/03/1940	£1,000,000	
SS Duchess of Bedford	28/03/1940	£1,000,000	
SS Duchess of Atholl	25/03/1940	£1,000,000	*to Halifax*
SS Scythia	03/04/1940	£2,234,816	
SS Duchess of Richmond	08/04/1940	£1,000,000	
HMS Ranpura	18/04/1940	£3,000,000	*from Plymouth*
HMS Emerald	28/04/1940	£5,000,000	*from Greenock*
SS Duchess of York	11/04/1940	£1,000,000	
SS Antonia	17/04/1940	£1,000,000	
SS Duchess of Bedford	26/04/1940	£1,500,000	

NAME OF SHIP	DATE	QUANTITY	
SS Duchess of Richmond	02/05/1940	£1,500,000	
SS Duchess of York	09/05/1940	£1,500,000	
SS Scythia	14/05/1940	£1,500,000	
SS Manchester Merchant	23/05/1940	£1,750,000	*from Manchester*
SS Silver Fir	24/05/1940	£1,500,000	
SS Erin	24/05/1940	£1,500,000	
SS Duchess of Bedford	24/05/1940	£4,500,000	
SS Dorelian	25/05/1940	£1,500,000	
SS City of Pittsburgh	27/05/1940	£3,000,000	*from Glasgow*
SS Manchester Brigade	29/05/1940	£2,000,000	*from Manchester*
SS Aracataca	29/05/1940	£1,500,000	
SS Duchess of Richmond	30/05/1940	£4,500,000	
SS Port Hunter	01/06/1940	£2,000,000	*from Southampton*
SS Gregalia	01/06/1940	£2,000,000	*from Glasgow*
SS Europa	01/06/1940	£3,000,000	*to Montreal*
SS Antonia	02/06/1940	£10,000,000	*from Greenock*
SS Duchess of Liverpool	02/06/1940	£10,000,000	*from Greenock*
HMS Revenge	02/06/1940	£40,000,000	*from Greenock*
SS City of Athens	03/06/1940	£2,000,000	*from Tilbury; port of destination unknown*
SS Manchester Exporter	04/06/1940	£2,000,000	*from Manchester*
SS Montreal City	04/06/1940	£1,000,000	*from Bristol; some question over whether this ship actually sailed with gold*
SS Bra Kar	05/06/1940	£2,000,000	*port of origin unknown; to Montreal*
SS Norma	05/06/1940	£2,000,000	*port of origin unknown; to Montreal*
SS Manchester Progress	07/06/1940	£2,000,000	*from Manchester*
SS Delilian	07/06/1940	£2,000,000	*from Glasgow*
SS Britannic	07/06/1940	£5,000,000	
HMS Alaunia	12/06/1940	£5,500,000	*from Southampton*
SS Silverelm	13/06/1940	£2,000,000	
SS Manchester Division	14/06/1940	£2,000,000	*from Manchester*
SS Sulaira	14/06/1940	£2,000,000	*from Glasgow*
SS Newfoundland	16/06/1940	£3,000,000	
HMS Furious	17/06/1940	£20,000,000	*from Greenock*
SS Bayano	17/06/1940	£3,000,000	
SS Norwegian	18/06/1940	£2,000,000	*from Swansea*
SS Port Hobart	18/06/1940	£3,000,000	*from Avonmouth*
SS Duchess of York	19/06/1940	£6,500,000	
SS Manchester Port	21/06/1940	£2,000,000	*from Manchester*
SS Duchess of Bedford	21/06/1940	£10,000,000	
SS Erin	21/06/1940	£4,000,000	
SS Camito	22/06/1940	£2,000,000	*Glasgow–Montreal*
SS San Andres	23/06/1940	£1,250,000	*Falmouth–Montreal*
SS Ida Bakke	23/06/1940	£1,750,000	*to Montreal*
SS Melmore Head	23/06/1940	£2,750,000	*from Glasgow*
HMS Montclare	24/06/1940	£5,000,000	*from Greenock*
HMS Emerald	24/06/1940	£30,000,000	*from Greenock*
SS Port Alma	24/06/1940	£3,000,000	*port of destination unknown*
SS Scythia	24/06/1940	£10,000,000	*port of destination unknown*
SS Duchess of Atholl	24/06/1940	£10,000,000	
SS Duchess of Richmond	27/06/1940	£10,000,000	
SS Manchester Citizen	28/06/1940	£3,000,000	*from Manchester*
SS Pacific Pioneer	28/06/1940	£3,000,000	*from Manchester*
SS Batia	28/06/1940	£2,000,000	
SS Parthenia	29/06/1940	£2,000,000	*from Glasgow*
SS Eastern Prince	29/06/1940	£3,000,000	*port of destination unknown*
SS Beaverhill	07/1940	£6,000,000	*from Southampton*
SS Batory	04/07/1940	£40,000,000	*Greenock–Halifax*
SS Sobieski	04/07/1940	£40,000,000	*Greenock–Halifax*
SS Monarch of Bermuda	04/07/1940	£40,000,000	*Greenock–Halifax*
HMS Revenge	04/07/1940	£47,000,000	*Greenock–Halifax*
HMS Bonaventure	04/07/1940	£25,000,000	*Greenock–Halifax*
SS Duchess of York	04/07/1940	£10,000,000	
SS Antonia	06/07/1940	£6,000,000	
SS City of Lille	09/07/1940	£3,000,000	*from Bristol*
SS Kenbane Head	10/07/1940	£2,000,000	*from Fowey*
SS Torr Head	10/07/1940	£2,000,000	*from Glasgow*
SS City of Singapore	11/07/1940	£3,000,000	*from Glasgow*
SS Manchester Commerce	12/07/1940	£2,250,000	*from Manchester*
HMS Esperance Bay	13/07/1940	£5,000,000	*from Southampton; returned to port as a result of damage*

NAME OF SHIP	DATE	QUANTITY	
SS Duchess of Bedford	15/07/1940	£6,000,000	
SS Beaverdale	16/07/1940	£6,000,000	*from Southampton*
SS Manchester Merchant	19/07/1940	£2,000,000	*from Manchester*
SS New York City	20/07/1940	£2,000,000	*from Swansea*
SS Duchess of Atholl	20/07/1940	£6,000,000	
SS Beaverford	22/07/1940	£6,000,000	*from Southampton*
SS Duchess of Richmond	26/07/1940	£6,000,000	
SS Manchester Brigade	26/07/1940	£2,000,000	*from Manchester*
SS Danaff Head	26/07/1940	£2,000,000	*from Glasgow*
SS Manchester Spinner	28/07/1940	£2,000,000	*from Manchester, port of destination unknown*
SS Duchess of Bedford	08/1940	£6,000,000	*port of destination unknown*
SS Manchester Progress	01/08/1940	£750,000	*from Manchester – port of destination unknown*
SS Antonia	06/08/1940	32,000 oz	*port of destination unknown*
SS Samaria	08/08/1940	69,000 oz	*port of destination unknown*
SS Duchess of Atholl	14/08/1940	£500,000	
SS Scythia	18/09/1940	15,000 oz	*port of destination unknown*
SS Samaria	18/09/1940	15,000 oz	*port of destination unknown*
SS Cameronia	17/10/1940	15,000 oz	*from Glasgow – port of destination unknown*
SS Samaria	09/11/1940	15,000 oz	*port of destination unknown*
HMS Ramillies	10/01/1941	£3,500,000	*from Greenock – port of destination unknown*
SS Georgic	27/01/1941	30,000 oz	*port of destination unknown*
HMS Forth	26/02/1941	£1,750,000	*ports of origin and destination unknown*
HMS Resolution	08/04/1941	£3,000,000	*ports of origin and destination unknown*
HMS Worcestershire	02/08/1941	31 *boxes*	*ports of origin and destination unknown*

SOUTH AFRICA–AUSTRALIA
(Cape Town to Sydney, unless otherwise stated)

NAME OF SHIP	DATE	QUANTITY
SS Waimara	25/11/1939	£2,000,000
SS Port Jackson	13/12/1939	£500,000
SS Ulysses	17/12/1939	£1,500,000
SS Coptic	29/12/1939	£1,000,000
SS Karamea	29/12/1939	£1,000,000
SS Huntingdon	03/01/1940	£1,000,000
SS Port Townsville	09/01/1940	£1,000,000
SS Dominion Monarch	19/01/1940	£2,500,000
SS Sussex	22/01/1940	£1,000,000
SS Ascanius	25/01/1940	£1,000,000
SS Essex	05/02/1940	£1,000,000
SS Port Hobart	14/02/1940	£500,000
SS Wairangi	18/02/1940	£1,500,000
SS Opawa	20/02/1940	£1,500,000
SS Nestor	23/02/1940	£1,500,000
SS Ceramic	08/03/1940	£1,500,000
SS Suffolk	06/04/1940	£1,000,000
SS Port Denison	08/04/1940	£500,000
SS Anchises	09/04/1940	£1,000,000
SS Waimara	15/04/1940	£1,000,000
SS Waistira	29/04/1940	£1,000,000
SS Dominion Monarch	11/05/1940	£2,500,000
SS Port Jackson	11/05/1940	£500,000
SS Port Fairey	30/05/1940	£500,000
SS Ulysses	02/06/1940	£1,500,000
SS Tangariro	07/06/1940	£500,000
SS Waipawa	12/06/1940	£1,000,000
SS Dorset	30/06/1940	£1,000,000
SS Menelaus	30/06/1940	£1,500,000
SS Tyndareus	07/1940	£1,500,000
SS Sussex	07/1940	£1,000,000
SS Coptic	07/1940	£1,000,000
SS Essex	07/1940	£1,000,000
SS Perseus	07/1940	£1,500,000
SS Ceramic	07/1940	£1,500,000
SS Zealandic	07/1940	£1,000,000
SS Port Huron	07/1940	£1,000,000
SS Northumberland	07/1940	£500,000
SS Port Gisborne	06/07/1940	£500,000
SS Empire Trader	13/07/1940	£500,000

NAME OF SHIP	DATE	QUANTITY	
SS Idomeneus	08/1940	£500,000	
SS Westmorland	10/09/1940	£500,000	
SS Nestor	13/09/1940	£1,000,000	
SS Somerset	18/09/1940	£500,000	
SS Diomed	06/10/1940	£500,000	
SS Autolycus	09/10/1940	£500,000	
SS Largo Bay	17/10/1940	£500,000	
SS Karamea	20/10/1940	£500,000	
SS Ulysses	11/1940	£500,000	

SOUTH AFRICA–INDIA

SS Khandalia	04/03/1944	37 boxes	
SS Kutsang	12/07/1944	74 boxes	
SS Khandalia	28/07/1944	71 boxes	
SS Rhajput	05/08/1944	76 boxes	

SOUTH AFRICA–UK

HMS Hawkins	00/10/1941	£3,000,000	
HMS Dauntless	00/12/1941	£3,000,000	
HMS Carthage	00/03/1942	£2,000,000	
HMS Farndale	02/04/1942	£1,000,000	
HMS Colombo	03/05/1942	£3,000,000	
HMS Carlisle	25/05/1942	£3,000,000	
HMS Archer	07/06/1942	£2,000,000	
HMS Abdiel	10/06/1942	£3,000,000	
HMS Canton	23/06/1942	£2,000,000	
HMS Cilicia	23/06/1942	£2,000,000	
HMS Danae	01/07/1942	£3,000,000	
HMS Emerald	01/07/1942	£3,000,000	
HMS Caledon	12/08/1942	£3,000,000	
HMS Formidable	00/09/1942	135 boxes	
HMS Griffin	12/09/1942	£1,000,000	
HMS Decoy	12/08/1942	£1,000,000	
HMS Duncan	20/09/1942	£1,000,000	
HMS Anthony	20/09/1942	£1,000,000	
HMS Dragon	02/11/1942	£3,000,000	

AUSTRALIA/NEW ZEALAND–CANADA/USA

SS Niagara	15/02/1940	£2,000,000	
SS Limerick	23/02/1940	£500,000	
SS Aorangi	11/03/1940	£2,000,000	
SS Cape Horn	13/03/1940	£500,000	
SS Niagara	11/04/1940	£2,000,000	
SS Waiotapu	10/05/1940	£500,000	
SS Aorangi	17/05/1940	£2,000,000	
SS Hauraki	24/05/1940	£500,000	
SS Niagara	13/06/1940	£2,500,000	*lost en route*
SS Aorangi	07/1940	£2,000,000	
SS Cape Horn	07/1940	£500,000	
SS Mariposa	08/1940	£2,000,000	
SS Waiotapu	09/1940	£500,000	
SS Awatea	09/1940	£2,000,000	
SS Monterey	09/1940	£2,000,000	
SS Aorangi	10/1940	£2,000,000	
SS Hauraki	10/1940	£500,000	
SS Mariposa	16/10/1940	£2,000,000	*transhipped onto SS Lurline at Honolulu*
SS Awatea	16/10/1940	£2,000,000	
SS Monterey	00/11/1940	£2,000,000	
SS Aorangi	00/12/1940	£2,000,000	
SS Limerick	00/12/1940	£500,000	
SS Empress of Russia	00/12/1940	£2,000,000	
SS Maui	00/12/1940	£1,000,000	
SS Wairuna	19/12/1940	£1,500,000	
SS Waiotapu	24/12/1940	£500,000	

INDIA–HONG KONG
(Bombay to Hong Kong)

SS Alipore	17/11/1939	£1,000,000	
SS Narkunda	07/12/1939	£1,000,000	
SS Somali	23/12/1939	£1,000,000	
SS Burdwan	23/12/1939	£1,000,000	

NAME OF SHIP	DATE	QUANTITY	
SS Viceroy of India	25/01/1940	£1,000,000	
SS Bangalore	31/01/1940	£1,000,000	
SS Behar	15/02/1940	£1,000,000	
SS Somali	17/04/1940	£1,000,000	
SS Burdwan	30/04/1940	£1,000,000	
SS Bangalore	01/06/1940	£1,000,000	
SS Narkunda	07/1940	£1,000,000	

INDIA–UNITED STATES

USS President Hayes	10/11/1939	Unknown	*Bombay–New York*

HONG KONG–CANADA
(Hong Kong to Vancouver)

SS Empress of Russia	12/1939	£1,000,000	
SS Talthybius	12/1939	£1,000,000	
SS Empress of Asia	12/1939	£1,000,000	
SS Empress of Russia	28/02/1940	£1,000,000	
SS Empress of Asia	27/03/1940	£1,000,000	
SS Talthybius	08/04/1940	£1,000,000	
SS Empress of Russia	19/04/1940	£1,000,000	
SS Empress of Russia	24/05/1940	£1,000,000	
SS Empress of Russia	08/1940	£1,000,000	

SINGAPORE–US

HMS Liverpool	05/1941	£400,000	*to San Francisco*

SINGAPORE–HONG KONG

SS Somali	22/12/1939	Unknown	

SINGAPORE–AUSTRALIA

SS Pingwo	Unknown	Unknown	*further shipments of gold taken out by Quantas airlines to Australia before Singapore fell to the Japanese*

SOUTH AFRICA–US

USS Louisville	05/01/1941	£35,000,000	
USS Vincennes	29/03/1941	£30,000,000	
SS West Chetac	00/08/1941	100,000 ozs	*probably Belgium gold*

NORWAY–UK

HMS Galatea	24/04/1940	200 parcels	
HMS Glasgow	29/04/1940	795 parcels	
HMS Enterprise	29/05/1940	547 parcels	

WEST AFRICA–UK

HMS Hawkins	19/01/1942	£3,000,000	
HMS Dauntless	19/01/1942	£3,000,000	
HMS Welshman	21/01/1942	174 boxes	
HMS Woodruff	26/01/1942	74 boxes	
HMS Prinses Beatrix	13/02/1942	42 boxes	
HMS Bulolo	00/03/1942	36 boxes	
HMS California	00/03/1942	62 boxes	
HMS Ajax	06/04/1942	Unknown	
HMS Totland	05/06/1942	40 boxes	
HMS Weston	05/06/1942	36 boxes	
HMS Wellington	05/06/1942	36 boxes	
HMS Gorleston	05/06/1942	34 boxes	
HMS Abdiel	28/06/1942	442 cases	
HMS Ibis	18/07/1942	74 boxes	
HMS Aberdeen	18/07/1942	74 boxes	
HMS Enchantress	18/07/1942	74 boxes	
HMS Walney	18/07/1942	74 boxes	
HMS Totland	05/10/1942	41 boxes	
HMS Honeysuckle	05/10/1942	56 boxes	
HMS Weston	05/10/1942	52 boxes	
HMS Hyderabad	05/10/1942	55 boxes	
HMS Woodruff	18/10/1942	43 boxes	
HMS Cowslip	04/03/1944	130 boxes	
HMS Aberdeen	04/04/1944	44 boxes	

NAME OF SHIP	DATE	QUANTITY	
HMS Lowestoff	12/06/1944	112 cases	
HMS Wear	28/04/1944	Unknown	
HMS Wolverine	28/04/1944	Unknown	
HMS Malcolm	28/04/1944	Unknown	
HMS Prince Rupert	23/05/1944	67 boxes	
HMS Exe	10/06/1944	70 cases	
HMS Lowestoft	12/06/1944	112 cases	
HMS Leith	12/06/1944	30 boxes	Polish gold
HMS Sandwich	12/06/1944	30 boxes	Polish gold
HMS Kilmartin	12/06/1944	30 boxes	Polish gold
HMS Cotton	21/06/1944	35 boxes	
HMS Gardiner	21/06/1944	35 boxes	
HMS Rushen Castle	21/06/1944	40 boxes	
HMS Flint Castle	21/06/1944	40 boxes	
HMS Foley	27/06/1944	20 boxes	
HMS Helmsdale	27/06/1944	50 boxes	
HMS Kilbride	02/07/1944	10 boxes	
HMS Odzani	02/07/1944	30 boxes	Polish gold
HMS Aire	02/07/1944	30 boxes	Polish gold
HMS Ballinderry	11/07/1944	30 boxes	
HMS Kilmelford	11/07/1944	50 boxes	
HMS Snowdrop	11/07/1944	30 boxes	
HMS Flint Castle	30/07/1944	30 boxes	
HMS Rushen Castle	30/07/1944	15 boxes	
HMS Snowdrop	30/07/1944	30 boxes	
HMS Odzani	10/08/1944	25 boxes	Polish gold
HMS Aire	10/08/1944	25 boxes	Polish gold
HMS Kilmington	10/08/1944	20 boxes	Polish gold
HMS Ballinderry	18/08/1944	30 boxes	
HMS Inver	18/08/1944	20 boxes	
HMS Kilmelford	18/08/1944	20 boxes	Polish gold
HMS Leith	31/08/1944	30 boxes	Polish gold
HMS Kilmartin	31/08/1944	20 boxes	Polish gold
HMS Kilmarnock	31/08/1944	20 boxes	Polish gold
HMS Amaranthus	31/08/1944	50 boxes	Polish gold
HMS Hadleigh Castle	01/09/1944	20 boxes	
HMS Ascension	01/09/1944	25 boxes	
HMS Goodall	01/09/1944	25 boxes	
HMS Folkestone	09/09/1944	40 boxes	Polish gold
HMS Nairana	12/09/1944	92 boxes	
HMS Reaper	12/09/1944	50 boxes	
HMS Dovey	12/09/1944	22 boxes	
HMS Prince Rupert	13/09/1944	40 boxes	
HMS Ettrick	13/09/1944	40 boxes	
HMS St Thomas	13/09/1944	24 boxes	
HMS Forest hill	13/09/1944	23 boxes	
HMS Cotton	20/09/1944	30 boxes	
HMS Morpeth Castle	20/09/1944	20 boxes	
HMS Oxford Castle	20/09/1944	20 boxes	
HMS Rother	21/09/1944	50 boxes	Polish gold
HMS Kilmelford	28/09/1944	23 boxes	
HMS Inver	28/09/1944	24 boxes	
HMS Enchantress	10/10/1944	14 boxes	
HMS Kilmarnock	10/10/1944	14 boxes	
HMS Kilmartin	10/10/1944	14 boxes	
HMS Tortola	29/10/1944	28 boxes	
HMS Bahamas	30/10/1944	14 boxes	
HMS Valiant	07/01/1945	747 boxes	
HMS Fritillary	11/01/1945	1 box	
HMS Kenya	25/04/1945	447 boxes	
HMS Mauretania	23/05/1945	298 boxes	

RUSSIA – UK

NAME OF SHIP	DATE	QUANTITY	
HMS Norman	00/10/1941	3 bars	
HMS Suffolk	14/10/1941	10 tons	
HMS Faulknor	03/02/1942	6 tons	
HMS Intrepid	03/02/1942	6 tons	
HMS Cairo	18/02/1942	12 tons	
HMS Kenya	14/03/1942	10 tons	
HMS Liverpool	12/04/1942	21 tons	
HMS Somali	17/05/1942	1.5 tons	
HMS Edinburgh	29/04/1942	4.5 tons	lost en route
HMS Intrepid	06/1942	500 sovereigns	
HMS Alynbank	28/06/1942	1539 cases	

NAME OF SHIP	DATE	QUANTITY	
HMS Suffolk	10/1943	10 tons	
HMS Inglefield	25/02/1944	1.5 tons	
HMS Black Prince	03/1944	10.5 tons	
HMS Rodney	10/1944	2.5 tons	
HMS Dido	11/1944	6.5 tons	
HMS Queen	05/1945	24 tons	

GIBRALTAR–UK

NAME OF SHIP	DATE	QUANTITY
HMS Wolverine	15/12/1943	63 boxes

UK–EGYPT
(These six ships sailed from Londonderry, Northern Ireland in convoy KMF 25. Gold was transhipped at Algiers)

NAME OF SHIP	DATE	QUANTITY
HMS Pelican	10/1943	51 boxes
HMS Jed	10/1943	51 boxes
HMS Spey	10/1943	51 boxes
HMS Rother	10/1943	51 boxes
HMS Evenlode	10/1943	52 boxes
HMS Rajah	10/1944	2 boxes

UK–INDIA

NAME OF SHIP	DATE	QUANTITY	
SS Fort Stikine	00/02/1944	£1m	lost at Bombay
SS Teucer	17/06/1944	£834,694	
(3m ozs shipped in total, further details not known)			

CANADA/US–UK

NAME OF SHIP	DATE	QUANTITY
HMS Arethusa	12/1943	650 bars
HMS Indomitable	04/1944	20 tons
HMS Manners	12/1944	13 bags

WEST AFRICA–SOUTH AFRICA
(Takoradi to Cape Town)

NAME OF SHIP	DATE	QUANTITY
SS Tyndareus	12/08/1940	22,251 oz
SS Cochrane	07/09/1940	23,078 oz
SS Cochrane	07/09/1940	31,625 oz
SS Ulysses	00/09/1940	23,273 oz
SS Nestor	13/09/1940	35,081 oz
SS Phrontis	06/10/1940	55,509 oz
SS Tyndareus	00/10/1940	42,168 oz
SS Mattawin	00/10/1940	67,849 oz
SS Calumet	04/11/1940	43,537 oz
SS Ulysses	30/11/1940	45,407 oz
SS Calgary	05/12/1940	32,932 oz
SS Mattawin	18/12/1940	53,700 oz
SS Perseus	15/03/1941	298,104 oz
SS Orestes	06/04/1941	25,347 oz
SS Cochrane	10/04/1941	57,215 oz
SS Calumet	13/06/1941	149,107 oz
SS Mattawin	15/07/1941	80,507 oz
SS Rhexenor	21/10/1941	18,499 oz

HOLLAND–UK

NAME OF SHIP	DATE	QUANTITY
HMS Titus	12/05/1940	527 boxes
		484 bags
HMS Iris	13/05/1940	828 boxes

EGYPT–SOUTH AFRICA

NAME OF SHIP	DATE	QUANTITY	
SS Empress of Russia	18/06/1941	£3,000,000	Greek gold
SS Strathaird	20/06/1941	£3,000,000	Greek gold

GLOSSARY

Aft The stern or rear part of a ship.

Amidships The central area of the ship between both port and starboard and bow and stern.

Beam The measurement of a ship across its widest part. Also the name given to the large timbers that went laterally across the ship and supported the decks.

Bends The condition experienced by a diver who surfaces too quickly, causing the nitrogen that has dissolved in the blood under pressure to start rapidly bubbling into the muscle tissue. Intense pain results, and in severe cases injury or even death.

Bulkhead An internal division of the hull by means of a vertical wall either longitudinally or more usually laterally to limit the ingress of water in the event of holing.

Calling Letters The coded identification used by a ship sending signals to other ships.

Compound Engines Engines that used the steam twice over by passing it through a second low-pressure cylinder, thus obtaining a greater efficiency per ton of coal. Introduced in the 1860s and 1870s.

Compressed air Air which is at a greater pressure than normal atmospheric pressure so that a diver can breathe comfortably when submerged in water. When a diver is at a depth of 60 feet he needs to breathe air at a pressure of three atmospheres.

Davits Iron or steel cranes fitted with hoisting gear for the lowering of a ship's lifeboats.

Decompression The process by which a diver comes to the surface in stages so that the dissolved nitrogen in his blood does not bubble out. This process can be carried out in more controlled conditions inside a specially designed decompression chamber.

Derelict Destroyer A ship that is used to get rid of pieces of wrecked or abandoned ships that float on the sea and are a threat to safe navigation.

Dive Support Vessel A ship used to support divers, usually working in saturation. The ship is equipped with special chambers that can be raised and lowered through a moon pool and is capable of staying on station by means of thrusters linked into a computer controlled satellite positioning system.

Droits of Admiralty The ancient rights under which the Admiralty or Crown could claim ownership of any goods or wreckage that were washed up on the shore or salvaged in territorial waters where there was no proof of ownership.

Escudos Portuguese gold coins.

Falls The raising and lowering tackle for the lifeboats.

Flotilla Small fleet.

Four Point Mooring The securing of a ship in position with the use of four anchors rather than the more usual two; frequently used by salvage ships in exposed situations.

Freighters Ship used to carry freight or cargo,

Galley An open rowing boat, or the small boat usually reserved for the captain on a warship. It can also mean the ship's kitchen.

Grab Mechanical tool sometimes used by salvors when lifting heavy objects.

Gross Tonnage The capacity of a ship below the upper deck in cubic feet, divided by 100.

Hatch The opening in a deck through which people or cargo can gain access to the ship's interior.

Hatch coaming The raised sides of the hatch above the level of the deck to prevent water running down the hatchway and also provide a structure for the attachment of hatch covers, tarpaulins and battening.

Hawser A thick rope used for a variety of shipboard purposes, such as attaching an anchor.

Helm The wheel or tiller by which a boat or ship is steered.

Hydrophones Listening devices by means of which an operator on a submarine could hear surface propeller noise.

Knot The speed of a ship, one knot being one nautical mile per hour or 6,080 feet.

Lead A lead weight attached to a line used for the measuring of water depths in traditional navigation.

Moon Pool A well in the centre of the ship through which diving or oil drilling equipment can be raised and lowered. The design allows for greater ship stability than is possible with lowering equipment over the ship's side.

'No cure, no pay' A term used to state that if no salvage takes place, then the salvors do not receive any payment.

Ordnance Munitions and artillery.

Pilot A qualified navigator experienced in a particular port or stretch of waterway. The pilot joins a ship at an appropriate point to assist with the navigation.

Pilot boat Small boat used to navigate difficult waterways.

Port The left hand side of a ship looking forwards.

Prize Crew The crew put on board a ship that has been captured from the enemy during times of war.

Recompression The process of forcing nitrogen that has begun to bubble out into a diver's tissues too rapidly back into solution. This is done by the diver either descending to a greater depth of water or entering a specially designed chamber where he is put under greater pressure.

RoV (Remote Operated Vehicle) Unmanned piece of machinery used in salvage that is controlled from the ship.

Rupee An Indian coin as well as a denomination of value. One pound was worth about 8 rupees throughout most of its history.

Satellite navigation The modern method of navigating a ship by means of information relayed from a satellite which tells the navigator exactly where the ship is on the Earth's surface at any one time to within a few meters of accuracy.

Saturation diving A professional diving system by which the diver lives and works out of a specially designed chamber on the seabed for up to a week at a time, his body remaining under pressure throughout the period.

Scow A wide, flat-bottomed boat that is used to carry men or cargo a short distance

Screw Steamer A steamer that is powered by a propeller at the stern of the ship rather than a paddle wheel.

Sextant A navigational instrument developed from the quadrant in the mid-eighteenth century and used for lunar observations as well as solar observations to assist with the determining of longitude. It can measure angles of up to 120°.

Side-scan sonar Equipment that is used to survey the seabed, usually by towing a sonar fish a few metres above the seabed. The echo of the sound of the waves emitted are received by transducers and converted into electrical pulses, which are then printed out in graphic form.

Slack Water The period around high water and low water when the tide changes from flow to ebb and vice versa and when the force of the stream is reduced thereby reducing the current. This is usually the best time for all salvage operations whether using divers, RoVs or grabs.

Spar Any timber used in association with the rigging of a ship such as masts or yards.

Spar deck The highest deck at the front of a ship or sometimes the upper deck of a modern ship.

Starboard The right hand side of a ship looking forwards.

Steerage The area of a liner low down in the ship towards the stern above the propellers reserved for those paying for the cheapest tickets and often fitted out with bunk beds in a large communal dormitory.

Supply ship A ship the main function of which is to supply other ships in the fleet with necessaries such as fuel, water, food, etc.

Surface raider Heavily armed ships that cruise by themselves and prey on enemy merchant shipping.

Thrusters Independently controlled propellers that are usually linked into a computer that is itself linked into a satellite navigation system enabling a ship to stay almost exactly in one place without having to moor.

BIBLIOGRAPHY

Archival Sources:
Much of the information was taken from personal archive material – letters, reports and interviews gathered during the last fifty years of shipwreck research carried out by my father and myself. In addition the following public files were of particular use: Public Record Office: ADM 116/1690, ADM 116/1691, ADM 116/5484, ADM 116/4679, ADM 116/4680, ADM 116/4681, ADM 137/1014, ADM 137/696; Bank of England Archive: C40/, C43/, C51/.

Printed Books:
Ballard, Dr Robert D., *Exploring the Lusitania*, London, 1995; *The Discovery of the Titanic* London, 1989; *Lost Liners*, London, 1997
Bennett, Captain Geoffrey, *By Human Error*, London, 1961
Besant, John, *Stalin's Silver*, London, 1995
Corbett, Sir Julian S. and Newbolt, Sir Henry, *History of the Great War Naval Operations (five volumes)*, London, 1920–31
Courtney, Charles, *Unlocking Adventure*, London, 1951
Davis, Robert H., *Deep Diving and Submarine Operations*, London, 1935
Dingman, Roger, *Ghost of War*, Annapolis, 1997
Dohna, Count Schlodien, *SMS Möwe*, Germany, 1916
Draper, Alfred, *Operation Fish*, London, 1979
Droste, C. L., *The Lusitania Case*, London, 1972
Dugan, J., *Man Explores the Sea*, London, 1956
Eaton, John P. and Haas, Charles A., *Falling Star*, Wellingborough, 1989
Eaton, John P. and Haas, Charles A., *Titanic Triumph and Tragedy*, Yeovil, 1994
Ennis, John, *Bombay Explosion*, London, 1959
Godley, John, *Living Like a Lord*, London, 1955

Haine, Edgar, *A Disaster at Sea*, New York, 1983
Her Majesty's Stationery Office, *British Vessels Lost at Sea 1939–1945*, London, 1947
Hinds, Fergus, *Riches from Wrecks*, Glasgow, 1995
Hocking, Charles, *Dictionary of Disasters at Sea During the Age of Steam (two volumes)*, London, 1969
Hoehling, A. A. & Mary, *The Last Voyage of the Lusitania*, London, 1956
Jane, Fred T., *The Imperial Russian Navy*, London, 1983
Kemp, Peter, *The Oxford Companion to Ships and the Sea*, Oxford, 1976
McCormick, D., *The Mystery of Lord Kitchener's Death*, London, 1959
Musk, George, *Canadian Pacific*, London, 1981
Penrose, Barry, *Stalin's Gold*, London, 1982
Pickford, Nigel, *The Atlas of Shipwreck & Treasure*, London, 1994
Protasio, J., *To the Bottom of the Sea*, London, 1991
Rohwer, Jurgen, *Axis Submarine Successes*, Cambridge, 1983
Seamer, Robert, *The Floating Inferno*, Wellingborough, 1990
Simpson, Colin, *Lusitania*, London, 1983
Tennent, A. J., *British Merchant Ships Sunk by U Boats in the 1914–1918 War*, Newport, 1990
Walter, John, *The Kaiser's Pirates*, London, 1994
Yusupov, Feliks, *Lost Splendour*, London, 1953

Serials:
The Shipbuilder, Manchester; *Lloyds List*, London; *New York Times*, New York; *The Times*, London; *Time*, Chicago; *Newsweek*, New York; *Corse Matin*, Bastia, Corsica; *Daily Mail*, London; *Evening Tribune*, San Diego, California; *Mainichi Daily News*, Tokyo

ACKNOWLEDGEMENTS

There are many to whom I owe a debt of gratitude for their assistance over the years and without their help this book could never have been written.

In particular, I would like to thank Lyle Craigie-Halkett, who has a wide knowledge of everything pertaining to shipwrecks and the sea and who has worked as a salvor on more of them than anyone else I know; Tony Matthews for his technical expertise and constant enthusiasm; Andrea Cordani, who has been deeper than most into this subject; Charles Haas for his encyclopaedic knowledge relating to all things *Titanic*; Bob Hudson and all those at Blue Water Recoveries, particularly in relation to the *John Barry*; Tom Spong for his fascinating accounts of diving in saturation on several of the huge liners that are included here; Rick Wharton for his helpful information on the *Edinburgh*; Martin Bayerle for supplying material on the *Republic*; Priit Vesilind for his incredibly prompt e-mails; Dr Theo Schulte for his assistance with the *I.52* chapter; and all those fellow authors whose books are mentioned in the bibliography. I would also like to thank Steve Dobell for his invaluable help and advice with the text and David Williams my editor at Pavilion. Most especially I would like to thank my wife, Ros, for her constant support and encouragement.

Finally, I would like to express my admiration of and gratitude for all the rich documentation produced by the brave members of the armed forces and merchant navies during this century and throughout the nations of the world. Without this rich source material, often produced at times of great stress and concerning events that were frequently extremely harrowing, this book could never have been discovered. In this connection I would also like to thank the staff of the Bank of England Archive, London, the Public Record Office, Kew; the British Library, Kings Cross; the Maritime Museum, Greenwich and the University Library, Cambridge.

Nigel Pickford

The publishers would like to thank the following copyright holders for permission to reproduce illustrations. Every possible effort has been made to trace and acknowledge the copyright holders. However, should any photographs not be correctly attributed, the publisher will undertake any appropriate changes in future editions of the book.
2 Public Record Office; 5 Wharton Holdings Ltd; 6, 24, 57, 58, 63 Christie's Images Ltd; 7, 79, 87 Private Collections; 8 Harland & Wolff Collection © National Museums and Galleries of Northern Ireland, Ulster Folk Museum; 9, 10, 36 (bottom), 37 Mary Evans Picture Library; 12 Cousteau Society/Image Bank; 14 Emory Kristof/National Geographic Society Image Collection; 15 Jonathan Blair/National Geographic Society Image Collection; 16, 23, 62 (top) Woods Hole Oceanographic Institution/Robert Ballard and Martin Bowen; 19, 159 (top), 160, 161, 162, 163, 164 Blue Water Recoveries; 21 Imperial War Museum/photo Paul Reeve; 26 Harry Pollard Collection, Provincial

Museums and Archives, Alberta; 27 (top) Special Collections, University of Washington Libraries; 27 (bottom) National Archives of Canada; 28 Special Collections, University of Washington Libraries; 29 (top) Ernest Brown Collection, Provincial Museum and Archives of Alberta; 29 (bottom), 42, 48, 53, 65, 67, 68, 72 (left), 73, 75 (bottom) 86, 112–13 Illustrated London News Picture Library; 30, 31 Special Collections, University of Washington Libraries, photo by E. A. Hegg; 32, 33 George F. Mobley/National Geographic Society Image Collection; 34, 39, 40, 80, 159 (bottom) Nigel Pickford Collection/photo Roger Vlitos; 35, 77, 84, 85, 93, 94, 97, 100, 105, 106, 114, 115, 116, 117, 118, 120, 125, 127, 129, 135, 136, 143, 144, 145, 156 The Trustees of the Imperial War Museum, London; 36 (top), 95, 101, 108, 126, 139, 140 National Maritime Museum, London; 41 (top) Matsumoto/Sipa/Rex Features; 41 (bottom) Johnson Matthey; 43 (top), 44, 47, 99 From *Falling Star: Misadventures of the White Star Line Ships* © 1989 by John P. Eaton and Charles A. Haas, Haynes Publishing Group/ W. W. Norton Inc. Reprinted by permission of the authors ; 43 (bottom), 96, 134, 146 Topham Picturepoint; 45 Harland & Wolff Collection © National Museums and Galleries of Northern Ireland, Ulster Folk and Transport Museum; 49, 83 Hulton Getty Collection; 50 Courtesy RMS-Republic.Com, Inc © 1987, 1999. All rights reserved.; 51 (top) 51 (bottom), 98, 103 (left), 104, 122 (top) Paul Louden-Brown Collection; 52, 54, 55 (top), 56, 59, 60, 62 (bottom) Onslows Auctions, London; 55 (bottom), 64, 69, 71, 74, 92 Public Records Office, Kew; 61 Pierre Mion/National Geographic Society Image Collection; 66 Corbis Bettmann; 70 Bundesarchiv, Germany; 72 (right), 76, 82, 120 Department of Art, Imperial War Museum, London; 75 (right) National Merseyside Maritime Museum/Christian Smith; 78 Cambridge University plc; 81 Maritiem Museum Prins Hendrik, Rotterdam; 88, 89, 91, 138 Courtesy of the Imperial War Museum/ Angelo Hornak; 102, 103 (right) Cambridge University plc, courtesy Siebe plc, publishers; 110 Canadian Pacific Archives, Montreal. Image No. A.6044; 111 Canadian Pacific Archives, Montreal. Image No. A.15320; 115 Imperial War Museum/collection of Captain Letty; 121 (left) Canadian Pacific Archives, Montreal. Image no. BR 204; 122 (bottom), 123 Designaztec Limited, MarineSalvage and Investment; 124 Sunday Times, London/ News International Syndication; 131 (top), 131 (bottom), 132, 133 Sunday Times Magazine, London/photos Ian Yeomans; 141, 142 By permission of Macmillan Inc. from John Ennis Bombay Explosion © 1959; 147 US National Archives (080-G-300488); 148 US National Archives (038/370/15/23/3); 149 US National Archives (080-G-266581); 151, 152, 170 Corbis; 153 Andrea Cordani; 154 The New York Times/Marty Schinz; 165 (top) US National Archives/Naval Historical Foundation Collection (080-G-398230); 165 (bottom) Us National Archives/Naval Historical Foundation Collection (080-G-233791); 166, 169 Captain John E. Bennett USN (Retd); 167 Nonomura Masao, Awa Maru Bereaved Families Association; 171 Professor Roger Dingman

INDEX

Note: Page numbers in *italics* refer to the captions for illustrations; page numbers in **bold type** refer to the A-Z listing details of lost ships.